Religion 2101 A.D.

Religion 2101 A.D.

by HILEY H. WARD

DOUBLEDAY & COMPANY, INC.
GARDEN CITY, NEW YORK
1975

Grateful acknowledgment is made to the following for permission to reprint their material:

"More Long Weekends: A Relatively Modest Proposal" by Andrew M. Greeley in the September 5, 1973 issue of THE CHRISTIAN CENTURY, copyright © 1973 by The Christian Century Foundation. Reprinted by permission of the Christian Century Foundation.

Excerpts from MAN INTO SUPERMAN by Robert C. Ettinger. Copyright © 1972 by Robert C. Ettinger. Reprinted by permission of St. Martin's Press.

Excerpts from "Balloons Belong in Church" by Ann Weems in the October 15, 1971 issue of PRESBYTERIAN LIFE. Copyright © by Presbyterian Life. Reprinted by permission.

Library of Congress Cataloging in Publication Data

Ward, Hiley H
    Religion 2101 A.D.

    Includes index.
    1. Christianity—20th century. 2. Twenty-second
century—Forecasts. I. Title.
BR124.W37   200'.973
ISBN 0-385-00981-X
Library of Congress Catalog Card Number 73–10864

Contents

vi   *Contents*

Introduction

If you woke up in the year A.D. 2101, what would religion be like? What would be the main religion on the scene? And where and how would people be worshipping?

By looking at changes and expectations in society, a variety of futures can be anticipated. And then the challenge is to look back to today, and ask just what will really be important in the future. In the long run, some things we hold dear may not seem important. These things may be church buildings, meeting times, and cultural ideas that now pass for doctrine. A serious interest in the future, as well as in the past, can shape attitudes and doctrines now.

It is instructive to look at the future. How much church history to date might have been altered had the heresy-minded church fathers of the first four centuries A.D. or the punctilious scholastic theologians or Medieval tormentors or the narrow council deliberators at Trent in the sixteenth century been looking to an age of co-operation and tolerance? That which can seriously be questioned can be altered. The future—with its questions, if faced with the aid of either futurists or men of private visions—can change the present.

Unfortunately, people do not look beyond the present or immediate past. Which only makes more necessary a book such as this. The future has its own value. Being open to the future provides a dimension that will help men of faith and seekers in all disciplines to a greater creative life.

This book follows certain premises that are reasonable, if not self-evident. They are mostly conservative premises, but beware, the directions from conservative premises do not merely point backwards. There is, however, some history on the side of each of these propositions:

(1) *Christianity is likely to be around for a long time in some form.* The same could be said for other major religions. With his-

tories going back two, three, and four thousand years, a disappearance of any one religion is not likely, although possible. Then there is the route of faith itself. Robert Torbert, leading American Baptist church historian, commented, "I do not despair of the future. The promises of God himself are that the gates of hell will not prevail against the church (Matt. 16:18). It is reasonable to expect religions of the past, including Christianity and Judaism, to be around in some form. But watch out for the word "form." It is a tricky word.

(2) *The present-day fluctuations are not really important to the long-range future.* A whole book could worry about the ups and downs of membership, financial crises, organizational shifting, etc. One year the churches look as if they are in trouble. Staffs are cut. National budgets are down. But wait, the local church is showing strength. And some main-line denominations are finding new zest, often in imitation of the more conservative brethren. Conservatism is in. Various emphases in religion can be expected to come and go many times.

(3) *Youth viewpoints and youth fads also do not make the future.* This book generally ignores the Jesus People movement, for several reasons. Their importance has been chronicled elsewhere.[1] However, it must be said, the youth are to be listened to, as the future is likely to be one of many voices. Youth are closer to the long-range future (in age) and to the past (in simple sentiments). Yet they are neither the wave of the future nor the crest of the past.

(4) *The future holds surprises and "discontinuities."* While most events have their causes and no longer look like surprises in retrospect, they appear unexpected at the time. "Continuing trends, however important, are only one dimension of the future, only one aspect of reality," says Peter F. Drucker in *The Age of Discontinuity*. This turns attention to the element of surprise. "The future is, of course, always 'guerrilla country' in which the unsuspected and apparently insignificant derail the massive and seemingly invincible trends of today . . . . Discontinuities, rather than the massive

[1] Cf. Ward, Hiley H., *The Far-Out Saints of the Jesus Communes* (New York: Association Press, 1972).

momentum of the apparent trends, are likely to mold and shape our tomorrow."[2]

(5) *Renewal is not the whole story of the future of religion.* Rebirth may occur, such as rediscovering tenets of the past in new forms. Or, simply, there may be *new* birth. Much of the debate concerning the future of the church comes down to the question of renewal vs. rebirth. Renewal zeros in on the past and present, with an interest in how things were done in the past or were intended to be. Rebirth allows a greater freedom and plays down attachments. Yet there may not be all that much difference between the two. As one seeks radical change, he may recover the past. Anthropologist Margaret Mead's point is worth noting: The more one gets into visions of the future, the more one gets into the past. "We found," she said, "that as more science fiction went into the future, young people got more interested in archaeology and very early man and stretched their thinking way back. By anchoring yourself far enough back, you are able to look into a far-enough future."[3]

(6) *There will be a status quo religion in the future.* This is not to say there will be one dominant religion or a national or international religion. Nor is it to cause consternation for groups who feel that their way is the best, if not the only, way and that the future holds a place for them. There will likely be room for remnants. It is possible that the main religion may be some kind of remnant. As we talk about a "new religion," we are talking about what might be the most prominent religion in the distant future, not necessarily at the expense of any current group. It is possible, too, that going far ahead to considerations of the year A.D. 2101, a remnant does not necessarily mean a remnant of "exactly what we have today."

(7) *The world is going to be more unified in the future.* This pragmatic unity results from new communication techniques, population growth, and new interdependence caused by crises such as

[2] (New York: Harper & Row, 1969, c. 1968), pp. ix, xii.
[3] "Finding Anchors for the Future," discussion between Margaret Mead and Roger Shinn of Union Theological Seminary, New York, co-leaders of a U.S. task force exploring the future and the church's role in a technological world, in *The Episcopalian,* May 1973, reprinted from *Youth,* December 1972, c. United Church Press.

shortages of oil and food, etc. Some form of "one world" looms ahead and may exist already with the practice of the constraint of power. This book assumes that some form of socialization without opting for the totalitarian big brother or Communist state may exist. Surely, at least as a minimal control, there will be an egalitarian or beneficent socialism—a concern for the collective good, with built-in absolute, sometimes harsh, if not utterly cruel means of controlling mass populations. Travels in Eastern Europe—Poland, East Germany, the Soviet Union, Hungary, Romania, Czechoslovakia—acquaint one with the climate under which much of religion now operates. Not that the future model parrots Eastern Europe. But some form of central control (which most nations, East and West, demonstrate anyway) may exist—defined not so much by new political philosophy but by the demands of mass populations with advanced technology.

(8) *The orneriness of man cannot be overlooked.* Certainly the twentieth century hasn't shown man to be a nice creature. Man is a savage. Gene Roddenberry, former airplane pilot and creator of TV's "Star Trek" and close to concerns of the future, expects a new dark age may be the more likely course of history. "Man takes three steps forward, then two backwards, and so on," he said. Roberto Vacca in his *The Coming Dark Age* (Doubleday & Co., Inc., 1973) expects the worst to happen, and so does Andrew Lipinski, of the Institute of the Future, commenting in an interview in Menlo Park, Calif. Both Vacca and Lipinski entertain the possibility that man's orneriness and a "holocaust" might reduce the earth back to a primitive stage. Vacca talks of new monastic communities to preserve knowledge in coming dark times. Lipinski merely sees a rerun possibility of history—a new Dark Ages calling for old primitive ascetic forms of religion to reemerge and develop along with society.

Political scientist Yehezkel Dror, of the Hebrew University of Jerusalem, believes firmly in the negative bent of human nature. In a speech to fellow futurists at Frascati, Italy, in 1973:

It is not very difficult to justify a pessimistic view of present humanity, which in its action should be regarded as *Homo Sapiens Falsa*. The history of humanity is one of suffering, misery and unhappiness on the individual level, with accumulated slow progress and some accelerated jumps. *Homo Sapiens Falsa* can be diagnosed as having serious inbuilt errors, such as: (1) Tendency to oscillate between collective madness and individual egocentrism; (2) inability to satisfy basic drives without hurting others; (3) limited intellect; (4) a tragic tendency to show self-sacrifice mainly for collective goals involving aggression towards others; and (5) inability to handle moral dilemmas. Social cooperation seems unable to overcome these weaknesses without substituting for them even worse phenomena, mainly collective crime of larger proportions. It is hard to see in history any trend at work which provides a factual basis for hope that these features are accidental and will disappear somehow.

In some opinions, more serious may be the inbuilt incapacity of the human mind to handle fundamental issues concerning the nature of the universe, the nature and purposes of life and the origin of existence.

Billy Graham puts it simply: "There is a little bit of Watergate in us all."[4] In interviews with Graham over the years—in Berlin, New York, etc.—he has told me the same, as he has preached it—man is a sinner. Yet Graham optimistically believes in a remnant—even a house church form of religion—that will persist into the year 2000. The end may not be around the corner, Graham told me in a New York interview as he put a pillow over the phone to muffle the intrusion of its ringing so loudly in the early morning. But God's punishment in an essentially negative scenario awaits all, he said, and the really faithful may be reduced to only a few, in numbers.

Just before Kurt Vonnegut, Jr., turned his "momentous" age fifty and feeling gloomy about it all, I asked this doom-minded critic of the past, present and future about the year 2101. He said, "There isn't any future. There won't be any earth then." I persisted, and so did he. "There isn't any—go ask the scientist," he said, and so we turned to other questions as he flipped over a coffee table and started glueing some loose parts.

Rudolf Bultmann, noted theologian from Marburg, West Germany, warned on his eighty-ninth birthday in 1973, that the church and mankind are always on the brink of over-all disaster. "Western churches must realize that the freedoms they prize can be de-

---

[4] *Religious News Service,* in *Michigan Christian Advocate,* October 25, 1973, p. 7.

stroyed by politics and can only be maintained by determined political action. The church must do more to encourage its members to be informed and to act responsibly."[5] Says theologian Wolfhart Pannenberg: "A convincing interpretation of the human situation has to take into account also the negative aspects of human experience and behavior. Otherwise no balanced evaluation of the reality of man would be achieved."[6]

This book agrees with the Reverend Dr. Earl D. C. Brewer, professor of sociology and religion, Candler School of Theology, Emory University, Atlanta, who says it is very important that religionists recover vision in terms of the scenario in looking to the future. He defines a scenario as "an imaginative narrative of possible futures based upon certain assumptions regarding trends or events." He says:

Scenarios regarding alternative possibilities for the place of religion in the future of societies could provide insights into possible sequences, dynamics, and options. . . . In spite of the traditional futuristic thrust of religion through various forms of writings, the contemporary religionist seems unimaginative and poverty-stricken in terms of possible alternative futures. Perhaps this is the reason why the artist is so much more capable of capturing the mood of modern man and his possible futures. At any rate, those with disciplined understanding of the present and part of religious phenomena should join in the tradition of seers, prophets, apocalyptic writers and others in producing, comparing, and assessing critically the implications of alternative futures.[7]

Such is the task of this book: Pointing to directions on which narratives can be constructed and concluding with an imaginative scenario, a scene or setting, "based upon certain assumptions regarding trends or events."

The reader is invited not to delegate the process of creating or

[5] "Dr. Bultmann Cites Lack of Christian Vigilance," in *The Living Church*, October 14, 1973, p. 27.
[6] "Postscript," in Tupper, Frank, *The Theology of Wolfhart Pannenberg* (Philadelphia: Westminster, 1973), p. 304.
[7] "Some Suggestions About Future-Oriented Research in Religion," a paper, later published in *Review of Religious Research*, fall, 1971, Vol. 13, No. 1, pp. 13–17.

envisioning futures to others. Let him merely learn from others, and then see his own visions.

Visions—and a lot of visions—are needed as the human race seeks its way through new ages of altered cities, life styles, new mental capacities, and changed humanness.

The future is exciting, and it can make the present exciting, too!

Religion 2101 A.D.

CHAPTER I

The THINGS of the Future

Early one Sunday morning in the spring of 1965 churchmen in business suits rode a bus out to a little log-cabin church near Paris, Kentucky. The men, representing their denominations at merger explorations in Lexington, Kentucky, walked among tombstones across moss-covered grounds. The Cane Ridge log cabin, built in 1791, gave birth to the Disciples of Christ denomination. The tall obelisk tombstone of one of the founders, Barton Stone, leaned toward the cabin. Inside the cabin, the churchmen, arriving before other tourists, sat on thick plank benches, looking at rough-hewn logs that formed pulpit, rails, and walls.

Representatives of six denominations, meeting in nearby Lexington and seeking the roots of their faith, had decided to share in a simple communion rite at the historic cabin. It was so different from the hustle, bustle of a big city suburban church of rumbling pipe organs and parking lot crowding.

In the day of fast-accelerated change, the real significance of that little church in the country may be the fact that it is still there at all. It has survived into a modern age. Perhaps it does not matter that it serves now really as a museum, or as a symbol of a history. It is a living testimony to a continuity with the past.

People don't worship in log cabin churches anymore, of course. But it's not because of any departure from doctrine: Disciples of Christ who began at Cane Ridge like to believe they hold true to the teachings of their forefathers. Also, the shifting of population does not make a log cabin obsolete. Actually, there has been a move back to the country. Rural non-farm population has nearly doubled from 24 million in 1930 to more than 55 million in 1968.[1] And as

[1] Cf. Schaller, Lyle E., *The Impact of the Future* (Nashville: Abingdon, 1969), p. 152.

Reverend Father John McRath, co-director of the National Catholic Rural Life Conference, in Des Moines, Iowa, told a conference of rural clergy at East Lansing, Michigan, rural churches are "not only a problem but a solution." They mix young and old, rural and city members, and provide more effective opportunities for worship and counseling. So the little country churches by the cornfields are not dead. The old churches can sometimes still be used in a new age.

Age alone does not make a church unserviceable, but the lack of modern equipment can. Old materials, dated pictures, outmoded equipment—these give it a museum status. But that "oldness" can be only a few years removed. I remember to my surprise finding the "equipment" like that of my childhood as museum objects in Henry Ford's Greenfield museum village in Dearborn, Michigan. The old lanterns, the coal and cob stoves, harnesses, ice boxes, separators, butter crocks, threshing machines—things I grew up with in the summer on the farm thirty years removed from my life, but now objects of curiosity in a museum setting. Not age; rather the coming of new things made my childhood world obsolete.

What really antiquates the Cane Ridge log-cabin church are the "things" of society: the new gadget (door handles, for example), building materials, new musical instruments (pipe organs, Moog synthesizers, and electric pianos and guitars), plumbing, air conditioning, sliding doors, cushions, display lighting, plexiglass, synthetic marble, plastics, prefab paneling, etc. Had logs remained in vogue as a main building material, for example, the Cane Ridge church might not appear anachronistic at all. But people have demanded for their churches the same new products they have in their homes.

Consider some of the things now on the horizon: microelectronics—pocket radios, telephones and computers; new high-strength structural materials; super-duty fabrics; 3-D photography; group television conferences; robot lawn mowers set to cut grass by themselves; duplicating machines that print-out color; locks that open at the sound of your voice; seven-feet-high "monster" TV screens; official moons giving light at night; picture-phones; mechanical "maids" to dust and set the table.

NEW GADGETS OF THE FUTURE

The eventual influence of the new gadgetry on religion might lead to a scenario like Charles Henderson's "An Electric Circus of the Spirit," published in the Methodist *World Outlook*. His scenario, appearing progressive, is compatible with conservative religion and historic doctrines. Already you can find light shows (at Glide Memorial, San Francisco); electronic music (as rock and folk-rock groups perform in churches across the country); blue and black lights (chalk artist lecturers in churches have depicted the moods of Jesus and the events of his life with special color lighting effects). With a shift only in things, and not doctrine, Henderson's future—and all too present church—comes out like this:

As the smooth steel doors slide open, you enter a large auditorium bathed in dim blue light. The room is filled with rows of seats which seem to be floating, without apparent means of support, in thin air. . . .

Notice, by the way, that these seats are held in place by a magnetic field force and can be moved automatically into any position we desire, simply by sending the proper signals from the central switchboard. . . . My guide then demonstrated the mechanics of these fascinating chairs. They could be raised or lowered, tilted forward or back. "Notice that they are designed to be used in a reclining position. A good deal of the action takes place overhead. They can be turned 360 degrees," he said. And his seat began to rotate slowly. "Members of the congregation can follow the action going on at any point in the sanctuary. Have a seat and let me demonstrate. I'll give you one of our favorite readings from Genesis 1. Please sit down." My host then walked over to the central projection unit and made several adjustments. In a few moments he came back and seated himself in the seat next to mine. And then it began.

The lights slowly dimmed, the room darkened, and for a few seconds there was nothing but silence. Then out of the darkness came the first sounds: music, but music like nothing I had ever heard. Music that evoked a sense of mystery; strange sounds that seemed to come from another world and another time. And that was how it felt: like being transported into a region of the unknown. Then out of the darkness I could see ghostlike forms of light, a variety of shapes and colors. Some were eerie wisps of luminous smoke, others were bright, flickering streaks of light. This combination of music and light created the impression of a tremendous, pent-up power. I felt as though I were floating in a sea of inhuman forms, of undulating lights and colored shadows. And at that moment a voice spoke out, and I heard those familiar words:

> "In the beginning God created the heavens and the earth. The earth was without form and void; and darkness was upon the face of the deep . . ."

The images projected on the dome overhead began to fade, the sound fled into silence, and I realized for the first time in minutes that I was not a spectator at the genesis of our world but a visitor at a Christian church in the year 2001.[2]

It is the desire for the new gadgets, such as the instruments that control central heating and air conditioning, that makes log cabins out of date. The pursuit of newness, comfort, and relevance—aided by a measure of affluence—makes the Cane Ridge church obsolete. Not the church's place in time, or its geography, or the doctrinal pattern that grew from it, or the reverence for leaders buried near it. Of course, the memory of the past, the lack of land development, and respect for doctrines are reasons for preserving a site. But these reasons are not sufficient to render a unit obsolete. I have slept in a four hundred-year-old monastery in the heart of Rome, sharing facilities with Protestant observers during the Second Vatican Council. I could look up at night to an ancient fresco in the ceiling. Old, yes, but the building was more than a fifteenth-century museum piece. It was serviceable with new plumbing and elevator. New "things" kept it from just being a museum.

When a church—a building or institution—is cut off from new things in society, it charts a narrow, limited course indeed for itself. Not only does it risk becoming smaller (which is not necessarily bad) as it cuts itself off, but it risks becoming a museum. Curiously, some of the most isolated, conservative churches are the most gadget conscious. They must have the jazzy songs and gimmicks (I remember one that fired a simulated rocket along a wire to the front of the congregation to demonstrate progress in an attendance drive). Without some gadgetry, their isolation would be complete. Isolated, and quiet, they would be museums.

THE CHURCH AS A MUSEUM

The Soviet Union has been successful in cutting off and isolating old churches, making them into museums for tourists. In the eyes of

[2] Vol. LIX, No. 4, April 1969, p. 15.

some, the Vatican is a museum piece. Delegates at the World Conference on Futures Research, suburban Rome, in Frascati, Italy, trekked in to keep a rendezvouz with Pope Paul VI. They came back generally unimpressed. They talked as if they had been to an aging zoo or museum. A Catholic, Dr. Anne Jaumine Ponsar, who teaches political science at the Catholic University of Louvain, in Louvain, Belgium, objected to the antiquated setting of the papal audience. "I am against the kind of show we saw at the Vatican," she said. "It is completely false. In the technical world we need true spiritualism, not exhibitionism." Dr. Leonard Duhl, psychiatrist and professor of urban social policy and public health at the University of California, told the religious section at the Frascati meeting, "the Pope was cold and unresponsive. He becomes conservative and destructive of the future." The Pope, who was led out from behind a curtain, spoke antiquatedly, some thought, as he told the delegates the church "already possesses a science concerning future and final realities, the science of eschatology." One woman complained to the Frascati conference religion section that the Pope missed the whole spirit of the conference by talking of rewards for the righteous at the end of the world. Another, walking back to the bus, pointed overhead: "There is more energy in that wire than in the papacy."

John McHale, director of the Center for Integrative Studies at the State University of New York in Binghamton, commented at the Frascati meeting that indeed religion buildings may be reduced to only a series of museums in the far-distant future. The form of worship and religious devotion might not be any more than a form of tourism, he said. "Just as people tour historic monuments now," he said, in the future they might "tour spiritual monuments. For instance, you could vacation in Hinduism or some other religion. We might recreate some images as we recreated Williamsburg. There could be living museums, communities or enclaves, like, for instance, the Amish or Mennonites. (Mormons in 1973 drew 600,000 visitors to a Polynesian cultural center at a Mormon college in Hawaii, an indication at least of a certain religious "touring" spirit in society.) The Reverend Dr. John McCollister, chairman of religion at Olivet College (Michigan), believes Christianity might be a "remnant of simplicity," which would be its appeal in a complex age. "Every phase of life will be updated—computerized—predictable. Within this type of society, one source of universal 'retreat' will be available—the Church. Because of the sophisticated manner of living in every respect, the appeal of the church will be one which is spelled out by the motto: 'Back to the Basics.'"

Yet the history of the church has been one of keeping up with things, some of which it transformed. A form of a tree, a cross, transformed into a symbol of salvation, is central in Christianity. The special day of the sun, with its emblems, taken over from the sun worship of Constantine and his soldiers, became Sunday. Chalices and other common utensils have their places in rites. And some centers of Christendom are collections of art and various things of historical and esthetic interest, from the Vatican to Westminster Abbey to great stained-glass edifices in the United States.

THE THEOLOGY OF THINGS

Things, or concreteness, are central to the theology of Christianity. Pierre Teilhard de Chardin articulated "Christ in matter" as well as any, and for him matter of all form took on the mystical awesomeness that Hermann Hesse wrote about as being in a stone in "Siddhartha." And further, the incarnation described in 1 John has a special meaning if Conrad Bonifazi's discussion of the "theology of Things" is considered. "In the beginning was the Word . . . All things were made by him" (John 1: 1,3). Bonifazi argues that a "word" is a "thing" also.

"A *thing* means any action, speech or thought with which we are concerned; it is any object of perception or knowledge; it is both idea and event. But our sense of discontinuity between thinking and doing makes us judge of this usage as ambiguous. The Hebrews find no ambiguity here: idea, word and event are a continuous whole."[3] Things are not distinct from commands or words. Life—matter and spirit—has its unity and continuity.

Mission fields have demonstrated the relation of theology to things. For example, a church can be colonialist and expansionist minded as it opens and settles an area. A church (denominational, missionary society, etc.) can be reactionary and visionary as it negates things conservatively in favor of "heaven up there" concepts; or it can build dozens of buildings, often after Western concepts, thus indicating its mind is on buildings and brick and mortar; or the group can associate with medical equipment or books, etc., thus indicating the service character of the church involved.

[3] *A Theology of Things* (New York: Lippincott, 1967), p. 186.

Negative reactions to things in particular are called for, too. On the one hand, tanks and guns can elicit a response for some, an anti-war viewpoint. The sudden dawning of the energy crisis on the nation at the end of 1973 also demanded a response. Adjustment to the status of things in the energy crisis was demanded of the churches, which proceeded to cut back lighting and heating. They pooled resources and lumped meetings on a single night in order to better use resources.

The very existence of things themselves, Alvin Toffler argues in *Future Shock,* symbolize change and acceleration. "All 'things'— from the tiniest virus to the greatest galaxy—are, in reality, not things at all, but processes. There is no static point, no nirvana-like un-change, against which to measure change."[4] Change is uneven and unpredictable, he argues. Its ascendance is not constant, and in the sweep of change, brings the input—or neglect—of the past thundering on mankind. "Indeed, not only do *contemporary* events radiate instantaneously—now we can be said to be feeling the impact of all *past* events in a new way. For the past is doubling back on us. We are caught in what might be called a 'time skip.' "[5]

THE LIMITS TO GROWTH THEORY

Fear of the growing pace of things, which concerns churchmen also, finds further support in the controversial *The Limits to Growth* study edited by Dennis Meadows and three other members of a team from the Massachusetts Institute of Technology. The study began under Jay Forrester, of MIT under whom Meadows, recently moved to Dartmouth, worked at MIT. The study which involved seventeen international scientists was sponsored and promoted by the Club of Rome, a group of thirty persons from ten countries brought together by Dr. Aurelio Peccei, an Italian economist and industrial manager.

Central to the *Limits* theory is the belief that economic growth and the proliferation of new products cannot continue without "bumping into the limits." Also, there is a limit as to how much pollution the earth can absorb, and, too, there is a limit to the number of people the earth can sustain. "There may be much disagreement with the statement that population and capital growth must stop

4 (New York: Bantam, 1971, c. 1970), p. 20.
5 Ibid., p. 16.

soon. But virtually no one will argue that material growth on this planet can go on forever."[6] Nevertheless, the Club of Rome's sequel to "Limits," called *Mankind at the Turning Point* (Dutton), published in November 1974, appears more optimistic as it points out that aroused populaces could prevent disaster if enlightened action is taken in the future.

John S. Platt, associate director of the Mental Health Research Institute at the University of Michigan, writing in *The Science Teacher,* notes that the "Limits to Growth" people do suggest some policies to help level off growth even though many of the policies would be difficult to adopt. In an appended report in the *Limits* study, incentives, and "adjustment mechanisms" are encouraged. But even these, according to Carl Kaysen, in his discussion of *Limits* in the *Foreign Affairs Quarterly,* of July 1972, are difficult to bring about because of the lack of knowledge to implement decisions or to gauge long-term effects of curbs. Platt maintains there are some practical ways to curb growth. He starts with the TV set. "Several trends in life styles today show ways in which our society might move toward resource conservation, in many cases with a gain in real values," he says. "One trend, which may be more desirable than it sounds, is toward the 'TV Society.' TV costs only about one cent per person per day, and if it became more educational, with richer material, culturally and intellectually, it might fill up our days and our leisure time with education and broadened experience very cheaply."[7]

Churchmen were introduced to "The Limits of Growth" theory in Chicago in January 1973, at "Insearch: The Future of Religion in America," a meeting sponsored by the George Dayton Foundation of Minneapolis. While a presentation by Jørgen Randers, a young researcher in the "Limits" project, was thorough, using audio-visual materials and a computer hitched up to a Cambridge data bank, the churchmen did not respond specifically to the "Limits" presentation. Some comments were prepared by Poikail J. George, of Kerala, India, but his remarks remained of a general nature. George, a member of the staff of the NCC in the Office of Planning and Program, warned that the "Limits" theory might become no more than another way for the rich to control the poor. "Our present institutions are set up and

---

[6] Meadows, Donella H.; Meadows, Dennis L.; Randers, Jørgen; Behrens III. William W., *The Limits to Growth* (New York: Signet, 1972), p. 159.

[7] "Science for Human Survival," *The Science Teacher,* Vol. 40, No. 1, January 1973.

sustained by the rich and powerful to meet their needs and sustain power," he said. "As long as these institutions are unchanged, it is clear that any limits to growth which might be imposed will be arbitrary and another means of controlling the majority of the earth's people."

As a group, the churchmen and women failed to deal with any of the aspects of the "Limits" theories and fell back onto projecting present experimental ministries (see Chapter IV) as their creative input into the future. They proceeded to look at films of young Jesus People communes and shared team ministries. All of which led the Reverend Dr. R. H. Edwin Espy, retiring general secretary of the National Council of Churches, to say, "It is not necessarily true that that which is new today will prevail for the future." Declared Jeffrey Hadden, sociology professor at the University of Virginia in Charlottesville, Virginia: "Looking at fringe groups is no way to shape the future. My God, this conference shows the sheer bankruptcy of the church."

Nevertheless, in interviews some of the churchmen at the conference appeared ready to face up to the negative aspect of "things" in society, including scarcity, which the church was soon to face, along with the rest of society. The Reverend Dr. Robert Marshall, head of the Lutheran Church in America, said: "Every decade there has been a different trend in the church, since World War I. In the 1920s, there were the liberals and the theme of *prosperity*. In the 1930s, it was *neo-orthodoxy;* in the 1940s, the world and *global concerns;* in the 1950s, there was the great emphasis on a *religious* (building) *boom,* and *evangelistic pragmatism.* In the 1960s, *social action;* the 1970s, a recoiling from social action to the *personal.*"

These reflected special needs of the time, he said, and now "present models are responsive to the current needs of people. All we do is adapt a form of the church to the present time. The 'Limits to Growth' theory is valid if it makes people more responsible. The whole society must respond responsibly. And there must be more cooperation of all segments of society and an agreement concerning goals."

THE FUEL CRISIS

Among society's new goals are some possible new alternatives to the fuel crisis. And the churches will be likely expected to take part in the new "things" of fuel, and, in some ways, might reflect some of the new things in the things of its ritual. Consider the possible new fuels. A presidential commission headed by William S. Paley, chairman of CBS, in 1952 studied possible new energy sources after predicting an energy crisis. The commission noted that the United States has enough oil, slate, and coal for the production of liquid and gaseous fuels to last for centuries, and likely in a decade considerable relief will come from this source. But whether this can be tapped and whether there is all that much to be found is questioned in a New York *Times* report of November 11, 1973, by Linda Charlton. She notes that "gas is getting more difficult to find and that producers say they are discouraged by regulation from seeking and exploiting it" and environmentalists are worried about developing fuel out of "high pollutants" such as coal.[8]

An atomic "breeder" fission reactor could give "essentially unlimited energy supply" to the nation, according to the Atomic Energy Commission. The director of research for Northern States Power Co., in Minneapolis, Leslie C. Weber, believes the effort won't get underway effectively until 1990. A task force of the NSP believes that by the year 2000 the breeders will provide about 12 per cent of the nation's energy. The "breeder" equipment turns uranium into plutonium by absorbing neutrons made available in the chain reaction. Only one neutron is needed to continue the reaction, so the remaining are absorbed by the uranium and turn out more fuel than is used.[9] There are, however, hazards. Besides danger of storage, plutonium is extremely toxic and a speck of it causes cancer in animals, warns a book, *Energy and the Future,* of the American Association for the Advancement of Science. High-powered laser beams may be used to create fusion reactions. Light pulses burst small pellets of deuterium, and tritium, forms of hydrogen. Fast-traveling neutrons emerge and are captured in a liquid metal such as lithium, and the hot metal produces steam which drives a generator.[10]

Hydrogen, the fuel that took up the top stages of the Saturn 5

[8] "Things Will Get Worse Before They Get Better," p. E-3.

[9] Cf. Strick, Stan, part four in a series, "Energy: The Alternative," the Minneapolis *Star,* February 14, 1974, p. 1. Cf. also "The Breeder Reactor," fourth in a series, "Closing the Energy Gap," Simak, Clifford D., in the Minneapolis *Tribune,* May 29, 1974, p. 6A.

[10] Cf. "Laser Energy," *Newsweek,* May 27, 1974, pp. 58–59. Also, "The Genius Behind What May Be a New Energy Era," story of KMS Industries, *The Sunday* (Detroit) *News Magazine,* July 14, 1974, p. 12.

rocket in Project Apollo, is also discussed. "It is potentially limitless because it can be produced by decomposing water. It is non-polluting because hydrogen unites with oxygen when it burns to create pure water."[11] (However, critics note that the energy needed to decompose the water will be obtained from alternate energy sources which may be polluting.) Already two of the cars that won in the National Urban Vehicle Design Competition in 1972 used hydrogen.

Under consideration also are plans to harness the winds, sun, and ocean currents. Dyna Technology, Inc., of Sioux City, Iowa, has produced a 200-watt model wind generator. The National Oceanic and Atmospheric Administration (NOAA) has found that turbines functioning as "windmills" underwater capture and transmit energy from Gulfstream currents which sometimes reach speeds of 5.5 miles an hour. Textron corporation in Providence, Rhode Island, is already using solar energy for navigational aids on vessels and in ground-based communication systems. The National Science Foundation (NSF) and the National Aeronautics and Space Administration (NASA) in the summer of 1973 called on the federal government to develop solar power technology at the cost of $3.5 billion in the next fifteen years. The scientists in these two groups predicted that by 2020 there could be an output of solar energy that equals the nation's entire use of power in 1970.

The possibilities of sun power are overwhelming, for in every fifteen minutes, the sun radiates as much energy to the earth as humans consume around the globe in all other forms in a whole year. Experts believe that up to 4 per cent of the power in the United States by 1990 could be supplied by the sun, and more after the turn of the century. An emphasis on the sun is not strange to religion. Christianity itself as we have noted, adapted to the sun worship patterns in its early years, as it took over the date of the annual sun festival for its birthday for Jesus, and the "day of the sun" to which the Romans looked became the Sunday of Christianity. Recently I went to a dedication of a big, new marble synagogue. The *bimah* and pulpit were set focally to capture the rays of the sun at early morning sabbath. Most Christian churches have altars facing east, toward the sun. It is not possible to imagine what a new emphasis on the sun would do to religion, but such an emphasis may well have some effect: more sun-centered programs—camping and

11 Edelson, Edward, New York Times Service, "Hydrogen: Energy Crisis Solution?" in the Detroit *Free Press,* December 6, 1973, p. 10B.

other outdoor activities on the one hand, or on the other, ritualistic revival of early Christian and Orthodox forms which described Jesus as the "sun of righteousness." Orthodox, of course, even now proceed in their processions with their great sunburst emblem.

THE SCARCITY OF FOOD

The "things" we eat will affect the future of religion. As food prices climb—especially in light of any real long-term scarcity in the nation—this kind of crisis can leave its mark on religion. If the globe is taken as a whole, then the food crisis is here. There are 390 million persons already who live on the brink of starvation, and 1,300 million who suffer from malnutrition. It is estimated there are an additional 190,000 more mouths to feed each day in the world. And in a twelve-month period, there may be from 10 million to 30 million deaths from starvation and diseases stemming from malnutrition. A combination of things brought the mounting food crisis to the fore at the end of 1974. Floods and drought had taken their toll in Asia, Africa, and the United States, and the energy crisis brought a cutback in fertilizer and rocketing costs in farm equipment. Grain supply deficits in developing countries will reach about 85 million tons by 1985, U. S. Secretary of State Henry Kissinger told the World Food Conference in Rome in November 1974.

The Third World may play a greater role in administration of church matters. In an interview in his Vatican office, John Cardinal Wright, prefect for the Sacred Congregation for the Clergy, said: "I would not be surprised in a 100 years there had flourished a full century of lay saints and it would not be surprising if the vital center of Christianity had shifted to Africa, but the head of it [papacy, etc.] would still be hanging around Rome as in the Fourth Century [Pope Victor I who reigned from A.D. 189 to 199 and Pope Melchiades who reigned from 311 to 314 were born in Africa]. Now in the rest of Africa there is an insurgent culture which is to the Twentieth Century as the England of Beckett and the Lion-Hearted was to that period—a mission to preach faith to Europe. I don't know whether the world will be democratic, socialist, monarchial or what, and I do not much care, but it will be more united, a kind of little neighborhood seen from space."

If churches in a united world became as concerned with food shortages as they are with energy, there could be a move for some symbolism of sharing food with the deprived. In liberal churches, this could mean a move to symbolic rather than actual bread in communion. In conservative, some cutbacks in the excesses of the potluck might emerge. And the very use of food materials and water in religion could take on deeper significance.

Scarcity can add depth to a communion service. Not only the spiritual meaning but the elements themselves have some "transignificance," more Catholic in tone. Food substitutes might be used in rites.

Add to food shortages and some input also from disciplinary Eastern religion and conservative diet patterns, there might be a renewed interest in fasting. Argues Dr. Marcus Bach, founder of the Fellowship for Spiritual Understanding, of Palos Verdes Estates, California: "Christendom should restore the practice of fasting during the forty days of Lent. One day a week without food, liquid diet only, would be the best thing that could happen for the total health of the total person."

THE NEW WAYS OF TRAVELING

The things by which men travel can affect his religion. A travel crisis, spurred by fuel shortages for passenger vehicles, has its implications for the church. First of all, if walking and bicycling become all that prevalent, the neighborhood parish—as well as the meetings in houses—may get a new boost, as people become interested again in "walk-to" churches. Fuel cutbacks affect church conventions already under fire, as localism is popular and regional meetings and new councils (e.g., the Presbyterian Synod of the Covenant in the Midwest) are organized. Less conventions and a cutback in broad-based representation and communication can lead to power shifts.

One thing that a visitor to Ray Bradbury, author of books on Mars and future worlds, finds interesting: His eighth floor office, at the edge of Hollywood, has a bicycle parked in the outer office room. He rides it to work every day, puts it on the elevator, and parks it in the skyscraper. Bradbury, hard at work in a white tennis outfit, at 8 in the morning, says he has never driven, and why should he, "they [cars] have killed three million persons already." He has never driven his wife's Jaguar. Energy crises and travel restrictions may produce more "Ray Bradbury's" when it comes to future travel.

The parking-lot conscious church may look to putting in bicycle stalls, or equip Sunday-school rooms with bicycle foyers in which to roll the bike in for Sunday school. And that every-member canvass, in which people go out two by two's to call on parishioners—in the future, bicycles built for two?

An electric car with a top speed of only forty miles an hour is now in the works. Five thousand of the T3 jeeplike models are to be ready by 1977, according to Electromotion, Inc., of Bedford, Massachusetts. Such lower speed vehicles if they could catch on would further help slow the pace of church life as all areas are slowed. Yet new forms of rapid transportation are likely to emerge. Karl M. Ruppenthal writing on "Future Transportation: Some Environmental Considerations" in C. S. Wall's, *Toward Century 21,* believes helicopters and related forms of travel "will begin to come into their own. Think of the metropolitan areas that could be well-served with large helicopters moving above the traffic from downtown to airport to residential areas."[12]

In 1974, the city of Detroit launched a new police "armada" of helicopters. They hover over scenes of a crime and monitor locations of criminals until ground units can get there at their slower pace. Transportation that becomes vertical as well as horizontal could conceivably effect the design of future churches as they put in landing ports or schedule high-level conventions. Detroit also has a five-story Sunday-school building with a roof-top terrace at the Second Baptist Church, a historic black church downtown. Such structures might be encouraged if travel takes to the air as well as on the ground.

There is talk of "people pipelines" (Cf. Ruppenthal's chapter) and individual "cartridge" transportation, as a person planning a flight enters a cartridge at the downtown station. It is shipped to the airport and plugged into the aircraft. "There could be hundreds or more of these sections," to fit into a people cargo plane, says R. Buckminster Fuller. The cartridges would be routed to the airport by helicopter, assembled much like a yardman assembles a train, routing cars to their future assignments. All the time the person is comfortable, even sleeping in a pull-out-bed in his cartridge. "At destination airport, the passenger cartridge sections would be helicopter-lifted or vacuum-tube-sucked to the nearest downtown disembarkation

12 (New York: Basic Books, 1970), p. 159.

points. The same world travel and freight traffic computerization would also take care of all hotel and dwelling accommodations."[13] How about churches that remain in the city, and maintain a sort of cathedral ministry to the whole area, drawing from people pipelines that are interwoven into the suburbs? The bedridden, perhaps with a hook-up bed cartridge in their home or apartment, could, via computer action, be programmed and hustled from a room to a church pew or church cartridge holder in a church.

Arthur Clarke in his *Profiles of the Future* discusses many travel possibilities . . . Ground Effect Machines (G.E.M.'s) and hovercraft riding on air thrusts; elaborate conveyor belts; dense powders or liquids like rivers to support man and to ease him from shore to current easily; computerized automobiles—you dial a direction or speak to it, etc. Whatever devices are developed, the day of the car is not for long into the future: "It is becoming obvious that vehicles —except public utility ones—cannot be permitted much longer in urban areas. We have taken some time to face this fact; more than two thousand years have passed since increasing traffic congestion in Rome compelled Julius Caesar to ban all wheeled vehicles during the hours of daylight, and the situation has become slightly worse since 46 B.C. If private cars are to continue to operate inside the cities, we will have to put all the buildings on stilts so that the entire ground area can be used for highways and parking lots—and even this may not solve the problem."[14]

SPARE PARTS FOR PEOPLE

In a discussion of new things, the new "people things," namely, spare parts, can hardly be overlooked. There is a growing literature of talk about transplants. The Paulist fathers and others are putting out books on the ethics of transplants. Who gets the available kidney or heart, when one is available, and twelve people are waiting in line —when the decision means life for one, death for others? Certainly the new parts form ethical questions for the future religionist. And beyond "who gets what" in the available parts, the "great brain" discussions hinted at in Chapter 2 raise more and more questions for

[13] "Why Not Roofs Over Our Cities?" *Think* magazine, International Business Machine Corp., Jan.–Feb., Vol. 34, No. 1, pp. 10, 11. Copyright 1968 by R. Buckminster Fuller.
[14] (New York: Harper & Row, 1973), pp. 25, 26.

religionists—how about free will and responsibility when decisions are made by computers or "plug-in" brains, etc.?

There is new discussion these days, too, about man himself—and not just new substitute parts. Is man himself a machine? To Kurt Vonnegut, Jr., man is merely a machine, often a malfunctioning one at that. Vonnegut's mechanistic view of man gives his novels much of their humor. A clumsy man, a nosy teen-age girl in a drug store, or a dog once hit by a car, or a salesman or a senator—or a Nazi sympathizer or a defender of the right—all behave the way they do because they are machines. In his new *Breakfast of Champions* he admits a "suspicion I express in this book, that human beings are robots, are machines," and Vonnegut proceeds to describe stiff-back men on a curb in Indianapolis: "He shuddered gently, as though he had a small motor which was idling inside. Here was his problem: his brains, where the instructions to his legs originated, were being eaten by corkscrews (syphilitic germs). The wires which had to carry the instructions weren't insulated anymore, or were eaten clear through. Switches along the way were welded open or shut. This man looked like an old, old man, although he might have been only thirty years old. He thought and thought. And then he kicked two times like a chorus girl. He certainly looked like a machine to me when I was a boy."[15] In his earlier *Player Piano,* Vonnegut has a hero, a factory manager, balk against being programmed like a machine. But at the end of that 1952 novel, people are behaving the same as always, still no different than the machines.

On a more serious note, V. L. Parsegian's *This Cybernetic World of Men, Machines, and Earth Systems* likewise coldly compares computers to the intricately wonderful but very machinelike human body. Parsegian, professor at the Rensselaer Polytechnic Institute in Troy, New York, describes the passing of a signal from a nerve into a synapse. He notes very mechanically "the signals that arrive from the peripheral nervous system or the internal organs of the body tend to have the nature of discrete electric pulses." And he finds there is no "dualism of body and mind. On meeting any situation, each individual brings to it a mental set, or objective set, which is determined by past experiences."[16] And as he deals with "knowledge and memory" as "conversion of information," he says: "One

[15] (New York: Delacorte, 1973), pp. 3, 4.
[16] (New York: Doubleday & Co., Inc., 1972), p. 106.

might compare the transformation with those that take place in television, wherein a view of physical objects is transformed by electromagnetic waves into the movements of an electron beam that records on a physical screen."[17] Man, the machine?

Man is a total unit, at least in terms that his moods, aspirations, and thoughts are tied in with bodily functions. Malfunctioning body parts can render him insane and self-destructive. His rationality and his spirit—his inner awareness—can be affected by his body. Terminate the body, and you put either an end to his inner awareness or you move his "soul" to another reality. Tamper with him as you would with a machine and you can change his outlook on life. And religion—the yearnings of man seeking meaning and purpose, in a present and in a future—will also be affected.

In dealing with religion of the future, man himself cannot be ignored as a "thing" that can be manipulated, programmed, restructured, and terminated. As the things around him and as man himself changes, religion changes. Religion relates to perception and conception as images are fed into the mind, and as man as a "machine" receives the input and relates to the ideas and images and allows for feedback, his religion takes form. Man, as machine in a world of things, determines the size and the shape of his church, as they are understood. He will also use the things around him for ritualistic expression.

The "things" of society—including man, as a thing, functioning and responding (although he may also be more)—are the construction blocks on which religious structure is built.

[17] Ibid., p. 142.

CHAPTER II

The People of the Future

Play the game with the child . . . put two fingers together, inter-lock the other fingers.

> "Look at the steeple."
> Open up your hands and "see all the people."

The Second Vatican Council, ending in 1965, said the church is people: "Among all the nations of earth there is but one People of God, which takes its citizens from every race. . . . The Church or People of God takes nothing away from the temporal welfare of any people."[1]

But to say the church is "people" means something more than to say the church offers a measure of democracy for people. It means also the church is people—who *change*. Individuals change, and the church has to respond to each one. The adult sitting in a pew is not the same wide-eyed Sunday-school youngster he was at ten.

If you have ever kept a diary, you will know how much you change when you compare what you wrote a few years back to what you write today. The events of the time take their toll. As change brings new demands, old pursuits and hobbies are dropped for new chal-lenges. I kept a diary when I was young. Most of the entries dealt with whether I practiced on my trumpet and what we had for supper. I keep a diary now, but I long ago gave up playing the trumpet and I have other more important concerns than "what's for supper." Every ten years, at the start of a new decade I write a letter to myself, and discuss—with myself—what I hold to be important, what are

[1] Abbott, Walter, *The Documents of Vatican II* (New York: Guild Press, American Press, Association Press, 1966), "The Dogmatic Constitution on the Church," Chap. II, Sec. 13, p. 31.

the beliefs that now guide me, etc. Comparing the start of one decade with another, it is obvious we are not the same person.

To say that the church is the people is to say also the church is changing. And the change element is more than an over-all creative development. The human being himself is changing and will change. And the change now may be more than a mere acculturation and aging process, more than the move from the starry dreamer to the conservative middle-ager. Consider the possibility that the human being's faculties change. Take his mind, for instance.

THE TELEPATHIC SERMON

Will the minds in the pews be the same? Even if the church stays the same—the sermon, the pews, the time of worship, the dogma— the person in the pew may be different. Harvey Cox of the Harvard Divinity School illustrated this for me in a Chicago interview. I asked him what might be some of the surprises of the future. Most thinkers, like Cox, stay pretty close to the present scene. But when pressed, Cox said there may be "some surprises" in the new capacity of human consciousness. "Things could happen in the study of the mind that might affect how people relate to one another," he said. For example, he said, an ability to understand one another's thoughts before words are spoken might be a new mental ability in the far distant future. Such an ability to transmit thoughts and feelings nonverbally, he said, could "cut down on the formal presentation of the sermons." With telepathic powers, what need would there be for a long verbalization of a sermon from the pulpit? Or the thoughts might be electronically transmitted by a silent pastor to a congregation that has telepathy-aided headgear. Lawrence Pinneo, of the Stanford Research Institute, Menlo Park, California, has demonstrated that a computer can translate thoughts from a human mind into action. Using an electroencephalograph, which records electrical currents from various parts of the brain, he identified the brain waves caused by certain thoughts. Using twenty-five people, Pinneo developed a 60 per cent accuracy of feeding the thought commands to the computer. The computer learned to respond to seven "thoughts"—down, up, left, right, fast, slow, and stop.

The language of the future itself might be a topic of interest some centuries from now. John W. Macvey in his exciting book, *Whispers From Space—Communications With Alien Civilizations of the*

Universe, discusses the possible emerging of a new "cosmic tongue." He rules out a common spoken language but considers a common "pictorial" language, "conveying a clear, unambiguous meaning."

"We will," he says, "assume that alien beings possess the power of sight since this is a sense of such obvious importance. The transmission, therefore, of a form of picture seems an eminently suitable way in which to pass intelligence from one star system to another."[2]

Suppose the day comes when there is interstellar communication and new sets of symbols for communication. Minds in churches would hardly be expected to be limited to the one-way verbal output orally of one man in the same confines.

Nobody knows, of course, in what direction physical and mental developments may go. But certainly a great unexplored field with many potential new secrets to be discovered is that of the brain. Each person's brain alone contains some 10 billion nerve cells that never sleep but constantly run a never-ending process of guiding the body. In some parts of the brain, some 100 million cells fit into a square inch, each cell linked to some 60,000 other cells, each one different. In a moment, the brain can process hundreds of bits of information. Besides storing incredible amounts of information, the brain can distinguish between reality and fantasy and curb desires and emotions. And man through language and other skills can add to and improve the natural storehouse of the brain.

While some believe the brain remains too great a mystery to be fully fathomed in the near future, James Dewey Watson, professor of biology at Harvard, winner of a Nobel prize with two Britishers for decoding the structure of genetic material in the brain, sees new progress concerning the brain. "Neurobiology will not be standing still," he writes. Creatures with simple nervous systems and large cells, such as snails or leeches, will continue to provide some answers, he believes. In twenty or thirty years, he says, "the insights gained from the lower animals may enable more scientific approaches toward the functioning of the brain of vertebraes."[3]

THE PROGRAMMED MEMORY

Scientists are looking for the "engram," or memory tape or "trace" of memory in the brain. With such a discovery, man could find a

[2] (New York: Macmillan, 1973), p. 161.
[3] "Five Challenges for the Biologist of the Future," in series, "The Next 100 Years," Detroit *News,* November 11, 1973, p. 2-E.

way to go far beyond his present mental capacity. He could build incredible foundations of knowledge in his mind without renewed retention efforts. In pursuit of the memory "tape," research has centered on the biochemical processes. Does the learning process trigger a chemical change in one or several brain cells?

Biologist Holger Hyden of Sweden in 1963 suggested that ribonucleic acid (RNA) in the cells acts as a memory molecule. James V. McConnell and Robert Thompson trained a worm to respond to light and electric shock conditions. When the worm was cut in half, retention of the learned responses was seen in both the tail and head halves, suggesting that retention is a part of cell activity. The evidence of this study with worms, and to some extent with rats, is inconclusive. But if this line of pursuit succeeds, chemical research could add a memory pill, which with certain educational input and timing, could be used to condition people.

Already society controls minds by drugs, hypnosis, and surgery. Tranquilizers relieve or prevent emotional distress; hypnosis is used by some doctors and dentists to put patients to sleep and mass evangelists and speakers know some mind-lulling techniques through the power of suggestion and repetition to achieve certain aims; and surgery has been altering minds through lobotomy and other operations for some time. Dr. Bertram S. Brown, director of the National Institute of Mental Health, told a Senate subcommittee in February 1973, that hundreds of brain operations to control human behavior go on every year and that government can do little to supervise doctors or protect patients. One doctor admitted to the committee that one of his patients after brain surgery was indeed "happier" although he suffered loss in intelligence.

George Lucas in his film, *THX 1138,* described a world in which all mankind was controlled by drugs. Heavy penalties awaited those who skipped their drugs. In Frank Herbert's *Dune* and *Dune Messiah,* great sand worms are bred for a mélange, an addictive drug or spice that adds to longevity and opens up dimensions of the future. People now rely on a variety of medicines and items that affect emotional control, among them birth control pills which affect both individual stability and depression levels in some and the mores and religion of a society in general. We may not be too far from the day when society might order special pills for its populace or certain groups of people—its scholars, combatants, and leaders. It was only forty years ago that Hitler used what know-how he could muster to try to develop a superior race, and former Vice-President Spiro T. Agnew in July 1970 was quoted in the Boston *Globe* calling for a new realism that says some people must be put aside: "We're always going to have a certain number of people in our community who have no desire to achieve or who have no desire to even fit in an amicable way with the rest of society. And these people should be separated from the community."

Memory is electrically controlled in Kurt Vonnegut's fantasy, *The Sirens of Titan,* as electrodes inside one's head makes it painful to remember certain things:

> Before Unk could remember anything, the head pain that had made him get on with the execution hurt him again. The pain did not stop, however, with the warning nip. While Boaz watched expressionlessly, the pain in Unk's head became a whanging flashing thing.
>
> Unk stood, dropped his rifle, clawed at his head, reeled, screamed, fainted. . . .
>
> "That's the worst thing you can *do,* Unk—remembering back," said Brackman. "That's what they put you in the hospital for in the first place—on account of you remembered too much."[4]

Harry Benson in Michael Crichton's novel, *The Terminal Man,* has a computer imbedded in his brain to control his emotions.

Now there comes Professor Edward M. Kosower from Tel Aviv University in Israel who describes an electrical stage in memory through the nerves in the body. Kosower believes that storage of information occurs at the synapses, or nerve cell "interfaces." Bonds, formed when neural impulses are transmitted, form a basis of short-termed memory, he says. He suggests that enlarging nerve ends "would increase synaptic effectiveness and would represent a stable information store, i.e., long-term memory." His experiments with rats show a synpatic growth as a result of learning processes, he says.[5]

The Reverend Dr. Thomas Kirkman, a Presbyterian pastor, in

4 (New York: Dell, c. 1959; Delta Book Printing, 1971), p. 113.
5 Boynton, Barbara, "Newsletter/Science" in *Intellectual Digest,* 1973, excerpted from "Proceedings of the National Academy of Sciences," Vol. 69, No. 11.

Royal Oak, Michigan, pointed out how difficult remembering is for man. "We find it difficult to remember the names of even our closest friends," he said. He cited the case of a TV talk show host in New York who even forgot his own name one night. Dr. Kirk said, "Our Lord, living almost 2000 years ago, understood the problem of the human memory. He knew how easily mankind forgets." Remembering became a main function of Jesus' Last Supper: "Take, eat . . . this do in remembrance of me" (1 Cor. 11:24).

But suppose memory could become a constant and programmed thing. A "set memory" would have some effect on the "memory rites" of religion. Could programmed memory make obsolete the rites and disciplines of Eastern religion that leads men through arduous paths to discover forgotten secrets? Could it even influence Judaism positively, aiding in Judaism's efforts to re-educate the young— and nations—not to forget the cataclysmic holocaust of the Hitler era? If there is memory fully achieved, what else will religion then do in its rites?

MIND OVER MATTER IN HEALING

Inevitably mind control comes down to the question, will man be able to exert mind over matter and enhance healing by will or faith? Will man control more illnesses by mind manipulation? Dr. Carl Simonton of Fort Worth, Texas, told a symposium on the "New Dimensions of Healing," in Chicago in 1973, how he uses "mind over matter" techniques in treating the sick. He believes that most people have cancer many times and get over it, as they fight it off before it comes to a person's attention. He enlists the patient's mental facilities to attack the cancer cells. He had a twelve-year-old boy imagine his white corpuscles were cowboys attacking the cancer; another patient saw her cells as an active snowstorm to be overcome; a Navy flier, the white corpuscles as Navy frogmen. He uses meditation along with these picture techniques to battle mental sicknesses.[6]

An Israeli, Uri Geller,[7] allegedly bends objects with his mind, and has testimony of several respected physicists to support his claims.

[6] Cf. Bowman, James, Chicago Daily News Wire Service, November 5, 1973.
[7] Cf. "A Mind that Bends Metal and Breaks the Laws of Nature," Schwabach, Robert, Knight newspaper writer, Philadelphia, in the Detroit *Free Press,* November 18, 1972, p. 19-A.

Alfred J. Cantor, M.D., maintains in a book on the healing possibilities of the mind that all disease is psychosomatic, from allergies to cancer. "Mind and body function together as a unity," he argues. "They are a unit. The division is a verbal one, arbitrary and contrary to fact. Therefore, even cancer has emotional components, as does every organic (somatic) disease."[8]

If science develops means of mind control and goes beyond the "trip" or meditation disciplines of the East, or the "faith" approaches of the West (such as Christian Science, Unity School, or Pentecostalism), the minister-church member relationship might become one of "channeling energies" and providing mind-over-matter techniques, rather than traditional counseling, once limited to listening and verbal thought implanting. Even the more staid Unitarians are getting into forms of mind suggestion if not control in their worship. There is a national Psi Symposium of four hundred persons, fifty of them clergy, in the Unitarian-Universalist denomination. Dr. Robert West, president of the 265,000-member denomination, states there has always been a wider dimension in the tradition of his denomination. "Ralph Waldo Emerson [poet and Unitarian leader in the nineteenth century] was influenced by Eastern thought and we have read from religions of the East in our services," Dr. West commented. "But I detect in recent months more interest in the feeling aspect of religion," a reflection of a youth culture and a "religious revival outside of organized religion."

Nowhere perhaps can the new Eastern and non-rational influences better be seen than in the First Unitarian-Universalist church in Detroit. The pastor, the Reverend Rudolf Gelsey, conducts an "energy circle," a form of "healing" rite in his church service. "He got awful close to Christian Science but stopped short of it," said one young member.

In Gelsey's futuristic Unitarian-Universalist "energy circle," the two hundred worshippers left their pews, joined hands around the church in the aisles, as Vienna-born Pastor Gelsey declared: "We will not develop psychosomatic, functional, or mental sicknesses."

He believes energy can flow from hand to hand, and out to help the sick who are mentioned. In smaller sessions in his home, he actually lays on hands during "energy" sessions, recalling ways of

[8] *Conscious Control of Your Subconscious Mind* (New York: Avon, 1970; c. 1965, Alfred Cantor, West Nyack, N.Y.: Parker Publishing Co.), p. 26.

more flamboyant faith healers. "When people are in groups—the same as in the old prayer groups—there is an immense kind of energy," he says. "If you concentrate on a person, the group can become a channel of healing for him."

He tells of one parishioner who had five heart attacks. The man entered the hospital for open heart surgery. "I led the congregation to send him energy, and the man later said he felt a tremendous surge of warmth," Pastor Gelsey says. He cites the story of the Syro-Phoenician woman in the Bible who touched Jesus and found instant healing. "Jesus told her that her faith healed her. It was the energy—the intense desire and expectancy of the woman which performed the healing."

Experiments may lead to an awareness that the mind can represent many personalities of a person within himself. Indeed, people take on different careers in a lifetime, different styles, different families, a result, the futurists say, of the complexities of life in a changing urban environment. But mind research might lead also to identifying different "people" and not just different paths in life. Certainly the book *Sybil,* with its account of a woman who had sixteen personalities, indicates one possibility over against those who see an integrative person of mind and body as one single expressive unit emerging.

Maya Pines, author of *The Brain Changers: Scientists and the New Mind Control,* argues that two persons exist in each of our heads. The implications for theologians, as Pines points out, are important. Noting that "brain scientists have begun to wonder whether our normal feeling of being just one person is also an illusion, even though our brains remain whole," Pines asks, "are the two halves of our brains integrated into a single soul? Is one hemisphere always dominant over the other? Or do the two persons in our brains take turns at directing our activities and thoughts?" Pines insists "two very different persons inhabit our heads, residing in the left and right hemispheres of our brains, the twin shells that cover the central brain stem. One of them is verbal, analytic, dominant. The other is artistic but mute, and still almost totally mysterious." One side leads to the rational approaches of Western religion, the other, to the Eastern mystics. Pines cites the work of Dr. Roger Sperry at the California Institute of Technology and Ronald Myers, head of a research section of the National Institute of Neurological Diseases and Stroke. Besides arousing theologians, Pines says, the research "has aroused the interest of many others who are concerned with human identity."[9]

THE RAISED IQ

In the long-range future, brain development might be achieved by very conscious breeding efforts, a theme that science fiction has not overlooked either. For example, besides the more familiar works of Herbert and Heinlein and interstellar breeding of superior consciousness, there is the lesser known *2150* by Don and Thea Plym. Their future hero has all the powers of telepathy, precognition, and psychokineses (power to move things by mind control). The Plyms, who work as counseling psychologists (he has a Ph.D.), believe that "unless man learns a new self concept which will permit him to use more of the 95 per cent of his mind which is presently dormant, he will become as extinct as the dinosaur in less than 100 years."

Says economist Burnham Beckwith: "By 2500 eugenic and education reforms will have raised the average American I.Q. above 140 (measured by 1960 tests). Males with an I.Q. below 130 will be subject to compulsory sterilization, before they have any children." Most children, he says, will be the result of artificial insemination with the sperm from superior males. The average I.Q. in the United States in 2500, he said, "will be superior to those of the best 0.1 percent in 1960."[10]

Brain development is not likely to go as far as predicted by Erich von Däniken who maintains that "man will more and more use his brain" and may see his legs and feet become less essential and fade away. "Maybe he'll communicate on mental waves. Maybe in 10,000 years man will be without a body," he said in an interview.

The late Dandridge Cole, space scientist in Houston, talked of "saucer men" with only their heads or brains remaining as they were, as other functions are taken over mechanically, and indeed Dr. Robert J. White has developed techniques to keep life functions of brains outside the body going. Animal brains and even severed heads

[9] "We Are Left-brained or Right-brained," condensation from *The Brain Changers: Scientists and the New Mind Control* (New York: Harcourt, Brace, Jovanovich, 1973), in the New York *Times Magazine,* September 9, 1973, p. 32.
[10] *The Next 500 Years* (New York: Exposition Press, 1967), p. 86.

have been kept alive for days. The idea may not be so strange in thirty years, White reports, and in a book discussing White's work, David Rorvik adds: "Of course, it may be possible eventually to link these disembodied brains to computers and other devices that would double for the missing body, permitting the brain to communicate and even direct action. This is an era of transplants. . . ."[11]

The "saucer men" or disembodied brain concepts are taken much further by physicist Robert C. W. Ettinger. "One can go even beyond this to the concept of 'extended bodies,'" he says. "The brain need not necessarily be mobile; in fact, it might be better protected and served if fixed at home base. The sensors and effectors—eyes, hands, etc.—could be far away, and even widely scattered, with communication by appropriate signals."[12] Ettinger suggests that such an "extended man" can keep and even increase "the animal pleasures. He can have a variety of remote-control bodies—either organic, mechanical, or a combination. . . . We cannot easily imagine what it would be like to enjoy such numerous and scattered limbs and organs." He explains:

> For those who find it hard to imagine a largely artificial or mechanized body, there are already some hints that one can, indeed, develop a feeling for it. Consider those pilots who 'fly by the seats of their pants, or the operators of bulldozers: they develop great sensitivity to the stresses and states of their machines, which may come to seem as much alive as a horse or even an extension of their body. When the perceptions become direct—when a clash of gears, for instance, produces a physical feeling of heartburn, or a sore elbow—then the machine will be as much a part of man as any piece of meat.[13]

Among "extended bodies," Ettinger, a professor of physics at Highland Park (Michigan) Community College, talks of "multicorporeal giants," which not only have "sensors and effectors but even brains distributed over large volumes of space." Giantism implies not only a proliferation of computers but a brain that grows on into infinity. (Ettinger, however, fails to discuss the fact that in a

---

[11] *Brave New Baby* (New York: Doubleday & Co., Inc., 1971), p. 149.
[12] *Man Into Superman* (New York: St. Martin's Press, 1972), p. 76.
[13] Ibid., p. 77.

way this "infinity" brain exists already, as humans, through heredity, proliferate and reproduce their brains in time.) He says:

> Actually, our information-stuffed brains will have to grow to provide more storage space, and the growth need be controlled; but if available space is infinite, only the annual percentage growth in brain tissue will have to decrease, not the tonnage.
>
> Now, a reader of decent sensibilities will be stunned by the word 'tonnage.' Tons of brain tissue? Of course: doubtlessly, some irreducible minimum amount of matter, in mass and volume, is required to store a unit of information, and if we jettison no memories, we must become gigantic. Even storing 'our' memories in a separate mechanical store or computer, plugged in at will, cannot avoid gigantism. . . ."[14]

Interested in "immortality" since he published his *The Prospect of Immortality* in 1962 (the book centered on liquid freezing of the dead for possible revival in the future as the cause of each death is conquered), Ettinger sees the extended or multiple body as immortal. But now Ettinger's idea of immortality, skirting the absurd, deals with giantism. "A society, if it spreads out fast enough, can have a non-zero probability of infinite life . . . Can an individual do the same?" he says. And:

> We should envisage a race of titans, each multicorporeal, his body divided into myriad components attenuated over a large and increasing volume of space, integrated by something like radio waves. . . .
>
> If you are spread over a trillion cubic light-years, and your nervous system signals from one part of you to another at the speed of light, it will take you a long while to think and act. It is interesting to speculate, however, that this may explain the mysterious absence of emissaries from higher civilizations: any culture much beyond the present human stage enters the macrocosmic phase and is more or less out of touch.[15]

There would be overlapping and intermingling of segments of people as their "bodies" are spread out through the galaxy. "A

14 Ibid., p. 79.
15 Ibid., p. 80.

galaxy, say, might support billions of individuals, each one scattered onto billions of planets and each planet supporting parts of billions of different people. People? Beings, rather. . . ."[16]

While these descriptions put him in the realm of fantasy, his one over-all conclusion, in the presence of ongoing change, is plausible: "It is doubtful that the present 'limiting' laws of physics—those of relatively and quantum mechanics—will retain their supposed fundamental character forever."[17]

THE VISION OF "MACRO LIFE"

The concept of "giantism," or "Macro Life," does have a realistic side to it—no less terrifying than imagining brains and parts of individuals spread out and interlinked by radio throughout a galaxy. "Macro Life" is a term used by Dandridge M. Cole, who at the time of his death at forty-five was a space programs analyst for the General Electric Missile and Space Division. *Macro* is the Greek term for "large." "Macro Life is to man as the body is to the cell," said Cole: "Macro Life is a new life form of gigantic size which has for its cells individual human beings, plants, animals, and machines."[18] Cole acknowledges the acceleration speed and growing complexity which others talk about, then asks what is next:

> The oft-noted stresses of modern life are increasing rapidly toward some unknown climax and we tolerate them only by learning the most complex and intricate behavior patterns. In fact, this accelerating frenzy is reaching such proportions that we may well wonder what cosmic orgasm is about to take place. And if we are indeed witnessing the preliminaries to a new birth, we may well ask what sort of new creature is our society about to spawn? In a sense, society can be said to be pregnant with a mutant creature which will be at the same time an extraterrestrial colony of human beings and a new large-scale life form.[19]

[16] Ibid., p. 80.
[17] Ibid., p. 81.
[18] "The Ultimate Human Society," in *Social and Political Implications of the Ultimate Human Society,* General Electric Company, Space Division, abridged, in *Social Speculations,* Kostelanetz, Richard (New York: William Morrow and Co., Inc., 1971), p. 241.
[19] Ibid., p. 240.

Cole foresees some "Queen Mary" of a space ship, with up to 100,000 people aboard, producing its own food supply, equipped with electronic sensing devices, and able to think "with the brain cells of its human colony and its electronic computers." It is indeed a total functioning body or Macro Life. The individual is just as dispensable as an infinitesimal cell. Yet the cells together as a unit are necessary for the corporate life.

Socially, mankind with its scheme of many people fitting into a large system, contributing to its function in some small way, already is Macro Life. Even theologically, the "koinonia" or fellowship or togetherness of the early church nearly 2,000 years ago is compatible with Macro Life. Jesus talked of "that they all may be one" (John 17:21) and he used various concepts to describe the unity of men of faith. A Macro Life in terms of unified living organisms describes his followers: "I am the vine, ye are the branches . . ." (John 15:5). He takes the elements at the Lord's Supper as his own body (1 Cor. 11:24): "Take, eat: this is my body, which is broken for you." Future theologians may see other wider applications of the analogies of a common group equal to one Divine body. The "other sheep I have, which are not of this fold" reference of Jesus, also in John's gospel (10:16), opens the way for an interpretation as wide as the universe, correlated in a one-body concept.

If as the world grows smaller, there emerges a wave of liberalism in theology, Jesus' concepts of brotherhood and co-existence of the good and the bad (Matt. 5:45) might allow for a theology of Macro Life that is global, maybe even galactic. Each man fits into the whole of creation, as the faithful constitute the body of galactic deity. In recent years, a film company prepared a successful version of the Gospel parables by making people look like ants. And man is compared to other small insects. The Reverend Father Charles J. Brady, of the University of Dayton, in Dayton, Ohio, discusses a plot of William Tenn (*Of Men and Monsters*) and concludes that Tenn is really saying in the tale of a few earthlings surviving earth on an alien ship: "Man survives as a hardy, cosmic louse infesting the universe!" An ant, a louse, an atom, a cell—is man only a speck in a larger entity?

A NEW COSMIC RELIGION

No matter how small man might be, the awareness that he is a part of the whole in any way whatever can be mind expanding and a broad step to new consciousness—a Consciousness III, as Charles Reich describes it in his *The Greening of America*. Consciousness III sees a new "liberation" versus the rugged independence and initiative of early Americans, values of Consciousness I, and beyond the values of Consciousness II, organization and institutionalism. Beyond the mere "liberation" of Consciousness III, the new awareness leads also to a Consciousness IV, according to Barbara Marx Hubbard, organizer of the Committee for the Future, Inc. "Consciousness IV people love the earth," she says. "They reject no one; they have no sense of division based on past categories of race, sex, color, ideology, or education. The only division they feel is a separation from those who reject the new option with hostility, those who would deny man an opportunity to open the frontier on the moon, those who are convinced that humanity is irrevocably earth-bound."[20] In an interview, she predicted "there will be a synthesis of the total potential of man in the future. Psychic power will combine with physical power to liberate man from his limits."

"We are moving toward a conscious change of the human body," she said. "Piece by piece we are backing into a new body," a reference to transplants and substitute body parts today. "We can consciously evolve out of this body." There is a "potential universal specieshood—a new man that can extend his life and use unlimited energy. It adds up to the vision of the mystics," she said. "All world religions are leading us to this point. We are one and have a cosmic destiny." In the year 2101, if she were alive then, she says, "I'd probably be living off of this planet and take advantage of an expanded life span, an option for those who want it. I'd probably be attached to or have access to a computer bank of awareness. It could answer any question."

Albert Rosenfeld, author of *The Second Genesis* and former science editor of *Life* magazine, also believes "man may be a more mystical creature" as human consciousness is expanded. Man will be more free, with a wider consciousness. "He will have a cosmic religion that negates or goes beyond the moral emphasis of current religion," he said. Future religion in terms of morality might be more concerned with man being asked to "share the energy of the universe," Rosenfeld believes. There could be "a sharing of a universal energy—a trusteeship in the cosmos could be set up to take care of

[20] "Consciousness IV," in *ARISE: A New Worlds Source Book*, prepared by the staff of the Committee for the Future, Philadelphia.

it." This super energy "could be psychic, electro-magnetic or bio-energy. I do not necessarily feel it has to be something totally new."

Says Edward Cornish, president of the World Future Society, Washington, and editor of *The Futurist:* "We'll see a new religious approach to life. We will see a greater identification with the universe. We'll assume things like love your neighbor. Morality and love will no longer be a particular religious issue. As technological questions become dull, then we will ask what should technology do and what is human life about. There will be a unified mankind."

But besides the discussion that man forms a larger "human" entity, in reality perhaps more social and mystical than literal, apart from the fantasies of Ettinger and others, what are some of the new imaginative approaches to a consideration of man himself? What might the new man be like?

Certainly he might live to be older. With durable spare parts and precision technology, man—more plastic and artificial than flesh and blood—might hold up much longer in the future. And a variety of experiments are going on to extend the life span by controlling the aging process. Dr. Clive M. McKay of Cornell has shown that the life span of rats could be increased by one third by reducing the calories in their diets. People who live in the valley of Vilcabamba in Ecuador on half the calories of Americans are noted for a long life span. The psychological aspects of growing old is being explored by Dr. Alexander Leaf of Harvard Medical School. Examining the village of Vilcabamba and several places in the Soviet Union, he believes attitudes are important. In those areas, the aged are esteemed and he says nobody retires but expects to live long. Scientists are also looking at temperature factors. At the University of California at Los Angeles, the life span of a fish, Cynolebias, was doubled by lowering the temperature of the water by about six degrees. Perhaps life spans of 150 years might not be too far afield in the future. In September 1973, a Russian, Shirali Mislimov, reputed to be 168 years old died in his mountain village of Barzavu. He was survived by his third wife, age 107, and 219 relatives. A celebration in Barzavu recently marked the hundredth birthday of one of his grandchildren.

The new man may not only have a longer lease on life, and be full of spare parts—new hearts, organs, even new "eyes" (tiny TV in a glass eye, tiny computer in glasses frame, electrodes in brain)—but he might have some new faces. Dr. Herbert Metz, a former dentist in Detroit, has a desk full of spare ears, eyes, noses, and jaw parts, among other things. He makes a mold of a person's face, then fills in the mold with a hard material. From this he makes a second mold of the area on which he will be working. With a silicone tinted material, he sculptures the face the way it "should" be, and the material stays intact with special adhesives. It is a step to the probability that the people of the future will likely look the way they want, and an Easter parade may involve more than comparing hats and new clothes.

Then the inevitable question comes: Beyond a certain point in the process of replacing human parts, and redesigning appearances, does a person become something other than human? A person with three-fourths artificial parts—is he man or humanoid, "like a human?" Take a man who is sub-level in mentality. He also has a plate in his head replacing skull damaged in an accident; his mental faculties are conditioned by remedial drugs; some or all of his limbs are replaced; he has a face job by somebody like Dr. Metz; internally, he has artificial parts . . . in all, 85 per cent synthetic and what mental response he has is conditioned. Is this a "man" or machine?

Dr. Kenneth Vaux of the Institute of Religion and Human Development at the Texas Medical Center in Houston, and author of *To Create a Different Future* believes: "By 2000, there will be a non-defective person. There will be life-time immunization against diseases. We will have wiped out airborne and water diseases. We are on the verge of wiping out cancer. Cybernetics are extending human functions with electronic devices. Also there are artificial organs, media extention of eyes and ears. The only way people will die will be by mental diseases such as forms not treated by drugs. Most people will have to kill themselves. They will not be able to die."

MERCY KILLING

Mercy killing has become a greater option. In the wake of the U. S. Supreme Court decision to allow abortions up to six months of pregnancy, anti-abortion advocates are warning if you kill at one stage you can kill at any stage of life. Dr. Richard Jaynes, president of an anti-abortion group in Michigan, said: "If you can destroy life at one point in development, there is no reason why a person can't be destroyed at another point. There is a definite relationship ethically between abortion and mercy killing."

Will it come to this, from a Kurt Vonnegut story:

When Nancy came into the suicide booth to see what he wanted, the Foxy Grandpa was lying on the mint-green Baralounger, where hundreds had died so peacefully over the years. He was studying the menu from the Howard Johnson's next door and beating time to the Muzak coming from the loudspeaker on the lemon-yellow wall. . . . There was a Howard Johnson's next door to every Ethical Suicide parlor, and vice versa. The Howard Johnson's had an orange roof and the Suicide Parlor had a purple roof. . . ."[21]

Robert Heinlein's *Stranger in a Strange Land* has a popular revivalistic religion that encourages people, once they have found peace with God and settled (and willed) their material assets, to "discorporate" on schedule and join the happy angelic world.

In real life, in the Netherlands recently, twenty-seven Dutch doctors admitted practicing euthanasia, or mercy killing, after two of their number, a man and a wife, admitted giving her incurably ill mother a lethal dose of tranquilizers. A foundation for voluntary euthanasia was started in Amsterdam with three thousand charter members. In the United States, the Euthanasia Educational Foundation, in New York, is encouraging people to write a "living will," a statement of intentions for a person. It says one wants to be allowed to die without interference by the medical profession if he reaches the point where he is unable to function as a human being. A new area of "marantology," from the Greek, for "withered" or "faded," has been suggested by an internist at Duke University, Dr. William D. Poe. He argues, in an article in the *New England Journal of Medicine,* that death can sometimes be regarded as a friend instead of always as an enemy.

In Florida last year, a physician who is a member of the Florida Legislature, introduced a "death with dignity" bill to allow adults to direct the discontinuation of medical treatment in cases of terminal illness or injury when such treatment is meant solely to sustain life. The doctor said he had allowed hundreds of terminally ill to die.

The editor of *The Journal of Religion and Health,* the Reverend Dr. Harry Meserve, in an interview counters critics of the "living

---

[21] Vonnegut, Jr., Kurt, "Welcome to the Monkey House," in *Welcome to the Monkey House* (New York: Dell, 1968, c. 1950), p. 32.

will" approach. "People who object to the 'living will' approach say you are not to interfere with the natural process," he said. "But I can't imagine any more interference in the natural process than the heroic efforts of doctors to keep some people alive." He noted that all medical efforts are interferences with natural processes.

But with questions of what is man and his termination aside, what about the quality of life of man? of the man-machine? Man, living in Macro Life, as human cells live in a body, aided also at times by modern chemicals and electrical assists, shares little vision beyond his functional usefulness.

A sense of entity or over-all purpose escapes the "vision" of the "cell" imprisoned in Macro Life. Yet there are "unitary men" who see process and connect events, says Lancelot Law Whyte in his *The Next Development in Man.* One such "unitary man" is William Irwin Thompson, a historian, who says:

If we . . . try to sort out the information from the noise, we come up with four propositions of a new world view.

1. There is intelligent life in the universe beyond earth.
2. The meeting we are expecting in front of us in linear time has already occurred, is now occurring, and will continue to occur. The gods do not talk *to* us, they play *through* us *with* our history.
3. There is more to our history than the meager record of six thousand years. Our religious myths are the detritus of the lost history of earth.
4. Our subjective-objective distinctions about reality are incorrect. As in the world view of the Hopi Indians, Matter, Energy, and Consciousness form a continuum. . . .

Which of us has the power and mobility to go into all the laboratories, multi-national corporation board rooms, and governmental cabinets to find out what is really going on on this planet? What the individual conscious ego does not know, however, does not limit the collective unconscious of mankind, and so one can make some intelligent guesses by paying attention to the seemingly unrelated works of art and mythologies at large.[22]

22 *Passages About Earth: An Exploration of the New Planetary Culture* (New York: Harper & Row, c. 1973, 1974, William Irwin Thompson), p. 139.

CLONING AND THE SOUL

On a more mundane level, man will answer some of the questions himself as he takes some godlike powers in his hands and even begins designing "man." "When we begin cloning," Albert Rosenfeld asks, "where will the soul be?" "Cloning," from the Greek *Klon*—a sprout or a twig—is the creation of something asexually, namely, by simply splitting of chromosomes or by grafting. It may be related by use of materials from other organisms, but its entity is due to the lab and not natural process. In contrast, cyborgs are "people" who have had parts of their subsystems replaced by artificial parts. And of course there are robots and humanoids, or simulated people. "What is the nature of man?" asks Rosenfeld further.

Will the new parts and structures of man add to his sensitivity— will special sensors and equipment put him in tune more with the quiet whispers and sounds of the universe, and thus be closer to God or being God himself? In a recent novel called *Clone,* Richard Cowper speaks of four "saintly" clones, with perfect memories. They "remember" the future, possess psychic and teleportational (space projection) abilities. In all visible appearances, man's creatures such as these clones may surpass himself in some way. If the "new" man achieves some levels of old anthropmorphic definitions of God— a man type with special cosmic powers—the "death of God" discussion might be revived in some way. The debate may be less of a linguistic matter and deal with the creating and shaping activity of both God and man-machine.

As man tampers with the body—from controlled breeding to reshaping and forming synthetic bodies—entirely new forms might emerge, a popular theme of much science fiction. The third volume of Isaac Asimov's *Foundation* trilogy deals with the "Mule," a mutant with strange powers to probe and control men's minds and how some more average people finally outsmart him (with the help unbeknown of some other obscure personalities). In Charles Harness' *The Ring of Ritornel,* a winged centaur who has superhuman powers is assigned to mate a human woman to repopulate a razed earth with a group of spider-type scientists. Dr. Miriam Anver, assistant professor of comparative pathology at the University of Michigan and a science fiction writer in Ypsilanti, Michigan, laughs as she describes her favorite character of the future in one of her stories, "The Enemy." He has a "bunch of legs, two eyes on stalks, white fur, a beak like a parrot, two orange sacks like a chicken; it's neat, and a tremendous tickle to see my animal," which she calls "George." In Richard Cowper's *Kuldesak,* hero Mel, a teen, is accompanied by Coney, a mutated animal with clairvoyant ability, and among the classes of humanlike creatures are the Plants (brain implants) and the Roberts (robots). In *Nowhere Earth,* Michael Elder's "mediums," telepathic people who can discover any rebellious thought on behalf of the "Thought Police," keep people thoroughly controlled. Isaac Asimov's "eternals" in *The End of Eternity* are emotionless types able to control man and conjure up past, present, or future.

Robert Silverberg has some interesting deviations or mutations of standard human forms:

> Thornhill eyed the others, curiously. There were five of them, three human, one humanoid, one nonhumanoid. The nonhumanoid, globular in its yellow-green phase just now but seeming ready to shift to its melancholy brownish-red guise, was a being of Spica. Tiny clawed feet peeked out from under the great melon-like body; dark grapes atop stalks studied Thornhill with unfathomable alien curiosity.
>
> The humanoid, Thornhill saw, hailed from one of the worlds of Regulus. He was keen-eyed, pale orange in color. The heavy flap of flesh swinging from his throat was the chief external alien characteristic of the being. Thornhill had met his kind before. . . ."[23]

EXOBIOLOGY

It would be narcissistic to limit a discussion of the people of the future to earth creatures, whatever they are or will become. Or to even infer that the proliferation of man—or controlling brains related to or evolved from man—might settle in galactic locations. There are two further considerations: (1) the fact that other kinds of creatures unrelated to man exist on other planets, and (2) other forms can evolve as well as man on this earth.

In Frankfurt, Germany, Dr. Heinrich Faust, a member of the research division of the German Meteorological Service, told the German Society for Space Research it could be "assumed without

[23] *Valley Beyond Time* (New York: Dell, 1973; c. Royal Publications, Inc., 1957), p. 16.

hesitation that there is life on one thousand trillion earth-like planets"
But, he said, only a small part, about one trillion, was inhabited by
"intelligent beings." Astronomers at the annual convention of the
American Association for the Advancement of Science, in San
Francisco, in 1974 talked in terms of 250 billion stars in our galaxy,
the Milky Way, and some billion trillion stars in the universe.

There continue to be scientific hints of other life out there. For example, radio astronomers and physicists have found molecules of
ammonia gas in some abundance in clouds of space dust near the
center of our galaxy. A University of California research team, reporting the discovery of the ammonia gas, says it is the first time
such ammonia compounds have been located in the space between
the stars. Ammonia, which along with water and methane, can be
linked into organic compounds essential to the emergence of basic
forms of life, is the most complex molecule so far to be found in interstellar space. Scientists at Cornell University and the Massachusetts Institute of Technology are reporting that satellites of some
planets in the solar system are covered with water, ice, or frost
which could support life. One is Titan, the biggest of the moons of
Saturn. Two others are the large moons of Jupiter, Europa, and
Ganymede.

There is now a special science, "exobiology"—the search for life
—in space research. One of the key researchers in this, Dr. Carl
Sagan, of Cornell University, author of *The Cosmic Connection: An
Extraterrestrial Perspective,* makes the point there is a whole new
approach to life if "chauvinistic" earth links up with the fabulous
cosmos. In isolation, he insists, "we live in the galactic boondocks,
where the action isn't." John W. Macvey in his *Whispers From
Space* makes the point that if minor planets or asteroids are counted,
there are something like 1,500 planets in the solar system alone.

Says Erich von Däniken in his own intimidable way: "Without
quoting fantastic figures or taking unknown galaxies into account, we
may surmise that there are 18,000 planets comparatively close to the
earth with conditions essential to life similar to those of our own
planet. Yet we can go even further and speculate that if only 1 percent of these 18,000 planets were actually inhabited, there would
still be 180 left!"[24]

Then there is the possibility of non-human evolution on earth or

[24] *Chariots of the Gods?* (New York: Bantam, 1973, c. 1968 Econ-Verlag
Gmbh.), p. 3.

elsewhere. Plants and other of the million-odd kinds of life forms on earth might hold some potential development. *Dune* has the giant worm on a sparse planet, and Joseph Green's *Conscience Interplanetary* has a worm that develops in the host and eats out a skull, then exists, becomes an insect and starts the cycle over again. Further, Green's book delves into the nature of possible evolved plants:

> At almost eye level with the human, one branch crossed beneath another. A saucer-shaped leaf, laced with silver threads, hung from the upper limb and grew into the lower . . . As Allan stared, almost unable to believe his eyes, the leaf vibrated and the thin voice uttered a string of gibberish.
>
> The leaf and coils formed an electrically operated speaker. The Cryer was the bush itself.[25]

The response to non-humans, aliens, or other evolved forms from earth will be a consideration. Just as the churches sought to respond on behalf of minorities in the '60s, minorities of the long-distance future may elicit response and support from religion. Andrew Lipinski, of the Institute for the Future, Menlo Park, California, in an interview wondered if religion would relate to the "mutant" minorities of the future. Would religion join in the active persecution as religion did in the medieval age, or would religion come to the defense of the minority against which society settles in nearly every generation? If there is a "genetic upheaval," as he puts it, "how will we consider people with three heads, for instance? How would we react to non-humans? Demonology will have a field day: kill them first . . . if we segregated the Indian, certainly will we separate people with two or more heads." Curiously, some of that kind of debate is already here. In Tucuman, Argentina, a child born with two heads was baptized as two persons. The child continued to live, according to reports, but no attempt was in sight to separate the two heads. Said the Reverend Father Albert Quijano, rector of St. Thomas University, in Tucuman, as he approved the two baptisms: "It was the intention to baptize two souls, since the heads showed they have their own separate characteristics."[26] However, Lipinski's thesis, based on history, is that if there become enough of this or any

[25] (Garden City, New York, Doubleday & Co., Inc., 1973), p. 69.
[26] National Catholic News Service, "Babies Share One Body, Baptized as Two Persons," Tucuman, Argentina, *The Catholic Weekly,* May 11, 1973, p. 9.

"oddity" to constitute a sizeable minority, the question of bias looms strong—for the church to acquiesce in or to stand up and fight the bias.

I like Frank Herbert's description of types that showed up for a political conference way out there in the future (and can you imagine these types at a church meeting of some sort in the future: a ghola or ghost, a fish-man, and a changing face type?):

> "Hayt is a multi-purpose ghola," Scytale said. "The Emperor's sister is of an age when she can be distracted by a charming male designed for that purpose. She will be attracted by his maleness and by his abilities as a mentat" [human computer].[27]
>
> Edric swam in a container of orange gas only a few paces away. His container sat in the center of the transparent dome which the Bene Gesserit had built for this meeting. The Guildsman was an elongated figure, vaguely humanoid with finned feet and hugely fanned membranous hands—a fish in a strange sea. . . .[28]
>
> Scytale shrugged. He had chosen a bland, round-faced appearance for this meeting, jolly features and vapid full lips, the body of a bloated dumpling. It occurred to him now, as he studied his fellow conspirators, that he had made an ideal choice —out of instinct perhaps. He alone in this group could manipulate fleshly appearance across a wide spectrum of bodily shapes and features. He was the human chameleon, a Face Dancer, and the shape he wore now invited others to judge him too lightly.[29]

And, as if the biological syndrome, including genetic and spare part manipulation, is not enough to consider, P. R. Bize's discussion at the Rome Special World Conference on Futures Research 1973 in Frascati, Italy, of a kind of "multiple" social man suggests that more than one kind of man is always involved beyond multiple appearances. "There is biological man, vulnerable man, sensimotor man, socio-affective man, existential man, mental man, hedonistic man, civil man, metaphysical man and specific man," said Bize,

---

honorary professor of medicine at the University of Paris and author of a dozen books on scientific and social issues (from a synopsis of his presentation distributed at the conference). These differentiations may amount to no more than the Sybil multiple personality types in social terms. Yet they may point to the multiple essences of man which hold some clues to the ultimate shaping of man.

But perhaps Bize has overlooked one man: "no-man," the child of the nihilists. Here is man who does not exist, not because he cannot be perceived, but rather the man who does not exist because he is no longer man. Man in Macro Life, lost as a cell in a life-stream and body, lost as an atom in an object, no longer expecting identity. By all rational indications, in terms of consciousness or any peculiar sense of identity, he is non-existent, just as a bacteria or virus or cell or atom is non-existent—as a being or as a man. A man who is so small that he is overlooked in any relation to a whole. A man who is not. The future forms of religion will have to deal with this kind of man.

CHAPTER III

A Matter of Time

A CONSIDERATION OF THE PAST

"I'm going to tell you the history of this planet, because that's where both the trouble and the solution lie," says Jason, the hero, in Harry Harrison's novel, *Deathworld I*.[1]

The planet in question is Pyrrus, where every form of life, from plant to animals, wage war against human beings. Jason comes to believe that there is something in the past actions of men that caused the creatures to be so hostile.

The townspeople are not so sure: "The past is unchangeable and we must fight in the present. That is enough to occupy all our energies,"[2] one of them says.

Jason's hunch proves to be right. After much travail, he heals the breach between the city people and the hostile lower forms, and between the city people and the Nordic-like tribes in the forests behind the attacking lines of creatures. He finds that the first inhabitants of the fictitious Pyrrus planet had attacked animals as the creatures were fleeing a forest fire. Later, the animals developed some mental powers of their own. But they did not forget the cruel humans. The forest animals linked the bipeds or humans with all forms of natural disasters, in the categories of fires, quakes, storms. A "psi" or psychic factor brought them all together to wage war against man. The anger of animals and plants toward man rings true, as modern ecologists seek to save earth's creatures from man.

Yet all the answers are not in the past, as indeed the future of Harrison's Pyrrus depends on many factors. There is more to life's patterns than cause and effect, or "whatsoever a man soweth, that shall he also reap" (Gal. 6:7). The past is only a part of the cause

[1] (London: Sphere Books Ltd., 1973; c. 1960, Harry Harrison), p. 46.
[2] Ibid., p. 75.

of the present and the future. There are other factors. For example, the most immediate events shape lives. A natural disaster, unexpected, will send people in all directions. But unaccomplished events take their toll, too. For example, a rumor of a strike of food truckers will send housewives to the store to stock up on goods. Expectations of glory have led Christians and Moslems and other holy men off to war. The expected, but not realized return of Jesus or His Mother, have motivated great crowds to assemble.

Events can also have future causes, as well as roots in the past. It is easy to blame past generations for alienating plant and animal life and using up resources without planning. It is easy nowadays to blame the white man for injustices to the Indian, the Japanese, the blacks, etc. But the present shapes the matter, too. Suddenly in the present, past injustices come to light and a concern for the future evokes efforts at change. Primitives and a progressing world are placed in confrontation in the present. There is a tension that causes Fred L. Polak, of The Netherlands, vice chairman of the International Society for Technology Assessment, to declare in one of his books, "previously, present day time had no independent significance or existence of its own . . . But now, on the contrary, the present sucks all existence in time up into itself."[3] He believes the present has "destroyed" the past and future. In the respect that the present dominates past and future, he may be right. But it would be difficult to follow him on a strictly negative jaunt. Actually in an interview at Frascati, he spoke of continuation of the past in some areas, such as the teachings of Jesus. "The content of Jesus teaching will be preserved without dogmatic covering. Words are influential," he said.

If the present sucks up the past and future, it becomes hard to blame the past or future on a deity. If the present is all that important as a point of correlation, systematic theology has less interest. The questions are not "why Jesus and the incarnation" or "why" concerning a future judgment, but "why" the present. Are confrontations between rich and poor in the present a part of a plan "on the way to the future" that got stopped in the present? Or must the present reflect a failure of an Intelligence to relate to humankind and to plan an earth big enough for all potentialities? If God is "sucked" up into the present, as Polak sees everything else is, then

[3] *The Image of the Future* (San Francisco: Jossey-Bass, Inc., 1973), p. 229.

there are very crucial problems in the God-encounter. Whatever designer there is in the world holds part of the responsibility for the present as well as the past and future. The future is never just the future, or the past just the past.

THE ACCELERATION OF CHANGE

Again, the rapid pace of change in society contributes to the confusion between past and present and present and future. History does not repeat itself; nor is there a predictable rate of change. Compare the events of history in terms of the incubation rate. Things that were a long time in jelling in past centuries jell overnight in the modern instant-communication age, or they don't jell at all. Dependence on the past for an "instant replay" and direction is not possible. It all happens so fast. "I've learned that the biggest liability is to be born in our century," says the Reverend Dr. Martin Marty, professor of modern church history at the University of Chicago. "In the past you could hide in the mountains for a century or two and make an impact. Now everyone exposes everything."

Toffler acknowledges that "the acceleration of change . . . radically alters the balance between novel and familiar situations. Rising rates of change thus compel us not merely to cope with a faster flow, but with more and more situations to which previous personal experience does not apply."[4] Besides the pace of change there are other factors that make it difficult to arbitrarily apply the lessons of history to the present—and future.

"The inhabitants of the earth are divided not only by race, nation, religion or ideology," says Toffler, "but also, in a sense, by their position in time."[5] For example, there are small groups who still hunt and forage for food "as men did millennia ago. Others, the vast majority of mankind, depend not on bear-hunting or berry-picking, but on agriculture. They live, in many respects, as their ancestors did centuries ago. These two groups taken together compose perhaps 70 per cent of all living human beings. They are the people of the past."[6] He notes some 25 per cent live in industrial areas. "They lead modern lives. They are products of the first half of the twentieth century, molded by mechanization and mass education, brought up

---

[4] *Future Shock*, p. 34.
[5] Ibid., p. 37.
[6] Ibid., p. 37.

with lingering memories of their own country's agricultural past. They are, in effect, the people of the present." The remaining 2 or 3 per cent fit neither into the past nor present:

> For within the main centers of technological centers of technological and cultural change, in Santa Monica, California and Cambridge, Massachusetts, in New York and London and Tokyo, are millions of men and women who can already be said to be living the way of life of the future. Trendmakers often without being aware of it, they live today as millions more will live tomorrow. And while they account for only a few percent of the global population today, they already form an international nation of the future in our midst. They are the advance agents of man, the earliest citizens of the world-wide super-industrial society now in the throes of birth.[7]

The past, present, and future are like three trains going in the same direction, but at different speeds. One could look at an earlier time in history and select his style, like a train, if conditions were equal. If growth factors and pace were the same, answers might also parallel lessons of the past. But they are not. There is extraordinary change all along the line. In quantity, the 1970 world population of 3.6 billion will more than double by 2000, according to United Nations estimates. The United Nations World Population conference in Bucharest, Romania, in August 1974, recognizing the people-growth crisis, called for a broad family-planning assistance and education program, endorsing contraception, abortion, and sterilization. The plan called for trying to curb birthrates in developing nations by 1985. There is also the unevenness of family life amid increasing new life styles; biological innovations and expanded life spans; instant—and disposable—new leaders; new total control systems; subliminal influences; different paces within a person's inner make-up (illustrated by meditation groups vs. main-line religion formal approaches). Jumping from the train of the past to the train in the present or future, even if the "trains" are headed in the same direction, can be disastrous. A person geared to a slow train can be "crushed" as he is thrown into sudden new eras. Old folks used to Latin and tradition at Mass often express how lost they feel in the new culture, for example.

[7] Ibid., pp. 37–38.

But despite a changed pace in culture, the past will always cast some kind of shadow ahead. Whatever differences or whatever mutations there may be, there remains some identity with the past. A future child may look like his grandfather, although he may talk a different language and live different ways and with different interests. But the grandfather's sphere might have been affected by certain things, such as losing his teeth, which the child of the future might not experience. A person of a minority group might have experienced extreme difficulty in one culture, but in another culture could experience the opposite, full acceptance and opportunity. But then in spite of all this, the continuity is there still in the looks and disciplines carried over.

WHAT IS THE PAST?

Consider the relation of the past to the future. Can the future be influenced favorably by the past or unfavorably, or indeed not at all? First of all, what is the past? Consider:

(1) *The past as a means of instruction.* Teachings of the past, words and Scripture recorded by great masters, continue down through time. The Ten Commandments are not forgotten, or the Golden Rule, although there may be some ambiguity in responding to them. People seem to forget the failures of some insurrection, or the failure of experiments in communality, such as the utopian societies of the Shakers or the perfectionist societies of Oneida and Wallingford. But the efforts of the fighters and the peacemakers exist for comparison by future historians. And though links are missed, there is a constancy of human nature that can always turn to the past when people are willing to look for instructional principles.

(2) *The past as coterminous to other times.* When the "stone-age" tree-walking Tasaday Indians, living in caves in the Philippines were discovered a few years ago, the decision was to leave them as they were. The past doesn't have to be eons removed. As we have seen, and as Toffler noted, people in industrial society live as though they are in the future (if we assume the future society is technologically oriented) while others live as primitives (which, contrary to Toffler, could be future man's status also if the world is largely destroyed). A person's life today skirts what looks like an ancient past

to our children, but one's life also skirts the present, and likely the future. One person holds past, present, and future. Various historical ruins around the world, from the elaborate ruins in Rome and around the Mediterranean, to more subtle ruins in Africa and Latin America, demonstrate the existence of civilizations up against one another. Ruscombe Lane, of Baltimore, Maryland, uses the "presence" of the past to justify the existence of the lost city of Atlantis. The fact the past can co-exist with the future means for him the presence of unknown worlds about us. For some, co-existence in time means that future worlds—inhabited by saucer men, and maybe a long time traveling—are about us. (Gregory Benford's novella, *Threads of Time*, has silent, evasive apelike creatures, aliens from another time and culture, hiding on earth, and destroying all who find them in isolated mountains with a rodlike laser gun.) Whether one should let his imagination run along or not is another thing, but socially and concretely segments of epochs of time over man's history do exist side by side.

(3) *The past as a component of a puzzle.* A puzzle is not complete without its parts. The past is a piece of a whole. You don't understand the lives of great people unless you understand something of their past. Lincoln's log-cabin past of humble origins is cited for understanding the great man. Hitler's possessive ambition and personality problems are useful in understanding the mad man in later years. The past here helps to complete a picture. Isaac Asimov's "psychohistory" in his *Foundation* trilogy makes all events contingent on others. His spheres are future directed, but the past and present are parts in a great plan. The plan is wholistic, but constituted of segments of known and predictable events.

(4) *The past as essential to the whole.* Here, again the past, present and future are interrelated, but the three are not dissected and put together. While a puzzle is descriptive, the essence is unity. There is only one pattern. Says Norman Spinrad, a young science fiction writer in his famous story-essay on time, in a sentence that flows like indivisible time: "I am an infant am a child am a youth am an old, old man dying on clean white sheets. I am all these me's, have always been all these me's will always be all these me's in the place where my mind dwells in an eternal moment divorced from

time. . . ."[8] And arguing, contrary to popular references to time, that what is unchangeable in a changing world is time itself, he adds: "Change is something that exists only as a function of the relationship between different moments in time and for me life is one eternal moment."[9] There is no past without a future, no future without the past, no present without past and future and no future without present and past. In this approach, there is no attempt to divide the three into categories. To define one, is to define the other. How can there be a past if there is no point of comparison? It is only a duration.

Even that which is discovered to replace something else may not be all that new. Lewis Mumford, author and historian, pointed out in a paper at the futures conference at Frascati that many innovations which seem to be entirely present day actually have their roots in "pre-history." He believes, for instance, the industrial revolution did not begin in the nineteenth century but in the eleventh. He points out that the invention of the mechanical clock in the fourteenth century did more to advance technology than the steam engine or automatic loom, the clock gave man a precise instrument for mathematical measurement, without which astronomy and moon-shots would have been impossible. An invention draws on previous knowledge. The moment of insight depends on the person trained to produce it. The background prepares for the insight. And the insight, once in the future, is also present and past. At what point was Edison's discovery of the light bulb future, present, and past? It was still in the future until accomplished, but the moment of insight was conceived in the past and presented in the present-past. The future becomes so soon the past.

Attempts to divide up time leads to the question: Can time be dissected down to the utmost particle, as atoms and molecules, etc.? Time defies absolute separation. What confuses people is that time is associated with matter. Certainly, time is treated as matter, as people live by "days" marked on a calendar. But take time from matter, and what is there—past, present, or future? The void before the creation—was it past, present, or future, and how can one tell until it is related to matter or a creation? This is to say that we get our con-

---

[8] "Weed of Time," in McCaffrey, Anne, compiler, *Alchemy and Academe* (Garden City, N.Y.: Doubleday & Co., Inc., 1970), p. 34.
[9] Ibid., p. 41.

cepts of past from our materialistic bent. As concrete or tangible creatures, we look to make objects around us seem real and tangible. And time itself is made into past, present, and future. But is it?

(5) *The past as future repetition.* Divide a life drama—singular or collective, individual or global—into three acts. Say the first act is over—the past exists, but it is incomplete, and as far as it is incomplete, it is not the past. Then come acts two and three. When the play is over, what is past, present, or future? There is still something more. Most plays are not over after the performance of all three acts in one evening. There are other evenings. Applied to a life cycle, a re-enacting of the drama could be regarded as reincarnation. But even if the drama changes and the actors go on to other projects, the continuation of the same existence is not terribly varied. Plots can be brought down to only a very few basic themes, less than forty, as the old short-story instruction books used to say. I thought it would be intriguing to do a play sometime on three levels, —one platform above another, constructed in such a way that an actor can go back and forth between the three levels. On one platform he is man, on another an animal, on another an insect. He changes costumes only slightly as he continues his role of survival and attainment on all three stages—as insect, animal, and man. There is a cohesion to any idea of reincarnation, and if time is one, the expressions of each "sequence" are not all that different from another. Various new books are bringing a discussion of reincarnation to greater popularity. *Reincarnation in the Twentieth Century* by Martin Ebon has readings from various mystics, East and West. Ebon declares: "Reincarnation is not a thing of the past. . . . A series of twentieth-century cases testify to its impact in our own time,"[10] and he describes people who feel they have traveled the same route before. Quincy Howe, Jr., in *Reincarnation for the Christian* believes the Christian life is enriched by a belief in reincarnation (Westminster, 1973). Indeed, there may be more than oblivion after death, and there is a chance for a sense of karma to balance out merits for good deeds, punishment for evil, as well as a Christian concept. If future religion becomes more eclectic and therefore less dogmatic, as it becomes perhaps more interested in universal right actions than geographical oriented doctrines, the demands of karma—the

[10] (New York: World Publishing Co., 1969, c. American Society for Psychical Research, 1960), p. 7.

accounting for every deed—could prevail. And with it, the continuing concern to right the wrongs.

"Karma is the cause of rebirth, and each birth is in turn followed by death," according to the teaching of one Eastern mystic, Sant Kirpal Singh Ji Maharaj, whose teachings, among others from the East, are being adapted by the young in the United States. ". . . No amount of integrity, intelligence or genius can absolve a man as long as there is the slightest trace of karma. . . . Prayers, confession and atonement may give temporary mental relief, but they cannot overcome karma. All karma must be wiped out completely before permanent salvation can be found."[11]

Irving Buchen, of the Dreyfuss College Division of the Future at Fairleigh Dickinson University, Madison, New Jersey, sees a psychological reincarnation of personalities within one life, a "constellation of selves," as Hermann Hesse said in his *Steppenwolf*. The doctrine of reincarnation could carry over, he said, as "various lives within lives are lived." Different careers, he said, could constitute "six to eight different lives" within a person.

MAN AS A MICRO CELL

An insignificant creature, even though he is ranked by the Psalmist as a little lower than the angels (Psalm 8:5), may be a more adequate description of man. This is especially so if the reincarnation people have their say about a person vacillating between higher and lower forms of existence according to his behavior in a previous life. Robert Theobald delves into the insignificance of man by discussing three science fiction stories in his *Futures Conditional*. On Isaac Asimov's "What If—" story, Theobald notes that it "suggests that if one chance event had not taken place it would have been replaced by other factors so that the end result would have been the same." And Theobald adds: "Other stories have argued that even the elimination of key historical figures—such as Napoleon—would be compensated by other factors."[12] These kinds of stories treat man as no more than a micro cell within a body politic. Things happen, but he cannot comprehend the nature of the entity. The consciousness of Spinrad's hero in "The Weed of Time" is conditioned by one act, the eating of the strange forbidden leaf of time—an act that makes

[11] *A Brief Life Sketch and Teachings of His Holiness Sant Kirpal Singh Ji Maharaj* (Delhi: Ruhani Satsang Publications, n.d.).
[12] (Indianapolis: Bobbs-Merrill, 1972), p. 3.

the 110-year span of a future man from birth to death indistinguish-able, forwards and backwards. "My life is immutable, invariant, for I have eaten of Temp, the Weed of Time. But you must not! . . . As this time-locus of March 4 'changes' my future, so too it 'changes' my past, expanding my Temp-consciousness to both extremes of my life-span. But once the past is changed, the previous past has never existed."[13]

In an interview, Spinrad said the "Weed of Time" story compares to Vonnegut's "Tralfamadore Time," in which Billy Pilgrim vacil-lates between a tragic earth existence and a sensuous but limited happy love cove on a distant planet. Certain conditions in life, such as induced by drugs, Spinrad said, can make "a whole life simul-taneous—all exists at the same time." Yet there is a pivotal point—the taking of the strange weed or drug, or in Christian terminology, a crisis event, or some other mind-expanding experience. An individual future hinges around a moment.

Theobald, discussing Ray Bradbury's "Sound of Thunder" story about a dinosaur hunting expedition via a time machine, notes his-tory can be influenced by the smallest "chance event—that there is no order to history at all. The decision to turn in one direction rather than another, to see a movie rather than to stay home, alters one's life."[14] And in Robert Heinlein's "Life-Line" tale about a gadget that tells how long a person will live, Theobald notes there is an "assumption that one's personal actions interact with existing trends to create new possibilities and that these possibilities are sub-ject to understanding and prediction. There is system to the universe and the result of each individual's acts can be important."[15] The past is therefore important, not in isolation, but in interrelation-ships. The past takes on its meaning and indeed its definition in relation to a present predicament or as part of a future summation or entity of events. The past, on the one hand, contributes to the future; on the other hand, it is merely absorbed by the present and future. But an appreciation of the past is always in terms of the future society and the future event.

TRADITION IS A PROCESS

Ives Congar, a pioneer in church unity, believes "tradition is liv-ing." Interviewed at his Dominican house residence in Paris, he

---

[13] Spinrad, op. cit., pp. 35, 42.
[14] Theobald, op. cit., pp. 3, 4.
[15] Ibid., p. 4.

pointed out tradition does not mean conservatism. "Tradition is not a repetition of the past," he said.

In Montreal, at a World Council of Churches Faith and Order meeting in 1963, a report distinguished between Tradition with a capital "T" and tradition with a small "t". "By the Tradition is meant the Gospel itself" . . . "tradition" is a process; traditions refer to "diversity of forms" and historical heritages of the various groups. "The testimony of prophets and apostles inaugurated the Tradition of his revelation," the leaders in Montreal said.[16] In Tradition, they saw past, present, and future linked together. The Divine Revelation Constitution of the Second Vatican Council said tradition, Scripture, and the teaching authority of the church are "so linked and joined together that one cannot stand without the others."[17]

The wider context of an event gives unity. If there were nothing to be accomplished later, there would be no direction or hope of judgment. Which may be the case. But in Orthodox Christian terms, at least, the context of an event is never complete until the future. "The meaning of any historical event can be known only from its context," says Carl E. Braaten in *The Future of God*. "One must know the full context. However, the full context is unavailable, since history is still going on and has not come to an end. The future perspective must be included in any contextual interpretation of an event's meaning. The context of the past or of the present is not enough."[18]

In trying to fathom the whole context, Christian theologians have come up with various concepts of sacred time. To Nicolas Berdyaev, there is metahistory or eternity and parallel to it is history or cosmic time. Existential time intersects and links metahistory and history. "Every creative act is performed in existential time and is merely projected in historical time." The moment of "creative impulse and ecstasy is outside objectivized and mathematical time."[19] Resurrection conquers time—past and future, Berdyaev says, but resurrection can be acknowledged in the moment of existential time. Man does not wait for the end of time, but prepares for it, and one day objective time will be absorbed into infinite, metahistorical time.

Oscar Cullmann, over dinner a few years ago in Rome, described

---

[16] Rodger, P. C., Vischer, Lukas, eds., Section II, "Scripture, Tradition and Traditions," *The Fourth World Conference on* Faith and Order (New York: Association Press, 1964), p. 51.
[17] *The Constitution on Divine Revelation,* NCWC translation, St. Paul edition.
[18] (New York: Harper & Row, 1969), pp. 23, 24.
[19] *Slavery and Freedom* (New York: Scribner's, 1944), p. 262.

to me his sense of time. Author of *Christ and Time* and a more recent big volume, *Heilsgeschichte* ("salvation history"), Cullmann, a French Lutheran theologian, believes the event of Christ is the pivot point of time and history. "For me, history of salvation is a series of events, a special history in which we integrate ourselves," he said. "It is still developing in our church. We belong to our history of our own people, but by faith we enter a special history." Yet this history, "holy history," is acted out not in subjectivism or metahistory, but in the observable realities of linear or calendar history.

Paul Tillich also talked of *kairos,* a Greek word for the "fullness of time." In his *The Interpretation of History,* Tillich explained *kairos* as finding partial realization in the human community, particularly some kind of religious socialism:

> The term is meant to express the fact that the struggle for a new social order cannot lead to a fulfillment such as is meant by the Kingdom of God, but that at a special time special tasks are demanded, and one special aspect of the Kingdom of God appears as a demand and expectation. The Kingdom of God will always remain as transcendent; but it appears as a judgment to a given form of society and as a norm to a coming one. Thus, the decision for Socialism during a definite period may be the decision for the Kingdom of God, even though the Socialist ideal remains infinitely distant from the Kingdom of God.[20]

RETHINKING CALENDAR TIME

Christians can expect considerable rethinking about "calendar" time in the future. Life in space dictates different kinds of attitudes toward sabbaths and holy days. Orbiting around the earth, astronauts experience a number of sunrises and sunsets in the span of an "earth" day. That strange technical inverted cylinder world of "Rama" in Arthur Clarke's new novel, *Rendezvous with Rama,* had a peculiar kind of "day" just as other locations in space have different kinds of "days." Says Clarke: "As Rama rotated, the shadows of the short enigmatic structures near the axis swept steadily across the metal plain. The northern face of Rama was a gigantic sundial, measuring the swift passage of its four-minute day."[21]

What churchmen will be up against in regard to calendar time in

[20] Part I, trans. by Rosetski, N. A. (New York: Scribner's, 1936), pp. 57, 58.
[21] (New York: Harcourt, Brace, Jovanovich, Inc., 1973), p. 17.

the far distant future is hinted at in a book of mine fifteen years ago. In *Space-Age Sunday,* I had "two space missionaries," the first to head for Venus, skid their space bullet to a stop on that planet:

CECIL: Whee! We made it!

HENRY: Let's see, now—our Bible, our manual, the exterminator in case the people here aren't what we think they are, rations for two months. . . .

CECIL: Say, Henry, I didn't see the sun go down.

HENRY: No, I didn't either.

CECIL: Let's get out the manual. (*He thumbs the pages.*) Venus . . . calendar . . . ah, here we are. . . .

HENRY: You know, we should have checked into this before we left.

CECIL: Yes, but you can't do everything. (*He pauses intently.*) Now . . . a day on Venus . . . can be as much as thirty earth days!

HENRY: You mean the sun may not go down for thirty days? Horrors! . . . Only a dozen days in a year?

CECIL: That's interesting. . . . Ha, ha . . . our two-months rations are for two days, then, instead of two months. . . . Who would have ever thought of coming way out here with only two days of food?

HENRY: Well, you know, we really have more.

CECIL: Yes, of course. But enough of that. Have you the program all planned for the first worship service?

HENRY: Yes, but . . . which day will be Sunday? These people won't know anything about our earth scheme of things; besides, how could you divide twelve days into 365? Where should we begin Sunday and where should we stop?

CECIL: (*Pondering*): A Sunday one month long . . . we can't have any of that. It would work us to death!

HENRY: We'll have to give some real thought to that, Cecil. But first let's see what this place is like. Maybe the people will have some ideas of their own.

CECIL: (*As they open door*): Ooops! I stepped on something.

HENRY: A bug, isn't it?

BUG-LIKE CREATURE: Ya, ya, ya, kee, kee, kee, koh, koh, koh, bok, bok, bok. GRRRRRRRRRRRRRRRRRRRRRRRR!

NARRATOR: And the two space missionaries are back in their space bullet, zinging toward earth, with their two-months—or was it two-days—rations.[22]

In Ceylon, where Arthur Clarke lives, Christians have adapted to a Sunday-less new calendar. Following the Buddhist lunar calendar, the new system, inaugurated in 1965, has "weekends" or "poya days" which can fall on weekdays on a Monday afternoon or Tuesday or a Wednesday afternoon or Thursday, for instance. Protestants and Catholics continue to schedule service on days that would have been Sundays and people come before or after work. A Religious News Service report filed from Colombo, Ceylon, in January 1971, said church attendance in most cases appeared to be up in spite of the rescheduling of time.

Arthur Clarke tells me that the Eastern influence is likely to spread. Citing a viewpoint in his *The Deep Range,* he said, "I assumed that Buddhism would be the only running 'religion' in a hundred years. But, of course, Buddhists don't believe in God."

Dr. Karl Friedrich Basedow, head of the Foundation for Eastern Wisdom and Western Science, near Munich, talks of a special "divine perception" and "living a divine life in the state of meditation time." The special rapport with something beyond in meditation or in prayer experience does give a sense of the further dimensions of time, if not a suspension of time. In Eastern philosophy, time exists only to be conquered. In Hermann Hesse's *Siddhartha:* "Was then not all sorrow in time, all self-torment and fear in time? Were not all difficulties and evil in the world conquered as soon as one conquered time, as soon as one dispelled time?" Siddhartha, the young man in India who has sought long and desperately for truth in old age finds solace in the river which "is everywhere at the same time . . . everywhere, and that the present only exists for it. . . ."[23] And Hesse has Siddhartha in his moment of enlightenment at the end of the book declare: "Time is not real, Govinda. I have realized this repeatedly. And if time is not real, then the dividing line that seems to lie between this world and eternity, between suffering and bliss, between good and evil, is also an illusion."[24]

Science fiction and fantasy writers emphasize the interrelatedness

[22] (New York: Macmillan, 1960), pp. 138–39.
[23] (New York: Bantam, 1971; c. 1951, New Directions, New York), p. 107.
[24] Ibid., p. 143.

of time. From Alley Oop, the caveman in the comics, to H. G. Wells's *The Time Machine* novel of 1895 to Ray Bradbury's *The Martian Chronicles,* and Robert Silverberg's *Valley Beyond Time,* people can go forward or backward in time.

Bradbury's "The Third Expedition" in *The Martian Chronicles* makes both space and time subjective. In this story, the latest wave of astronauts on Mars are delighted as they are entertained by people they knew back on earth, some of them deceased. It is a trick of the Martians who can convert memories telepathically into reality. Memory time becomes real, as of course it does in many psychoses.

"What does it matter who is Past or Future, if we are both alive," one Bradbury Martian says. "For what follows will follow, tomorrow or in ten thousand years. How do you know that those temples are not the temples of your own civilization one hundred centuries from now, tumbled and broken? You do not know. Then don't ask. But the night is very short. . . ."[25] And in the same "Night Meeting" story of A.D. 2002, time is as real and pliable as matter:

> There was a smell of Time in the air tonight. He smiled and turned the fancy in his mind. There was a thought. What did Time smell like? Like dust and clocks and people. And if you wondered what Time sounded like it sounded like water running in a dark cave and voices crying and dirt dropping down upon hollow box lids, and rain. And, going further, what did Time *look* like? Time looked like snow dropping silently into a black room or it looked like a silent film in an ancient theater, one hundred billion faces falling like those New Year balloons, down and down into nothing. That was how Time smelled and looked and sounded. And tonight—Tomás shoved a hand into the wind outside the truck—tonight you could almost *touch* Time.[26]

In Silverberg's novel time as past, future, present stands still. Nothing happens in the valley to which various creatures, human and humanoid, are cast from around the galaxy. Not only does time stand still in the valley, but once they escape, they return to the particular

[25] (New York: Bantam, 1970; c. Doubleday & Co., Inc., 1950), "Night Meeting," p. 86.
[26] Ibid., p. 80.

moment at which they were taken by a special force. One of the women is now receiving a call she was about to answer before taken to the time valley. Back from the valley, the call is from the lover she met in the valley. A futurity in an instant of present or past time. Asher Sutton, in Clifford Simak's *Time and Again,* finds an old book signed in his own name, but bearing a date in the future, and the book becomes a ticket to a galactic empire far in the future.

Shangri-La in James Hilton's novel and two film versions by Frank Capra and Ross Hunter, all called *Lost Horizon,* is a place where time stops. In this mysterious paradise at least; outside the paradise, chronological age returns, and history is caught up. There are some interesting ways of looking at *Lost Horizon* timewise. A British diplomat on a peace mission to an Asian country ends up on a hi-jacked plane. They crash-land somewhere in the middle of an icy nowhere. They are met by a caravan from Shangri-La. An icy cave leads the group into the fertile valley of Shangri-La, past lush pools, waterfalls, luxurious gardens, and into a palace. Here the story continues as the diplomat, his brother and others stranded with him enjoy the setting, but quarrel with each other as to whether they should seek to return to the outside world or not. The hero, Richard Conway (Peter Finch in the new film version), already fallen in love with Catherine, the resident beauty (Liv Ullmann), is granted an audience with the high lama of Shangri-La (Charles Boyer). It turns out that the high lama, a 300-plus-year-old Belgian priest, brought Conway there to be his successor. What is Conway to do? His brother, George (Michael York), believes it is all a trick.

Eventually, the viewer asks himself what is real. Are private fantasies as real as life, as Billy Pilgrim's world of the planet Tralfamadore is in Kurt Vonnegut's *Slaughterhouse-Five?* Or, in recalling seventeenth century Irish bishop George Berkeley, is all reality the figment of perception? Does anything exist by itself? Most would assume the viewpoint of the novel and film is that of the main character, diplomat Conway. But try to understand this movie from the viewpoint of the high lama. Aged, near death, wise and visionary (perhaps in an old-folks home in reality), could not *Lost Horizon* be his own story, and all the other characters are figments of the old dying high lama's imagination instead of Conway's? And to go further in a psychological direction, why not assume that Shangri-La is one big mind, and the people that walk around it and the ideas they represent are thoughts of somebody's—everybody's—mind?

Is this a twentieth century *Pilgrim's Progress,* walking through a vision and a terrain of ideas? "Everything seems so familiar," wonders Conway about Shangri-La in the latest film version. "Look inside yourself," intones Shangri-La's Catherine.

Movies open up some of the more profound questions of time. Alain Resnais, in his French new wave films, of the 1960s, mixed up time. In his *Last Year at Marienbad,* you have no idea as to what is real time or dream time. A number of things happen, but there is no way to know who is actually around or who is merely the creature of imagination. The events are clearer in his *Hiroshima Mon Amour,* but the flashbacks are so real and poignant you don't know whether the girl from France emotionally survived her lover, a war casualty in France, or on the other hand whether her new Japanese acquaintance ever survived the emotional ordeal of the holocaust of Hiroshima. Certain events dominate other events that occur in time. Among other films, Paramount's *Ulysses* of twenty years ago views in only a minute the actions of a day in the lives of two Irishmen, as if real time can be sifted down into a small crisp. Past, present, and future mix together in an old German film, *Secrets of the Soul,* as images are superimposed to suggest a dream world. Luis Buñuel's *The Discreet Charm of the Bourgeoisie* follows various plot directions, only to have the viewer see somebody wake up from a dream. Another line of action suddenly begins, very realistically, only to come out also as somebody's dream. Ingmar Bergman has a corpse sit up and talk (*Cries and Whispers*), a passer-by imagine that he is in a coffin (*Wild Strawberries*), a hero put off "death" with a game of chess (*The Seventh Seal*).

THE GOD-TIME RIDDLE

Bergman, particularly in a trilogy on silence in the universe (*Through a Glass Darkly, Winter Light,* and *The Silence*), delves in God concepts as he deals with time. God is always there—as the bearer of death and judgment or as a force to limit time. Time and God are both abstract, but when defined, both become concrete or material within time. A unique feature of Christianity is the effort to mix God and time. "God was in Christ, reconciling the world unto himself. . . ."

For Erich von Däniken, however, you cannot mix God and Time. Bound by classical definitions that God has to be above all and before all and beyond all, Von Däniken said in an interview: "This so-called Big God of Christianity must be timeless. If not, then he is not God. He has to be before, and after. For a true God to wait to see the results of something (which God has started) is ridiculous. A real God can never have human feelings. This timeless God created Adam and Eve, but knows they will sin. Free will or not, he knows the result, and he is mad, and punishes the rest of them and this true God is happy again! and his own son has to be killed in a terrible way! This is pure nonsense. So I have to ask myself how do you explain consciousness and the ego, what is the beginning of everything?" Or, you can go the way of a limited God, the God in the process of becoming, the limited God of Edgar Sheffield Brightman, who described God as "finite-infinite" in his books (*Personality and Religion, A Philosophy of Religion,* etc.)

Or you can go the way of the linguistic analysts who believe the name of God is literally meaningless or the way of other "death of God" theologians who believed that God "emptied" himself out in the person of Jesus Christ, and therefore is limited—in time. Whatever the course, theologians and popular writers alike have had difficulty facing the God-time riddle. Just how and why did God enter time? The birth of Jesus leaves more questions than it answers. God became man, out of love? Why? Does love entail death? Does time make God helpless in history, at crucifixions, etc.? In what way is God limited? How do you define a God-man?

Incarnation—an event of the intersection of eternal and historical time—must always remain a riddle. It may be true, but it is not explainable. But to opt solely for a limited God within time, for whatever reason, strips God of godly powers and makes him a non-God. Further, to opt for Von Däniken, courts a basic problem. Not only does a God that must always be above everything become nothing, or a substitute for a substitute, etc., but such a God becomes a victim of time. If deity or "something other" has no meaning time has no meaning. Time becomes then only a procession of marking off earth days. Time without God then is not thinkable. Time is meaningful in meditation, but meaningless in isolation. Like a prisoner in solitary confinement, you can mark progression. But slip up once, or forget where you are, then there is no "time," not even in a concrete sense (until a calendar is created again).

Besides the inadequate incarnation answers of Christian apologists on the one hand, and the overly demanding fantasies of Von Däniken and traditional deists, on the other hand, maybe a hint could be taken from Jesus' own phraseology concerning the meaning of the meshing of time and ultimate reality. He said: "I *am* the light of the world" (John 8:12) and "I *am* the bread of life" (John 6:35) and compared himself to the living water (John 4:10). And there is the analogy of God as light and love in 1 John (1:5; 4:8). "God *is* love. . . ." Perhaps, without pushing an analogy too far, one can also say, if God is love (what does that mean?) God is also time (what does that mean?), or God is like time, as God is also like love.

GOD AS TIME

God who has no boundaries can be compared to time which has no boundaries. God identifies with time. So time is best regarded widely. Otherwise God is limited, when time is limited. Yet you can think of God himself as the "matter" of eternal time. The "body" of God holds together all notions of time—linear, cyclical, progressive and goal directed, mystical, and even timelessness. God brings together and coalesces various kinds of time. A theology of the future, especially for Christians, might seek to hold together the various kinds of time, instead of going in fragmented directions with only one or several kinds of time concepts.

Christmas, for instance, would be more than an event of linear or historical time. Some new twilight dimensions, with new cosmic awareness and interplanetary births as well as new kinds of psychic births within a person's mind, may become areas of concerns for Christmases of the twenty-second century. God as (or like) time, and his Son, as (or like) time—pinpointed, ascended, returned, mystical, within a concept that is God himself. With God as, or like, "time," avatars, gurus, and even Christs can exist within or as part of such "Matter" of time. With God and time related, and both as all-inclusive, there can be little talk of the end of the world and an end of time for judgmental purposes. It's not merely that an end or consummation of the world is no longer a viable concept with God and time as all inclusive. But more immediately there remains little need for chronicling of progression. The evolutionists—the physical side with Charles Darwin and the spiritual side with Pierre Lecomte du Noüy and Père Teilhard de Chardin—have little meaning when there is no peak or pinnacle to which everything is moving at the tick of a clock. With God and time open ended and mutually inclusive neither the inconsistencies and fragmentations in history nor a future moment of consummation have any special meaning. For there will still be something beyond, even mankind and whatever other creatures that now or may exist. Further, counter to any rational sense of consummation, man may even destroy himself arbitrarily before any logical or evolved end of the world.

If God is time in a broad way, or like time, God is a mystery. Who being within time can fathom time? If God is ever fulfilled, he becomes a limited thing. If time is ever fulfilled, then there is nothingness or nihilism. Time and God need each other, so to speak, but if there is ever consummation or fulfillment, the act is fatal to the other. God and time are interrelated. And the Gospel of John hints just that: "In the *beginning* was the Word, and the Word was with God, and the Word was *God*" (John 1:1). God, and Incarnation, and Time—together, a mystery.

NOT PANTHEISM BUT PANENTHEISM

There are attempts to grapple with the "totality" of existence that go beyond the themes of progression and consummation. Once there was "pantheism," that God is everywhere and in everything. This left the direction of history open to theologizing and manipulation. God was just "there" and "in." Time was still plotted and pointed by theologians and philosophers to certain directions. But in Toronto at the annual International Convention of the Religious Education Association in November, 1973, there was talk of "pan*en*theism." Matthew Fox, a Dominican priest and chairman of the religious studies department of Barat College, Lake Forest, Illinois, led a workshop on "Panentheistic Spirituality: The Religious Education of Tomorrow?" He defined "panentheism" as "an experience of the whole." Beyond pantheism, which is a passive look at the universe, panentheism emphasizes experience, not of a doctrine or revelation or a Deity, but the experience of the whole.

Similarly, Gene Roddenberry, creator of "Star Trek" on TV, has a view of God that meshes with the view that links God and time in a total context. "God is not a being," Roddenberry said in his Warner Brothers studio, Burbank, California. "God is the sum of all intelligences, all operating now. If God is beyond time, he is not an entity. If God is matter, he is controlled by the things he created." Roddenberry goes on to suggest a "cyclical" theory of history different from a Greek cyclical political theory of history repeating itself.

Possibly, Roddenberry says, "we created ourselves." And man creates god. And God-man creates man, and so on. Certainly, biologically mankind creates itself. The process somehow is self-perpetuating.

If God is not limited to any special kind of time, space, or galaxy, the possibilities of God are greater. In a way, the Muslim concept of God hints at this "open" inclusiveness: "God will continue creating, and maybe recycling. Even after the death of the earth, he can continue creating," said Muhammad Tahir, of Washington, D.C., editor of *Islamic Items,* in an interview. Tahir, noting that the Koran says God created all creatures, adds, "They [creatures] could be on earth or other planets. Mankind is just a small segment of God's creation."

The past, the present, and the future thus become irrelevant. There is always more. And thus it makes sense to define God as or like "time," but not to leave "time" as merely past, present, or future, with pre-existence or post-existence. God is always something more (yet allowing for a character of God in history). Time remains open-ended, and most assuredly when that is so, then past, present, and future are open-ended also.

CHAPTER IV

The Experiments of the Present

"For us, the most interesting approach to the future of religion is to look at those experiments, new movements and renaissance of old myths and community forms which seem to be catching hold and pointing the way towards the future," said the Reverend Dr. John E. Biersdorf, former director of the department of ministry of the National Council of Churches at "Insearch: The Future of Religion in America" conference in Chicago in 1973.

Biersdorf, now director of the Advanced Pastoral Studies Institute in Cranbrook, Bloomfield Hills, Michigan, said in his keynote speech at the Chicago meeting a look at present happenings has its faults but may be more fruitful for religion than other attempts at forecasting. One of the other ways, he said, would be to side with the futurists and their scientific efforts, among them, a polling of experts (delphi method) and "envelope" forecasting, or mapping of a general curve based on "rates of speed" of development. Still another way, he said, could be to look at the trends in religion. "We can rely upon the future forecasting increasingly practiced in secular society to describe the societal constraints and value issues to which organized religion must respond," Biersdorf said, thus acknowledging that religion finds a part of its shape in reacting to culture. But, he added, the secular forecasters merely "draw lines into the future by continuing trends already known in the present . . . they are unable by definition to include any unknown trends and developments."

Forecasting on the basis of trends in religion falls into the same error as forecasts of futurists on present data in society, he says. "These projections [from trends] suffer from the same defects . . . they are surprise-free, and if there is anything predictable about the history of religion, it is that it will contain surprises. One need only imagine a commentator in A.D. 1500 forecasting the future of the church on the basis of existing data to realize the futility of relying solely on known trends." Today's trends, he says, include the slowdown in growth of religious organizations, the leveling off of membership, the fluctuating in the financial picture, cutbacks in staffs, dumping of social action programs. "The picture that results is one of decline in growth and support, increasing conservatism, dissatisfaction among clergy, decreasing confidence among laity, and increasing alienation among young people." A scenario based on such trends could be dismal indeed.

But Biersdorf adds: "Malaise and decline are not the whole story. . . . Here and there persons and groups are creating alternative futures. . . . They are modeling the future now, so that the surveys of 1980 will record their effectiveness in changing the shape of organized religion." They may be effective despite the fact that some of them will "go out of existence or persist only as marginal groups." Biersdorf proceeded to lead the Chicago conference to concentrate on the new exciting endeavors of churchmen.

SOME "VITAL EXAMPLES"

Biersdorf called attention to current categories of religious experience today, and found examples of a consciousness of the future in each. There were Pentecostal revivals, house churches, communal groups, liturgical experiments, etc. A list of two hundred groups was compiled, with fifty-six reported in detail to the Chicago conference. Biersdorf explained:

The aim was to study at least one vital example of each major variation on the four dimensions of theological tradition, organizational form, mission and strategy focus, and composition. The term "vital example" refers to the following criteria, used as appropriate in each case. First, reported power and authenticity of community experience as reported by members and outsiders. Secondly, effectiveness in changing lives of members and/or accomplishing mission tasks in the community around them as reported by members and outsiders. Third, clarity and visibility of group identity and goals. Fourth, when appropriate, the length of time the group has been able to sustain its vitality and existence. Fifth, when appropriate, growth in membership and budget.

Among groups cited in Biersdorf's report as setting future styles for religion in the United States:

—*Koinonia Missionary Baptist Church, Gary, Indiana.* Founded in 1971, the Koinonia Church began with fifty adults and a large group of youth after a dispute and split in another Gary church. The group, taking the name of "koinonia" from the Greek for "fellowship," bought a former Greek Orthodox church and community center. The Koinonia church launched a recreational program and an educational effort that included an "Opportunities Industrialization Center," which centered largely on vocational education. The center is linked with the Reverend Leon Sullivan's Opportunities Center. Founded in 1964 in Philadelphia, the OIC program has one hundred centers with a budget of $7 million in one hundred cities. The Gary church, seeking black empowerment, also has a co-operative buying program to "increase our self-reliance" and to "keep profits inside the Koinonia community that otherwise would be going to white merchants and not benefiting the black community."

—*Old Cambridge (Massachusetts) Baptist Church.* In the absence of a minister on leave, this "university" church in which Harvey Cox and others take part in the program, decided on a collective ministry in the pulpit and in other functions normally reserved to the minister. The church had its Lenten and other special meetings in the homes over the years. Task forces of laymen minister to prisoners or take part in civil rights demonstrations. A discussion group formed along vocational lines, called the Lay Associates, deals with issues related to the work week. A book of Celebrations and Concerns is the base for worship, with entertainers, for example, a cast of *Godspell,* taking part in the service.

—*The King's Temple, Seattle.* Founded by Charlotte Baker, who comes from a Pentecostal background, King's Temple has set its own course in the new charismatic movement. Most members are young, between twenty and thirty, and although there are no official restrictions, most do not dance, go to movies, use make-up, or smoke or drink. Faith healing and casting out of demons are part of the life of the church. People are chosen for work in the church through a process of "prophetic" blessing, an inspiration imparted and made known through the laying on of hands. Members accept these revelations of a special calling and proceed to serve in various pastoral ministries, plus visitation, music, intercessory prayer, mission work, etc. The temple has two services on Sunday, and one each on Tuesday and Thursday evenings. Besides a Sunday School, it also has a Bible academy, which meets four mornings a week, an evening Bible school on Mondays, and a young people's night on Friday. The worship is a lively form with "a semi-free flow" of "sung and spoken" words. An organ, piano, and a six-piece orchestra mix with the various chants and praises in strange tongues.

—*Open End, San Anselmo, California.* The 250 members of Open End, most of them middle-class and middle-aged, regard themselves as "a non-residential community that seeks to offer alternative and deeper levels of community to suburbanites." Sensitivity training is a part of the approach. There are group meetings, encounter groups, dance therapy, fun weekends of skiing and hiking. The group serves as the communication center for "Well Being," a national association of "human" community-building groups. The Open End programs and activities are headquartered in a large rented house and several other buildings. Open End has an "enabler" or co-ordinator, and group leaders, who meet once a month for training, hold sessions on various topics in homes. The organization has no creed, but attempts to meet "religious needs" through a "wide choice of community intensity."

—*First United Church, Newton, Massachusetts.* Three parishes of the United Church of Christ came together on a trial basis to see if they could operate as one parish. Problems included dwindling finances. The three churches included First Church, which dates back to 1664 and which since 1952 had lost two-thirds of its membership. The others were Second church, down one-third, and the Eliot church, which was facing a conflict between its old-timers and social-action-minded youth. In the combined program, a family service is held at 8:30 A.M. Sunday at the Eliot church and two services, traditional and contemporary, in two parts of the Second church at 11 A.M. A popular Friday night program of supper and activities for various age groups takes place at the Eliot church. Plans call for three "professionals" or clergy and one lay administrator to serve the joint parish.

Biersdorf's report for the Chicago conference also listed: *work communes* such as Earth Light in Cambridge, Massachusetts; Emmaus House, New York City; Lighthouse Ranch, Loleta, California. *Special agencies,* such as Teen Challenge, Riverside, California; the Love of Children Task Force of the Church of Our Savior, Washington, D.C.; Joint Health Venture, of Los Angeles; and the Chicago Center for Black Religious studies. *Meditative communities* such as the Abbey (Trappist) of New Clairveaux, Vina, California, and the Tail of the Tiger (Tibetan Buddhist) community, Barnet, Vermont. *Experimental congregations,* such as St. Francis Presbyterian, Ft. Worth, Texas; Now Church, San Jose, California; COACT (Community of Active Christians Today), Waco, Texas; Catholic Study and Discussion Group, Springfield, Massachusetts, and Church of the Celebration (Protestant), San Dimas, California.

Biersdorf, in a summary of these groups, noted one common denominator:

> Most of the groups, whatever their other goals, were preoccupied with the realization of an intimate community. The appeal of the applied behavorial sciences and the human potential movement is that they promise to make Judaeo-Christian teachings of love and community operational in the life of the group that adopts their methods. But Pentecostal or orthodox groups such as King's Temple also emphasize these values, and count the realization of a loving community as the most important sign of their fidelity to the gospel. The value of intimate community is so ubiquitous among the groups interviewed that it tends to overshadow other goals and interests. It would seem that these groups are responding, some even unwittingly, to a primary need and problem in contemporary culture. Prudent bets on growth potential can be placed by policy makers on those groups which meet that need most directly and powerfully.

Chicago priest-sociologist Andrew Greeley, speaking at the George Dayton Foundation Conference on the Future, Hudson, Wisconsin, in October 1969, also wondered whether the off-beat contra-status-quo groups might have a greater spark of life and perpetuity. "The critical question," he said, "is whether organized religion is ready to face the fact that some underground communities may indeed represent the authentic working of the Spirit who still blows whither He wills."

THE EMERGING CHURCH

The future of the church, denominations and all, proved to be the basis for an interesting exercise of the emotions at the Emerging Church Conference in Chicago, one of the five regional settings of the conference sparked by the Faith and Work movement. In a "game" to determine the nature of the church in the future, participants were given a cup. "This cup is the church as an institution; do to this cup as you feel, not as you think you ought to feel," said Lyman Coleman, director of the Halfway House, Newton, Pennsylvania, and author of *The Coffee House Itch, Acts Alive,* and other books.

The delegates to this all-clergy conference broke into small groups, and silently did to the cup as they felt moved. All tried to guess the meaning of the actions of the others. One man dropped it, then picked it up. He explained that you just can't drop the church. "You pick up what you love," he said.

The second man tore and punched holes in the cup. Meaning: "The Holy Spirit can't be confined. The church as an institution is still there even when it is full of holes, letting the spirit in and out." A third wrote, "understanding, joy, and humility" on the bottom of his cup. Meaning: "These words are the foundation of the church," and the "doormat" between church and world. A fourth, a college president, set the cup down and then moved it to his foot. Meaning: The institution can be set aside, but this is still where man stands, regardless of what he does to it. A fifth, black evangelist William Pannell, member of the Tom Skinner evangelism crusade team, drew a ladder inside the cup. Meaning: There is still hope for the church despite the bias and racial lily whiteness of the "cup."

A reporter took the cup, when it was his turn, wadded it up, and chewed it to a pulp. This thoroughly got the little group discussing until time for all small groups to come back for a general synthesis with the conference leaders. Meaning of the chewed-up cup: First, in the process of wadding up the cup, compressing it, the church is "up tight" and uneasy as it shares in society's tensions. Further, the gesture of eating the cup symbolized the potential total disappearance of an institution, even as Christ said of the visible institution in His day, "not one stone shall stand." Meaning, further: The church is a people of God, and institutions, while they must exist, can be started as new and are never absolute in themselves. The church as a permanent institution becomes as nothing.

All this activity about a cup typified the mood of the five "1970 National Clergy Conferences" which took up the question of the shape of the emerging church. Most participants were conservative, white, suburban clergymen. They created a rising new voice that the wind of change in the church is compatible with evangelical theology as well as with the radical theology of the non-church movement of the activists.

Initiating the conferences with the Faith at Work organization of New York City were various committees and groups handling the local arrangements in Atlanta, Dallas, Los Angeles, Kansas City, and New York, as well as Chicago. In Chicago, a new organization, Christian Laymen of Chicago, started by Dean Griffith, executive vice-president of Griffith Laboratories, and a Methodist, helped with the plans and promotion. Barry Rankin, forty-four, a former member of the Roman Catholic Passionist Fathers, with a Ph.D. from Angelicum University in Rome, is CLC associate executive director. Christian Laymen of Chicago, Rankin said in an interview, "promotes small groups of Christians who meet regularly to search out a deeper personal life." The goals are the same for the national Faith at Work, which promotes small groups, personal testimonies, and emphasizes the power of the Holy Spirit. In some Faith at Work local chapters, there is an interest in faith healing.

Those 1970 National Clergy Conferences on "The Emerging Church" foresaw a church entirely new, yet keeping (1) the same old doctrines of the "old time religion" and (2) institutional shells. But there would be little preoccupation with life after death. Like the radical modern reformers, who are more at home with non-church building task forces and home groups, the conservative renewalists are concerned with the here and now.

"Maybe we are not in the last days, but beginning a new day," said the Reverend Bruce Larson, a United Presbyterian and president of Faith at Work, in the Chicago keynote speech. "Instead of a holding operation, maybe we are to snatch a few brands from the fire, and come into a discovery of what we have been experimenting with, a sense of joy." He urged emphasizing in theology: (1) An active God. "We must allow God to function. We must discover God is with people, instead of only bringing Christ *to* people." (2) A relational principle. "People support that with which they can relate." Also, "There is a new facet of a relational, or incarnational, theology, emphasizing that Christ was made flesh, and that humanity is related and Christ's followers are related in one body." (3) A vulnerability. "The Christian stance is to be vulnerable," recognizing his weaknesses and inadequacies. Larson cited the humility of Pope John XXIII and Pope John's willingness to be "vulnerable" and his friendly style with all. "The Holy Spirit, if He convicts you [conservative term for being under the total power of the Holy Spirit], doesn't need for us to lay it on."

Evangelist Pannell described the new concern. "Jesus didn't drop Gospel tracts from the sky or shout from the back of a Gospel chariot," said Pannell. "Jesus came, looked a man square in the eye and said 'you are something else. I can't stand spending eternity without you. You and I have to get together.' And He did this effectively by becoming a 'nigger,' a term for the most opprobrious in society. My preacher friends wince at that. But that kind of God can get to me. That's why I'm here. It's a whole new ball game. We see a whole new brotherhood of people who hurt and let it all hang out and scream at once. All colors, shapes and hues are getting together. It's a whole new crowd of hurtin' damn niggers—people who hurt and see themselves as victims of a callous majority. Only thing we have in common is loneliness, hurt and alienation."

Larson, believing in "a two-legged gospel," predicted a new polarity in the church away from liberal vs. conservative, on doctrines, to a "new polarity of the personal vs. the impersonal. What is dead is impersonal evangelism vs. impersonal liberalism."

THE SHOPPING CENTER CHURCH

New attempts at outreach produced new forms, among them the shopping center church. Lutherans operated a youth drop-in center at one of the busy basement areas of the Northland Mall, Southfield, Michigan. The Salt Cellar served aimless and alienated teens, among others, who dropped in to sit and talk beneath wild art and photo and poetry displays, sometimes seeing a brief film. Eventual pressure from management of the shopping center, who regarded the youth as troublesome and contrary to the commercial intents of the mall, caused this one to close down.

However, some more traditional approaches in shopping centers have fared well. The churches of Arvada, Colorado, hold community Thanksgiving services outdoors in the hustle and bustle of pre-Christmas shopping in the concourse area of the Arvada Plaza Shopping Center. Processions from churches, the West High School band and pop club music, and sermons and litanies fill the scene. The Reverend Dr. Harvey Everett, of Valley Forge, Pennsylvania, parish development secretary of the American Baptist Convention, estimates that twenty different styles have sprung up with 150 to 250 new projects in the last several years. "There are some resemblances between these shopping center ministries and the 'church on the square' in the old New England town," Dr. Everett said. "But they're geared to people in a new age, among the new 'mall ministries.'"[1] Among the mall projects, there are Smith Haven Ministries, an ecumenical work with store owners and employees, at Lake Grove, New York; the Church on the Mall, ecumenical, in an enclosed mall at Plymouth Meeting, Pennsylvania; Agora, of the United Church of Christ, Oak Brook Shopping Center, Oak Brook, Illinois; and a ministry to high-rise apartment residents at Landmark Shopping Center, Alexandria, Virginia. One of the more elaborate shopping mall ministries has been in the Pittsburgh area. A Ministry in the Mall is financed by twenty churches and synagogues. Fifty volunteers direct people to find help for their special needs. The volunteers also run a Saturday night coffeehouse in the mall's community room. Director is Lyndon Whybrew, a young Presbyterian.

New retirement centers and complex high-rise and suburban housing developments offer new church possibilities. In Seal Beach, California, at the Leisure World retirement community of 22,000, the Southern California Council of Churches led in the organizing of a congregation. The Leisure World Community Church there now has 1,500 members from twenty-seven denominations. Forty-three retired ministers, missionaries and their wives help with the leadership. The oldsters do many things, from tutoring to saving stamps for buying thirty tons of food for hungry world children.

[1] Associated Press, George Cornell, January 7, 1970.

There are four men fellowship groups, and prayer-Bible study and "self-discovery" groups in the home units.

Churches and synagogues have rented apartments for services in some new high rises. These include the West End apartments in New York, and the Jeffries high-rise apartment buildings in Detroit. Detroit priests have rented apartments together in order to bring a witness to apartment buildings. On Milwaukee's east side near Lake Michigan is Juneau Village, 1,800 units in high-rise apartments serving 2,300 upper middle-class residents. The Board of American Missions of the Lutheran Church in America sent in the Reverend Dr. Eric J. Gustavson. Over 2,600 square feet of space between a bank and cocktail lounge in the adjoining shopping center was leased at $11,000 a year. Gustavson began recruiting, not by ringing door bells, but by showing up at village functions, the swimming pool, and in other settings. Most of the residents are retired couples. The rented church space is used for Sunday morning worship, discussions, dinners, exhibits, recitals, films, lectures, and plays. College students in the Milwaukee area take over to provide a coffeehouse, The Ark, on Saturday nights.

THE COFFEEHOUSE MINISTRY

The coffeehouse ministries continue to spring up and meet a need, although one of the pioneers in this movement, Malcolm Boyd, who rode to fame counseling and reading poetry in coffeehouses, churchly and secular, believes they are now generally passé. He says, "I do not have much to do with coffeehouses now. There is a lot of sincerity with them, and they are a place for teens who don't want to be at home. But there is a real need now for coffeehouses to go through an identity crisis. They are too easy and too predictable. There is not much radicalization. In the old days, they were not bland, but instruments of radicalization, and the church should be particularly a place of radicalization. Now they tend to represent conformity, the ones I see."

More than 2,000 coffeehouses were estimated to be in the United States by Religious News-Features at the start of the '70s. Sixty-five per cent of them were operated by churches. Methodists lead the number, but more than half of the coffeehouses are interfaith. Opening up in garages, church basements, boiler rooms, even in an icehouse, they have names such as "The Catacombs," "Içthus"

("Fish"), "The Needle's Eye," "Upper Room," "The Word," "Kontemplation," "The Lavender Mushroom," "The Last Drop," "Inn Security," and "The Trek." The coffeehouse was supposed to represent a kind of bridge between the secular and sacred without affront to each other. But a malaise has set in. "The Ark," a coffeehouse in the old parsonage of Zion Lutheran Church, Fort Wayne, Indiana, reported complaints from teens such as, "I've lost interest. We just can't get anybody involved. Maybe there are too many school things to do."[2]

THE THEATER IN THE CHURCH

Among innovations there is the theater church. Near the United Nations, in New York City, Lutherans had a theater cabaret at noontime in one of their churches. Also in New York Judson Memorial (American Baptist) Church, which has departed from the usual chance melodramatic plays, turned to serious new productions. Associate pastor Al Carmines, a full-faced actor, singer, composer, produced an off-Broadway hit, an adaptation of Gertrude Stein's *In Circles,* with music by Carmines, which won an off-Broadway best musical "Obie" award. The New York *Post* called the Judson theater effort "the most original and stimulating theater in all New York" and the New York *Times* said, "There is no livelier theater in New York than the Judson Memorial Church." On Sunday morning, there is a certain sense of spontaneity as people get up and talk or read clippings. But most startling is the physical arrangement—all pews are gone, the chancel area is stripped of furniture and carpeting and the people, freaks and straight alike, sit around in a circle. Many of the Jesus People, particularly in their early stages at the start of the '70s, had an abhorrence to pews. And there is a Jewish reaction against the formality and regimentation, too. The Stephen W. Wise Free Synagogue in Los Angeles features movable chairs instead of pews.

St. Mark's-in-the-Bouwerie in New York has a play-producing group, "Theater Genesis," started by a former film actor, Ralph Cook. He describes his theater program there as "a deeply subjective kind of realism." It is an "indigenous theater. The actors, directors and writers are members of a geographical community and

2 Thiele, Norma, "The Ark Coffee House Runs into Rough Seas," *Lutheran Witness Reporter,* February 16, 1969.

we are presenting plays for members of that community, not as a special gala event, but as an integral everyday part of the life of that community." Plays there have included *Fruit Salad,* an indictment of war, and a surrealistic rock-and-roll picture of Americans in another production.[3]

Glide Memorial, San Francisco, is probably the best known of the "show" churches, and critics of the pastor, Cecil Williams, who has been in the public eye in many ways, including a go-between in the Patty Hearst kidnapping in 1974, have described his appearances before Methodist and other conventions as a "road show." Williams depends heavily on the use of psychedelic lights, rock ensembles, and a packed sanctuary of youths who on Sunday morning lock arms and rock and dance in the aisles and chancel.

"There may still be a sanctuary or nave in the church in the future, but it will not be a place to be preached at," said Dale Rott, a professor of drama at Bethel College, St. Paul, Minnesota. The church service, he feels, should develop out of the experience of members. "The man in the pew may know more of the technological new world than the clergyman," he said. Both Rott, former president of the Religion Project of American Educational Theater Association, and his successor, James Young, professor of drama, University of Massachusetts, favor "happenings" or "improvising" in the aisles, along with standard plays or excerpt scenes to illustrate sermons. They told of one church drama on the theme of "A confession of violence." "A kid pantomimes a toy soldier to the tune of Victor Herbert's 'The Toy Soldier'; He 'kills' other toy soldiers [actors]; then there are actual battle sounds; the toy soldiers come to life, move people out of the front rows and build barricades, and 'kill' each other again; there follows a folk song of a prayer for peace; chairs in the drama used for barriers in the pretended war are restacked as an altar and the congregation comes forward to join in a prayer of confession."

All Saints (Pasadena) Episcopal Church has had a contemporary liturgy of a theatrical nature at 9 A.M. Sundays twice a month. "We long ago threw the Trial Liturgy [new Episcopalian ritual] aside and wrote our own," said the Reverend Father George R. Regas, rector. "We can't talk about responding to racial crises, poverty, and still use the Prayer Book worship," he said. "If we're going to be

[3] Hughes, Catharine, "The Church Is 'Where It's At,'" *The Catholic World,* Vol. 208, No. 1245, December 1968, p. 130.

alive to the contemporary world, we have to trust the black man, but also talk to God." In one liturgy, he said, "We brought in The Geronimo Black Band for All Saints' Day. He [the leader] wrote his own service about twenty contemporary saints such as Rachel Carson, Ghandi, Pope John, etc."[4]

THE "FLOATING PARISH"

"Floating parishes" or rotating parishes not assigned to one location are found across the country. In Cleveland, Ohio, the forty-five-member Congregation of the Reconciliation has a free-form liturgy once a month, usually combined with an afternoon retreat and Sunday dinner. In good weather, the program is sometimes held in a park. The congregation, which has a Presbyterian pastor was formed originally to express concern over racial issues.

Roman Catholics have been in the forefront of experimenting with "floating" parishes. Back in 1966, the "floating" John XXIII was launched in Oklahoma City, and six months later, in 1967, the Community of the Living Christ began in Tulsa. The John XXIII parish, described as "experimental" and "nonterritorial," had "the threefold aim of developing among its members a relevant, meaningful liturgy, more effective social action programs and a deepened sense of community—values which petitioners felt were lacking in local parishes."[5] Starting with thirty members, the group reached one hundred members in a year, and by 1973 had settled down in a rented church building. The parish went through three stages, a study shows: a concern with social issues, a turning inwardly to seek spiritual renewal, and more recently a "workshop" phase. "Usually held in a member's home, workshops have treated such issues as unfair real estate practices, penal reform, the person of Christ, interpersonal and marital communication and alternative life styles."[6]

The Community of the Living Christ in Tulsa paralleled the aims and the stages of development of its predecessor in Oklahoma City, but by 1973 had begun to decline drastically—a development blamed on a more rapid rate of transfer from the area of its mem-

---

[4] Foley, June, "All Saints', Pasadena," in a special issue on "The Parish," *The Episcopalian,* Vol. 135, No. 5, May 1970, p. 22.
[5] "Experimental Parishes—Two Case Histories," *National Catholic Reporter,* October 19, 1973, p. 7.
[6] Ibid.

bers who found their jobs sent them to other parts of the country. This second parish also had problems with changes in leadership as several priests, one ailing, sought to help it along.

In Detroit, the Cardinal Leger "floating" parish began in 1968, met in schools, parks, homes, and by lake sides. Liturgy was very informal, with communion distributed to all present in an informal, friendly setting. Although the Leger community, named after the Montreal cardinal who quit to go to Africa as a missionary, appears to be the only Detroit floating congregation to be constituted officially as a parish, the Archdiocese boasted a dozen experimental, floating kinds of parishes in the mid-1970s. A chancery official celebrates mass for one of the congregations in the War Memorial building in Grosse Pointe.

One of the newest "floating" parishes in the Detroit Archdiocese is the Living Worship community on the city's northwest side. Drawing members from a split from a more staid traditional parish, this group usually met in the home of one of the organizers. A young priest, the Reverend Father Joseph Schillmoeller, celebrated mass in the home in his plain blue suit, with white and blue tie, and a narrow stole, his only priestly garment thrown over his shoulders. He held a big Bible in his hands, as he gave a short sermon. Before him was a table altar draped with a cloth that said, "Community: Living Worship." During the mass nearly everybody had a part. The kids, who had been playing in the basement, were brought up to recite a pledge for peace for children. During the time usually allotted for the quick kiss of peace or hand shaking, members walked around, shook hands, chatted for a while before mass was resumed. Teens sat among them, sang and played guitars, and parents, many in sportswear, sat around on the floor.

OTHER ROMAN CATHOLIC EXPERIMENTS

In other Roman Catholic experiments, there is the "mini parish." A Redemptorist priest in the Diocese of Lansing, Michigan, for instance, organizes local parishes in small groups of ten families in each group, or "Communions," as the priest, the Reverend Father John R. McPhee, calls the groups. In each group, each member prays each day for the other members. In addition, a "correspondent couple," or chair couple, goes to a home and picks up an item such as a cross, Bible, or a banner and takes it from house to house, and then leaves it in the next key home, thus performing a link between the families. There is also the "mediator" who looks over several communions and serves as the link to the priest who in turn is a link to the bishop. The mediator also serves as a bulwark between a parish pastor or laymen from the parish council who might want to run it all.

And headquartered in Kansas City (where there is also the ecumenical St. Mark's parish with its new building involving three Protestant denominations and Roman Catholics) is the new semi-official Society of Our Lady of the Most Holy Trinity, traditional in theology (Marian and Trinitarian) but radical in membership (lay and clergy) and radical in its devotion to social needs. Founded in 1957 by the Reverend Father James A. Flanagan, a Boston priest, with the approval of Richard Cardinal Cushing, the Society was organized in Santa Fe, at the invitation of the Most Reverend Edwin Byrne, archbishop of New Mexico. The first members were women who had accompanied Father Flanagan to the rural Mora Valley in the Sangre de Cristo mountains a hundred miles from Santa Fe. Several single lay people came in the first fall to work in a parish school and to start a small clinic in a local parish with Father Flanagan. In 1960, the first family joined the Society. They had four children.

With the death of Archbishop Byrne in 1964, the group was asked to leave by his successor. They settled in Kansas City at the invitation of the Kansas City-St. Joseph bishop, the Most Reverend Charles Helmsing. Soon there were over seventy members, including three priests, fourteen sisters, six married couples and their children, eighteen single lay people, and nine seminarians. In 1970, a member of the first graduating class of perpetual (married) deacons, a renewed order in the Roman Catholic church, set out from Kansas City for the Society with plans to do mission work in Central America. Most of the Society members work in the United States with migrants and Indians (Sioux, in South Dakota). One sister is a midwife in Ethiopia. Those in the Kansas City area work at other jobs and contribute their salaries. In Kansas City they work with inmates in the Jackson County jail and conduct a suicide round-the-clock-prevention service, Human Rescue, Inc. They have a community mass on Saturday evening and vespers on Sunday.

The New York *Times* says there are now some sixty "new religious communities" in the United States existing "outside the legal and financial jurisdiction of the Roman Catholic and Protestant churches."[7] The *Times* article cites the Family Service Corps, a group of fourteen women, most of them former nuns. The Corps seeks to minister to various social needs in the city without the restrictions of the "rigidly organized orders."

NO MORE BRICKS AND MORTAR

A development very important to the emergence of new formats is the decrease of preoccupation with the church building. This is probably not noticed by most, as congregations continue to build or at least continue building committees for future hopes. Yet there are cases of giving up church buildings and refusing to build in an effort to save costs for other concerns and to avoid confusing the church as people of God with the church as brick and mortar. The Episcopal bishop of New York ended work on the huge Cathedral of St. John the Divine, in New York City, freeing funds for programs for the poor. Two new Washington, D.C., area churches decided that a church building is "unnecessary." The Church of the Apostles (Episcopalian), a year-and-a-half-old group meeting in a Falls Church, Virginia, school cafeteria, and the Lutheran-related Community of Christ, meeting in the downtown Dupont Circle area, Washington, in a basement, both declined to proceed with building a church. The evangelical independent Church of Our Savior, also near Dupont Circle, in an old mansion, has also passed up building a church. Downtown, the Episcopal Church of St. Stephen and the Incarnation, originally a white church, voted to give its $300,000 property to the black community around it. In Detroit, two small nearly vacant white United Methodist churches merged in 1970, and one of the congregations gave its $400,000 building to the black Scott Memorial United Methodist congregation for only $1.00. In Dallas, Texas, the 9,000-member Highland Park United Methodist Church finally turned thumbs down on a proposal to replace its forty-three-year-old Gothic church with a new $5 million contemporary building. The Cross Roads United Methodist Church and the Church of the Beatitudes (United Church of Christ), both in Phoenix, took similar action.

Then there is "Diakonia," (Greek: "a serving, relief"), a United Presbyterian Church at State College, in the Appalachians

[7] King, Seth, New York Times News Service, February 16, 1971.

in mid-Pennsylvania, started as a mission of the State College church. Organizers were thirty families who met in homes for study, worship, and planning of social action projects. They opposed church buildings, full-time ministers, and links with denominations. A worship service is made up of discussion, popular music, drama, and special events, such as a wedding of a church member.

Judaism is reflecting a reaction against big church buildings also. Dr. Malcolm H. Stern, curator for the American Jewish Historical Society, says, "I am not sure the big synagogue is valuable for even today, much less for the future. Everybody is a number today, and you look to the synagogue to recognize you as an individual. A huge congregation can't do it." He says the role of the rabbi has shifted from that of a "performer" to "co-officiant" with the "audience." Thus, he says, "The changes in Reform Judaism are demanding new architecture, as well as new forms of liturgical expression: new music, as well as new prayers."

A new kind of "relevant" mission of the church appeared in the 1960s; then all but faded out in the 1970s. These were the power-structure oriented missions to industry and city hall. The late Saul Alinsky, of Chicago, called attention to the power of protest at city hall. Before the angry demonstrations of the 1960s, churchmen had already begun to try to penetrate the secular "world of work." In Detroit, it was the Detroit Industrial Mission, mostly Presbyterian and Episcopalian, with its seminars with management and its several clergymen working on assembly lines trying to reach workers. Much of this had stopped by the early 1970s as DIM attention turned to ways to correct racism within the churches. Metropolitan Associates of Philadelphia promised penetration of city hall and urban departments through urban-planning scholars and others placed strategically on city staffs. But interest waned, and even the main promoter, the Reverend Dr. Jitsuo Morikawa, evangelism expert for the American Baptists, switched to a more personal evangelistic approach in keeping with the shifts in the times to a more personal faith. In Lansing, Michigan, a two-man office, the Ecumenical Associates, set up to try to influence government in favor of religious values, shut down in 1973. A "New Forms of Ministry List," put out by a division of the National Council of Churches toward the end of the 1960s, had listed some seventeen "industrial mission" types of activity plus a variety of project ministries, ranging from "community organizations," such as the Baltimore Street Ministry, to "leisure ministry" organizations, such as the Lake of the Ozarks Parish, Columbia, Missouri, and the Lake Texoma United Ministry, Denison, Texas.

The Directory of the Liberated Church in America, Berkeley, has listed 148 groups in thirty-six states and the District of Columbia. It is a project of the Free Church in Berkeley, a radical action group serving youths and others in need. The directory included farm co-op programs in the South guerrilla theater (Rapid Transit Guerrilla Communications, Chicago); black community organizations (Christian Homesteading Movement, Oxford, New York); clergy and laymen training centers (Center for Urban Encounter, Portland, Oregon); retreat and study centers (Kirkbridge, Bangor, Pennsylvania).

THE PARISH: ASSET OR MILLSTONE?

Three books in the early 1970s centered on renewing the parish. *Creative Congregations* by Edgar Trexler, an editor of *The Lutheran,* describes how nine congregations in rural Kansas developed a shared ministry with four pastors, how the Community of Christ the Servant holds service in a barn in Lombard, Illinois, without the usual formality and trappings of Sunday morning, how an ecumenical fellowship serves singles at the Fourth Presbyterian Church on Chicago's near-North Side. Lyle Schaller, a church planner, in the final chapter of the book seeks to correlate the decline in new congregations in the major denominations and the new forms of ministry. Over a dozen major denominations, he says, experienced cutbacks of a third or half in the number of new congregations at the start of the '70s compared to the start of the '60s. As seen earlier, more rural churches are staying open or being revived in light of an exodus to the country, and Schaller believes that this is where some of the new forms of mission to special needs and common groupings supplant the earlier trends toward new denominationally sponsored traditional congregations.

To Come Alive! by James Anderson, a parish-development aide to the Episcopal bishop of Washington, D.C., asks churchmen to regard the church as open-ended, as "an open socio-theological system" and the answer to many problems centered in an interdisciplinary approach. Anderson, a behavior scientist, charts ways for a parish to determine its problems and potentials. For instance, a leadership crisis, he says, may lie more in the concept of leadership in the congregation than in the lack of trained leaders.

Congregations in Change, by Elisa DesPortes, seeks to chart the ways new kinds of churches are being born, the kind that emerges to meet a task, rather than happening out of a negative split with a larger congregation or as a prestigious extension of the larger body. Her case histories include a number of inner city churches, in big cities, such as Chicago, which began to seek to meet the immediate needs of an area. Resulting are team ministries and special recreation, training, and resource centers. Cynthia Wedel, former president of the National Council of Churches, in the Foreword to the book, agrees that consultants and specialists who can analyze and test a congregation are going to be needed to carry people through the resistance of congregations, as the world, society, and people are changing.[8] The book holds that renewal and survival of institutional forms, or new approaches related to institutional forms, are desirable.

But the approach to the future, in terms of "congregations," as we noted at the start of this book, may not all be tied up with renewal, and in particular, the renewal of the parish. The Anglican Diocese of Birmingham, England, is proposing that the parish cease to be the chief planning and operative unit of the Church of England. The parish is described in the report as a "millstone 'round the necks" of both clergy and laity. The report, *Structures for Ministry,* suggests a replacing of the parish by a more flexible unit of ministry, comparable to a deanery or district. This unit would be the center of planning and administration, meeting varying needs in the community with special skills. "The idea would be to express unity not so much in the more familiar aims of joint worship and shared buildings as through shared skills and talents," an explanation of the report, conducted by a nine-member Commission on Needs and Resources, says. "The aim . . . is to facilitate a new type of leadership with the parson no longer trying to be the autocratic boss of the past . . . but one prepared to find and give scope to grass-roots leaders."[9]

CLUSTERING

Clustering has become a key word in describing many of the new formats. It is applied to groupings of agencies within a church or inter-

[8] (New York: Seabury, 1973), p. v.
[9] "Anglican Report Urges End of Central Role for Parish," a Religious News Service report from Birmingham, England, in the *National Catholic Reporter,* March 8, 1973.

church agencies, working together around a common emphasis or problem. Clusters also refer to churches or churchmen relating together to the community on various issues. In a sense, any grouping of people or organizations or committees for a common cause is clustering.

"Call it grassroots ecumenism; call it alliance for action; call it community coalition," says a United Church of Christ office of communication release. "Essentially, clustering is the effort by established churches to make alliances with neighboring churches and community organizations in order to meet local needs."

The Reverend Theodore H. Erickson, of the Evangelism Division of the UCC Board for Homeland Ministries, a member of a seven-man interdenominational committee studying clustering, says, "The process allows churches to maintain traditional activities while adding the new cooperative activities which bring in persons with new kinds of life styles."

The first national consultation on clustering was held in 1969 under American Baptist sponsorship. Erickson has joined with other national Protestant executives to prepare a booklet, *Guidelines for the Development of Local Clusters.*[10] The *Guidelines* suggests that "most clusters fit one of two broad categories: either they are part of a denominational linkage system or designed to relate local congregations to their communities." And: "All the evidence to date suggests that a cluster cannot be both an ecclesiastical intermediary and a community link for local congregations. It appears better for a congregation to be a part of two clusters, one ecclesiastical and the other community oriented, rather than to expect one cluster to meet dissimilar needs." Clusters are determined by specific needs, such as churches setting up immediate food and relief services following a rebellion of youth and/or blacks in cities and the suburbs. Clusters of different churches and denominations have set up camp programs, coffeehouses, lay conferences, night-school classes, etc. The new experimental clustering (such as a coffeehouse) the *Guidelines* call "transcendent cluster." The grouping of "programs that are reminiscent of the traditional activities of the church" (such as camping, retreats, youth rallies) are called an "efficient program cluster."

[10] Published jointly by the Division of Evangelism, Board of National Missions, United Presbyterian Church in the U.S.A., New York, and the Division of Evangelism, Board for Homeland Ministries, United Church of Christ, New York.

Blacks have had their own committees and organizations seeking empowerment and self-determination. One of the most ambitious is the Black Christian Nationalist Movement of the Reverend Albert Cleage, Jr., pastor of the United Church of Christ Shrine of the Black Madonna (formerly Central UCC Church), Detroit. His new movement, designed to relate black nationalist congregations in Cleveland, Detroit, New York (Harlem), Chicago, Philadelphia, and other cities, ordains its own men for social tasks, has its own manual of discipline, and presents its own theology of a black Jesus and activism. Cleage intends to keep his association with the UCC as long as the denomination doesn't get in his way. His route indicates the course some new groupings might go in the future, depending on the intensity of the issues and the degree of polarization in the churches.

NEW MODELS FOR COUNCILS

Councils of churches have been reorganizing. The National Council of Churches in Dallas in 1972 launched plans for a more flexible operating style while centralizing authority in the hands of an enlarged central committee, a 347-member Governing Board instead of a 250-member General Board. The next assembly of the World Council of Churches will consider five new models for reorganization of its general assembly. Most of these are procedural. One model suggests than the assembly is "a festival of the people of God."

Locally and regionally, the councils of churches are proceeding to new alliances and new kinds of organizations. Among some new models are: (1) *Christian Associates of Southwest Pennsylvania,* successor agency to the Pittsburgh Council of Churches. Administration centers in a twenty-member interfaith council (senate) and a forty-member board of delegates (house of representatives). One person from each member organization sits on the council; the board of delegates has representation in proportion to the size of the member organization or denomination. (2) *Metropolitan Area Church Board,* Columbus, Ohio. This grew out of the efforts of a young associate executive director of the Council of Churches who left the Council staff in 1966 and launched an Inter-Church Board for Metropolitan Affairs which included denominations and the Roman Catholic diocese. The Council grew weaker as the new group gained strength, and in 1967 the Council and Board merged to form the new Metropolitan Area Board. Membership includes not only the church bodies but other area councils which join while maintaining their local identity. The ministries of the new group parallel usual council task forces, training, and community projects, on a co-ordinated basis. The Board also backs a counseling center and a coffeehouse. (3) *Metropolitan Inter-Church Agency,* of Kansas City, Missouri. This is made up of representatives of both the denominations and the area councils of churches. However, as in the case of the two above plans, it became the successor organization to the local Council of Churches. The staff includes an executive co-ordinator, director of communications, director of planning, and an administrative assistant, plus two elected officers—a president and a treasurer. Program units are made up of task forces "which vary according to the community issues." The cabinet includes two representatives of each participating denomination or church body. The Kansas City organization includes Roman Catholics and the Reorganized Church of Jesus Christ of Latter Day Saints.

By and large, new organization schemes of councils of churches proved mostly to be paper tigers. Church councils became passé and showed little growth. One of the most active in previous years, the Metropolitan Detroit Council of Churches retreated into a "shell," sold its building, moved into smaller quarters, became largely silent on most issues, reported continued deficits, and generally gave the impression its death was near if not already achieved.

The much heralded Consultation on Church Union of the 1960s continued to flounder and stutter. It put aside grand plans, promised a rewriting of the plans to merge nine denominations, and offered new grass-root approaches to church merger. The shift was enough to win back the United Presbyterians who had pulled out, but all in all COCU could offer only a very muddied picture of the future shape of co-operative Christianity. Facing opposition to super-merger plans, rolling with the punches, and accepting a new "localism" approach in order to survive, COCU leaders agreed in Memphis in April 1973, "that viable proposals for organization and structure of the Church of Christ Uniting need to be developed out of the experience of living and working together. The Consultation, therefore, sees the next stages of its work as actively involving the churches in working together at the various levels of their life. Growing out of this experience, a full plan of union can be developed for a united church—catholic, evangelical, and reformed."

Procedurally, the Consultation said that "the Consultation welcomes and encourages both denominational and ecumenical exploration by the member churches of alternative models of church life on all levels, particularly at the middle judicatory level." And: "The Executive Committee authorize a task force to make a theological and sociological study of the forms of the church at the local level. This should include the 'parish' as a means by which to achieve a richer and more diverse Christian fellowship and liberation from institutional racism, and the local congregation which, because of its personal values, is regarded by many as the locus of Christian identity." It also calls for "generating communities," local creative efforts at merger that can test merger formats and also inspire others to expand the experiment until, hopefully, the churches are merged from the ground up. In its document on *A Proposal for Generating Communities,* COCU architects said the "generating community" would develop a "recognizable life-style" which "treasures the historic faith while encouraging its contemporary expression, celebrates this faith in regular eucharistic fellowship in common with other churches, structures itself for mission on all levels of its life, fosters flexibility and encourages experimentation, maintains an openness to further ecumenical relationships . . . regards all organization as provisional, and shares its learning with others through the Consultation on Church Union and related groups."

The Consultation then joined in offering eight "mission" models for congregational unity, but leaving their shape largely to "local initiative growing out of a renewed vision of the church's life and mission." The eight models are: (1) a cluster of congregations exploring or studying unity in a joint project, (2) a uniting of several congregations, (3) the combining of specific functions, (4) the developing of a congregation after the "COCU style" of "redefining" its aims to include "as many elements of inclusiveness as possible," (5) uniting around a task group made up of representatives from congregations and dealing with an issue or common topic, (6) a "cadre of professional staff" dealing with social issues and inequities in society, (7) a long-term task group seeking long-range commitments on issues out of which would come a worship style, and (8) a "neo-cathedral" drawing support from several congregations. "The cathedral need not have its own congregation or complete range of ministries. Congregations sponsoring such an ecumenical center for public worship, public witness, interim eucharistic fellowship, and community relations could together determine its most valuable activities for that specific community."[11]

SOME GRASS-ROOTS UNITY

Some of the new grass-roots church unity approaches began to emerge, much as the revised COCU scheme hoped it would. The energy crisis of 1974 gave some an assist, as in Mankato, Minnesota, where three congregations, meeting in one building to conserve fuel in the winter, considered coming together in shared facilities in one new building. In a vote, March 10, 1974, the First Congregational Church (United Church of Christ) and the Centenary Methodist accepted the proposal by majority vote, while First Baptist, requiring a two-thirds vote said "no" by only two votes. However, the Baptists voted again and, despite the easing of the energy crisis, agreed to join in building a unit to be shared by all three. "Churches cooperate in a lot of things, so there is no big theological issue involved," said the Reverend Eugene Allen, pastor of the American Baptist church. "We can build so much cheaper together and use the money saved for the mission of the church." The new $600,000 Baptist-Methodist-United Church of Christ building will have two sanctuaries; a Sunday morning will feature two Methodist services, one United Church of Christ, and one Baptist.

A variety of combined efforts emerged at the parish level in Michigan. Nine Protestant and Roman Catholic parishes in the Troy, Michigan, area north of Detroit formed a North Suburban Parish. These churches conduct camps, retreats, education programs together, led by nuns and Protestant clergy. The churches hold special liturgies together—at Easter, Thanksgiving, and for anniversaries of pastors or congregations. Co-ordinating this very loose federation is a committee chaired by an Episcopalian laywoman. Each church contributes one minister and two lay persons to the committee.

"We have a structured community working on the church of tomorrow today," says the Reverend John Malestein, pastor of the North Hills Christian Reformed Church, Troy, and vice-president of the North Suburban Parish. Tentative plans of the North Suburban Parish also call for developing an "ecumenical center" in the new Northfield Village housing development on a country road. The

---

[11] *Congregations Uniting for Mission,* A Working Paper of the Commission on Structures for Mission, Consultation on Church Union, Princeton, New Jersey, p. 13.

center would have offices for the pastors. There would be "some joint worship," says Mr. Malestein. With land at $15,000 an acre, he said, "we can't go in there and build a half-dozen churches." In Saline, forty miles west of Detroit, Faith Lutheran congregation, meeting in a school, moved into the same building with an Episcopal church and paid $45,000 to add a wing to the building.

In Ann Arbor, down in a glen, the St. Aidan's Episcopal and the Northside Presbyterian churches hold forth in the same building that looks more like a ski lodge than a church. The Presbyterians meet upstairs, and the Episcopalians on the main level, not symbolic, members say, as to who is closer to heaven or other realms. There are three boards, and three budgets—a nine-member board or "session" for the Presbyterians, and a twelve-member board or "vestry" for the Episcopalians. A joint twenty-one-member board or "assembly" forms the legal entity, the Northside Associated Ministries. The Presbyterians were there first and built the church at $185,000. The Episcopalians are "buying in" and are expected to pay half of the building costs eventually.

The two pastors, Episcopalian Richard Singleton and Presbyterian William Baker, alternate running both projects during summer vacations. Occasionally, during the year joint rites are held. Members then choose what kind of communion they will take, which led one member to refer to these joint communion services as "smorgasbord" communions. "I consecrate wafers and the chalice of wine, and Bill consecrates grape juice and bread," said Father Singleton. "And you take your choice."

Dress is informal. Katie Luther, seven, in sandals and granny dress, took up the offering. Kathy Roman, twenty-nine, stood in sunshine shorts and dark blouse and read the Old Testament Scripture. Ernie Manders, two and a half, in a red fireman's hat, crawled around and ended up at the altar during communion. Nine-week old John Davis Pointer, Jr., was baptized as he slept, as his mother stood in floppy hat, barefoot before the altar (to avoid making a lot of noise walking on the hard floor as she exited several times with the baby, she said).

Each of the two congregations in the Northside church number about fifty families. Many of the couples are mixed Presbyterian-Episcopalian. David Houseman, thirty, business administrator for an auto repair co-op, once studied for the Presbyterian ministry at Princeton (New Jersey) Theological School, but married an Episcopalian. "I am still actually a Presbyterian," he said, "but function as an Episcopalian. Actually there isn't that much difference. Both congregations here transcend denominationalism. We come more because of the type of ministry than because of any denominational background."

There are also three or four "merged" congregations of different denominational backgrounds in the same greater Detroit area. One of these is the North Oakland Community Church, east of Pontiac, Michigan. This church began when a group split off from the First Christian Church, Pontiac, six years ago. Both the Disciples of Christ and the United Church of Christ help with the budget of this combined church across the road from an upper-class real estate development.

Both forms of baptism—sprinkling infants, UCC style, and total immersion of youth and adults, Disciples style—are available to the congregation. At a communion service, the juice and bread are held and taken together, instead of in succession with more prayer in between as is generally common in both traditions.

First pastor at North Oakland Community Church was a Disciples of Christ minister, the next was duly ordained by both denominations, and the new pastor, just called by the congregation, is a Disciples of Christ, from Lexington, Kentucky.

A member, Edward Underwood, sixty-two, of Avon Township, retired from the GM Truck and Coach Division in Pontiac, Michigan, believes this combined church, which also has a list of various social-action projects, illustrates that "life style and what one does with his life is more important than creeds. I could never see the sense of a multiplicity of denominations. They seem unchristian and downright stupid. Denominational names have zero meaning."

CHAPTER V

The Coming New Cities

Since early times man has aspired to building castles, but usually settled for something less; namely, cities. His aspirations are seen on hills, from Jerusalem and the network of excavated cisterns and rooms at the Qumran community near the Dead Sea at Jericho to elaborate unearthed passageways and ornate churchly palaces in Rome. Turrets and towers in France and England and high gun-guarded harbors in Lisbon tell of a history of castles for war-making. America has its castles, too: old Pueblo Indian settlements in cliffs and strategic forts along the waterways, and today, big city pent-houses and mountain retreats, such as Robert Heinlein's mountain slope guarded by a high wire fence, like a moat, above Santa Cruz, California.

Malachi Martin's *The New Castle* argues that from the earliest Egyptian dynasties, the image of the castle has been used to describe an ideal human existence on earth. The castle is not heaven, but heaven on earth, the ideal place to live, and at the same time an emblem of man reaching up to spiritual powers. "The Castle for us is the consummation of all deepest wishes," Martin says. With a castle, "heaven was seen touching earth," a reference to Jerusalem and its walled castlelike city and sacred shrines high on a hill beneath the sun.[1]

A man's castle has been said to be his home, a place to which he can retreat. It is a womb, a place of refuge. Martin Luther found refuge at the Castle at Wartburg, protected by Frederick the Wise. But once a person finds a castle as a place of refuge, like Luther, he will also look further. Even in his home as castle, a person looks outside. For example, a family looks to a church as a castle in which

[1] (New York: E. P. Dutton, 1974), pp. 6, 25.

to worship and from there seeks something beyond in deity and heaven. Beyond a home, a woman looks to her clubs, a man to his office, a youth to his Scout troop. A castle is always something beyond.

A castle is also visible, whether it is within reach or not. "A city that is set on an hill cannot be hid," Jesus said (Matt. 5:14). The castle, usually on a hill, lends itself as a term to describe future cities. The new designs represent dreams, and something beyond, sometimes "up there," too. With cities, a completion of one phase of development only increases the hunger for more structure. Like a child building a castle in the sand, there is more to do. The creative urge demands refining the new structure with waterways and tunnels or moving on to new structures. A castle never means the fulfillment of a dream. Its armies are quick to go out and try to conquer other castles. A castle, despite its formidable iron gates and death moats, is never strictly a bastion of refuge. It implies a future.

Although a castle is inevitably a showcase, it also represents a dreamworld, a place to be coveted and achieved. But if it is achieved, the image of the castle will move on. If sociologists and others think the difficulties of today's cities, representing a "castle" to past generations, are monstrous, wait until they see the problems of the future cities, when even perfection itself may seem reason enough to censure a city before it paralyzes human thought and action. Too much or total beauty kills a city—this is the theme of Frank Herbert's story, "Death of a City." His city critics or doctors are looking down the hill into "the most beautiful city man has ever conceived." But at this point "absolutes were lethal. They provided no potential, no differences in tension that the species could employ as energy sources."[2]

The problems of too much harmony, on the one hand, or unchecked chaos and excessive death-dealing pollution on the other, are the problems of the future castle cities, just as cities have problems today. But the problems of future castle settings are beyond this discussion. Whether they work or not, sufficient for the moment is a consideration of the "better" dwellings that man aspires to—the castles that express creativity and demand allegiance.

What are some of the "castles" men might build for themselves as they seek to live in the future?

[2] In Elwood, Roger, *Future City* (New York: Trident, 1973), p. 154.

VERTICAL CITIES

Like a castle on a hill, there may be vertical cities. Already there are self-sustaining vertical units within the cities. The fifty-seven story IDS (Investors Diversified Services) tower complex linked by sky-way malls with other buildings in Minneapolis create a vast support system of shops, restaurants, offices, motels, pools, concourses. Boston has its skyscraper insurance building that links up with hotels and shops; Detroit is building a multi-million-dollar Renaissance center that will link many facilities. Elevators shoot to the top of new Hyatt hotels in Atlanta, Chicago, San Francisco. Rotating restaurants are on top, and rooms look down over flowers into a central concourse or atrium of shops, restaurants, and gardens, all indoors. The Four Seasons Sheraton Hotel in Toronto is a city in itself—with shops, waterfalls, etc.

The one hundred-story John Hancock Center on the near-North Side of Chicago is a "handsome, tapered tower" that "combines within it practically everything that is necessary for city life."[3] Walk into the Hancock Center and you find the lower floors contain a bank, a department store, parking for 1,200 cars, business and professional offices. Floors between 44 and 92 have 705 apartments, and on top there are restaurants, swimming pool, sauna, health club, lounge, etc. There is a self-sufficient power plant that can take over in the event of a power failure. An extension of the Chicago subway system is expected to link with the building, and with other comparable new buildings, such as the 110-story Sears tower and the eighty-story Standard Oil Building. In Montreal there is the Alexis Nihon Plaza. Here six hundred families can live, shop, go to the doctor or movies— and in some cases work in the building, without ever having to go outdoors. The complex includes a three-story shopping mall, a ten-story office building, a seven-story medical center and two apartment towers—one is twenty-four stories, the other is twenty-seven stories. Also on the connecting stretches beneath roofs are a playground, small golf unit, two pools, and three tennis courts.

Even farms may go "up." A drawing in the *National Geographic* in a discussion of farm revolution has "multi-level" cattle pens. These are towers nine stories high. A "bubble" of a farmhouse con-

[3] Hellman, Hal, *City in the World of the Future* (New York: M. Evans and Co. Inc., 1970), p. 141.

trols the tower pens (along with ten-mile automated fields that can be harvested with the push of a button). The cattle towers have tubes running from conical mills that blend the feed, plus other tubes running out for the breaking down of wastes into fertilizer.[4]

In Tokyo, Kenzo Tange has built the Shizuoka Press and Broadcasting Center, a tall cylinder tube stretching to the sky with rooms jutting out from the sides of the cylinders, giving the structure a totem pole look. It hints of possible future "tube" cities reaching skyward. Another kind of high-rise "city" covering more territory was demonstrated by "Habitat" at Expo 67 in Montreal. Habitat, arrangements of 158 box units, linked at varying heights over a hill area, achieved individuality of units in a great complex molecule of a structure. Its architect, Israeli Moshe Safdie, is putting together a similar cluster of three hundred concrete modules on a high hill in Puerto Rico. Robert Silverberg writes about a thousand-story-high "Urbmons" in his new novel, *The World Inside*.

Vertical cities that go a mile high are the dreams of Paolo Soleri, who is busy building a prototype of the vertical city that leaves the land as free as possible for shaping for the leisure and food needs of man. Soleri's effort is called "arcology." The word is his own, standing for an architectural structure that would take the place of man's natural ecology, a combination of the words "architecture and ecology." "Arcology, or ecological architecture," he says, is a structure that "would take the place of the natural landscape inasmuch as it would constitute the new topography to be dealt with." Differing from "natural topography," Soleri's all compact "multi-level" cities would control its own weather and have services for all the needs of man. Soleri, a native of Turin, Italy, draws his tall, upright models of a city from the image of man himself. "It is the wholeness of a biological organism that is sought in the making of the city," he says. If Soleri is correct, the cities themselves will unify man into a common body, and symbolically his cities will look like a great upright human —or humanoid.[5] "Arcology is both dimensionally . . . and functionally on the human scale without loss of its awesome force, indeed almost because of it."[6]

---

[4] "The Revolution in American Agriculture," Billard, Jules B., Vol. 137, No. 2, February 1970, pp. 184–85.
[5] *Arocology: The City in the Image of Man* (Cambridge, Mass.: MIT Press, 1969), p. 13.
[6] Ibid., p. 31.

Soleri, who has meager financing as he works with a few students on a windswept mesa seventy miles north of Phoenix, is not alone in his dream of a compact upright city of the future.

Edward Hall in a chapter, "Human Needs and Inhuman Cities," in a Smithsonian Institute study, says "a city can be seen as a total network of internal systems—systems for assuring people's health, mobility, and cleanliness, fighting fires, enforcing laws, providing shelter, educating children."[7] Hall cites architect John Eberhard's comparison of these systems to human biology. Eberhard says that a unified city system that takes in water, food, and fuel compares to the body's metabolic system; the complex corridors of transportation compare to the cardiovascular system; the information network and communication processes compare to the nervous system, and the enclosure system of a city compares to the body's skeletal system.[8]

I asked Nelson Rockefeller at the National Newspaper Association meeting in Toronto, Ontario, Canada, whether indeed cities would go up or might they go down into the earth. At the time, in July 1974, Rockefeller was chairman of the Commission on Critical Choices for Americans and the National Water Quality Commission. "From the sociological point of view to go up is very difficult" after the experience of "the tight ghettoes" that now exist, he said. Nevertheless, he felt "the cities of the future will be built up and wide, and spread out. There is the best living that way." He defined the best living conditions as providing "light, and air, and space."

THE UNDERGROUND BASE

But even the vertical cities rely heavily on underground expansion. Soleri's cities are deeply rooted in the ground, with storage, research centers, shipping and receiving, and various industries underground. The underground cities, like the above-ground skyscraper complexes, are more than a dream. Already many cities are beginning to expand underground. Atlanta has an entertainment district with shops, restaurants, and clubs in several blocks of underground facilities. Chicago 21, a project that would revamp downtown Chicago by the twenty-first century, calls for "sunken plazas" in addition to pedestrian "skyways." These networks would make even the ground level

[7] In Adams, Robert M., *Smithsonian Annual II: The Fitness of Man's Environment* (Washington: Smithsonian Institute Press, 1968), p. 181.
[8] Ibid. Cf. Eberhard, John, *Technology for the City, International Science and Technology,* September 1966.

seem underground. Planners and scientists meeting in Minneapolis in 1974 called for an "underground Minneapolis" section. The thirty-foot deep "city" dug from the sandstone below a firm layer of limestone would provide housing for shops, industry, parking, truck deliveries, storage, and offices. The advantages cited would include cutting heating costs, savings in maintenance and construction, noise-free settings for precision products manufacturing, a separation of pedestrians from traffic such as directing truck deliveries to another level, storage facilities easy to maintain at a constant temperature.[9]

The ultimate in underground cities is Isaac Asimov's description of the fictitious Trantor planet of 40 billion people who live under the surface in a contiguous chain of tunnels. The planet, given to administration of the galaxy, raised no food of its own but depended on the incoming ships from twenty agricultural worlds. A visit to Trantor begins Asimov's *Foundation* trilogy: "Gaal was not certain whether the sun shone, or, for that matter, whether it was day or night. He was ashamed to ask. All the planet seemed to live beneath metal. The meal of which he had just partaken had been labelled luncheon, but there were many planets which lived a standard time-scale that took no account of the perhaps inconvenient alternation of day and night."[10] And the visitor, Gaal Dornick, inquires at an underground hotel desk about a trip to the surface. He's told by the desk clerk who hands him a ticket to the tower elevator: "I don't bother with the outside myself. The last time I was in the open was three years ago. You see it once, you know, and that's all there is to it."[11]

Asimov discusses underground cities in an article, "The Next 100 Years," written in 1968. He believes man will noticeably be "burrow-ing underground by 2068" and "the future will be clear. Every city will already have its underground portion; many newer suburbs will be entirely underground." But he adds, "the underground dweller" will not "be deprived of the touch of nature. Quite the contrary. Where the modern city dweller may have to travel twenty miles to get out 'in the country,' the underground dweller will merely have to rise a few hundred feet in an elevator, for once a city is completely underground, the area above can be made into parkland."[12]

[9] Slovut, Gordon, " 'The Coming Thing': Real Underground Outlined for City," Minneapolis *Star,* March 15, 1974, p. 1A.
[10] (New York: Avon, 1972, c. 1951 by Isaac Asimov), p. 13.
[11] Ibid., p. 14.
[12] In *The World Almanac,* 1968, (c. Newspaper Enterprise Association, Inc., 1967), p. 40.

Of course, many science fiction writers believe nuclear holocaust will force man underground. Robert Foster's *The Rest Must Die* tells of life and new tribal warfare in the underground New York subway system after nuclear destruction. Robert Goldstone, Judith Merril, Lawrence Schoonever, Martin Caidin, and others deal with similar situations in post-nuclear survival.

THE MALL AND THE LINEAR CITY

On the ground surface, shopping malls and airports have been pace-setters in creative new designs. All across the country now enough services to support a small city can be found under one roof in malls that link big department stores, food chains, small shops, and recreation facilities. In St. Petersburg, Florida, the Tyrone Square Mall has 103 different stores, all under one roof. New "monster" airports are in the works. The Dallas-Fort Worth airport in Texas is being built in three stages; the first stage already completed, another stage to be ready in 1985, the third in 2001. Bigger than all of Manhattan Island in New York, it will have seventeen-inch-deep concrete landing strips that can be expanded to twenty-four inches to handle monstrous loads of the next century. Passengers can ride right up to the sixty-six gates or take "Airtrans," electric buslike trains riding on tires on cement "roller coaster" tracks. Phase I of the project cost $700 million. Eventually the airport will serve 50 million people a year in 2001. But even this "Texas-scale airport," as a New York *Times Magazine* article on September 16, 1973, called it, is going to be upstaged. A new Montreal airport is about to be built on 137.5 square miles. The Dallas-Fort Worth airport has 27.3 square miles.

Among new ideas in surface designs are "linear cities" that follow the lines of transportation. A plan for Brooklyn calls for schools and housing over an expressway. Already the toll roads around Chicago have "oases" built right above the Freeways. French architect Le Corbusier (real name, Charles Edouard Jenneret-Gris) forty years ago suggested a long hairlike building of fourteen stories, only eighty-five feet deep stretched out over an artery eight miles long. Built on stilts, it would have the highway on the upper level. Rivers may have their bridge cities. A "span" city has been suggested over the Thames River in London. It would have a hotel, dock, skating rink, and art gallery. The University of Minnesota has a sky-high enclosed mall and bicycle lanes over the Mississippi River linking East and West bank campuses.

Resort cities are rising in Arizona and Florida and other areas, often as "retirement" complexes that offer full services around a waterway or golf course. Disney World in Florida has plans for a residential-business complex called Experimental Prototype Community of Tomorrow (EPCOT). This city is expected to always be changing as new discoveries are introduced. There will be no traffic lights. Pedestrians will walk on the main level; traffic will be underground. A thirty-story hotel will jut out of the enclosed fifty-acre center of the town.

CITIES OF INTELLECT

Like former military bases, new universities are built like cities. Lloyd V. Berkner of the Graduate Research Center of the Southwest, Dallas, has predicted that in several decades the U.S. population will center in 150 city areas. Describing them as "cities of intellect," he says: "Each is a sprawling industrial and suburban complex, centered around one or more great graduate universities, which have been forced to provide the intellectual focus that guides the economic and cultural development of the city."[13]

Stephen R. Graubard, in a discussion of future "university cities," believes that in the year 2000 there will be the "university city" which "will be an urban area of some size and economic importance that will shelter a significant number of strong educational institutions, broadly defined; these institutions will co-operate in ways that are now only dimly perceived," and by the year 2000 "the business of certain cities will be education, in the broadest sense."[14] These will differ from the industrial cities of today, as modern cities differ from the cathedral cities of Europe in the Middle Ages. He argues that universities relate to many life functions, and says a University City Science Center in Philadelphia with 2,000 scientists may generate some 50,000 support jobs.

A whole new town is being planned around the University of California branch at Irvine. The city has a fifty-year master plan as it rises in stages on the 93,000 acres of a ranch, an area as big as

[13] "The Rise of the Metropolis," in Calder, N., *The World in 1984,* Vol. 2. (Baltimore: Penguin Books, 1965), p. 145.
[14] "University Cities in the Year 2000," in *Daedalus,* Vol. 96, No. 3, summer, 1967, pp. 817, 818.

Detroit. Hellman has suggested the possibility of "plug-in" cities related to the cores of the university cities. "Perhaps there will be a traveling or portable section of a household, containing clothing, beds, and other essentials, which will be picked up in toto, delivered on board a ship, then put on a train or trailer truck, and finally 'plugged in' to a preselected, prepared spot in the new university city."[15]

The July–August 1973, issue of the Southern Baptist *Home Missions* magazine discusses the mobility of Americans (pre-energy and inflation crisis) and how 8,000 families have registered to help develop ministries to campers. In a way, the trailers with all the modern equipment ready to move constitute a plug-in community. Toffler in *Future Shock* estimates that some 108,000,000 Americans took 360,000,000 trips more than 100 miles from home in 1967. These trips, he said, add up to 312,000,000,000 miles.

THE LATEST EXPERIMENTS

Some of the new cities, however, are designed in such a way that man has no need to travel. Which may be realistic if energy crises compound or other forces, political and economic, limit man to his community. Consider some fifty to 250 or so "new towns." Reston, Virginia, planned by a subsidiary of Gulf Oil, is combining resort and modern living facilities around the sizable Lake Anne. Most popular has been Columbia, Maryland, developed by a private builder on some 14,000 acres between Baltimore and Washington. The city is made up of a series of villages, each containing a school in the center, and the nine villages surround a central business area. A third of the project has lakes, woods, and parks. Such new towns have led churches to rethink their former excessive use of space. Columbia received special attention when the churches were required to use one common interfaith center. A second interfaith center to reach other religious groups, such as the Southern Baptists, interested in a ministry in the area, is expected to be built. Waiting for that day, the Southern Baptists are meeting in a school. Sun City, Arizona, has a non-denominational new community church; in Reston (Virginia), five Protestant groups have banded together to avoid "wasteful church development."[16] Soul City, in rural North

15 Hellman, Ibid., pp. 115, 116.
16 Nicholas, Tim, "No Room for Religion?" *Home Missions*, Vol. 43, No. 7, July–August 1973, p. 35.

Carolina, a gathering of mobile homes and offices around an old mansion, plans a multiple-unity religious center for churches.

"Experimental cities" are on the drawing boards in various parts of the country. These seek to structure a town of a controlled size to meet the needs of the residents. Building from scratch, they can be placed anywhere in the country, preferably away from urban complexes that will swallow up some of the "new towns" near big cities.

One 250,000-person Experimental City was talked about for rural Minnesota. A study report, which was never implemented, called for all utility services to be underground, and said buildings would be "portable," made of new lightweight materials and modular units that can be moved about as demands of the city change. Athelstan Spilhaus, of Palm Beach, Florida, former dean of the Institute for Technology at the University of Minnesota, points out that the Minnesota Experimental City plan might find it advisable to ask for "inflatable buildings, which can be instantly deflated." Precast rooms could be used as in Habitat at Expo 67, in Montreal, or in the new San Antonio Hilton Hotel. "The disassembly of a building will resemble the disassembly of an erector set. Reusable components of the building will be swallowed by the city's substructure. . . . An obsolete building will disappear like ice cream that melts and drains out through the truncated bottom of the cone. In building new structures, the process will be the reverse. Materials will be lifted from the substructure into the middle of the site. . . ."[17]

The size of the proposed Minnesota experimental city has helped to render it impractical. "To establish a new city of 250,000 population within a ten-year period would entail an organizational effort almost without parallel in our history," admits Walter K. Vivrett, reporting on the project. "Under the simplified assumption that the level of in-migration would be constant, an average of 25,000 people would have to be attracted to the City each year."[18] Some 8,000 to 11,000 new jobs would have to be generated each year, and some 7,000 to 9,000 new housing units each year. "The task would be further complicated by such problems as timing; the need to build critical infrastructure in advance of residential, industrial and

[17] "The Experimental City," in *Dialogue,* Vol. II, No. 1, 1969.
[18] "The Scenario for Minnesota's Experimental City," Paper No. 3, Office for Applied Social Science and the Future, Center for Urban and Regional Affairs, University of Minnesota, Minneapolis, January 1972, p. 12.

commercial facilities; and the need to match housing and job development."[19] Nevertheless, Vivrett concludes with a statement of faith in the availability of people who "have the necessary pioneering zeal" and an "unifying vision."[20]

One of the ambitious plans for a new city comes from Dr. Genevieve Marcus and Robert Lee Smith of Los Angeles. In an office on a slope just below the Beverly Hills homes of movie stars, the two are completing plans for launching the first phase of their Experimental Cities Inc. They say they have 5,000 persons lined up already. The city would expect to serve 50,000.

Marcus and Smith expect to choose between several desert sites they say are being offered by industries in exchange for experimenting with various industry programs. One of the programs would be raising and cultivating fish in new desert lakes. Smith is a former executive of a hotel chain and former head of a computer company. Dr. Marcus has her degree in contemporary music from the University of California in Los Angeles. She believes her arts background prepares her for creating a sensitive new community. "We are trying to find ways to insure the continuing of the human species and the individual to reach his highest growth," she said in an interview.

In the Marcus-Smith experimental city plan, the new city would have a fixed guaranteed income and all members would be required to put in a certain amount of work to preserve and improve the community. A planning document says: "Everyone will always be employed because the jobs maintaining the basic economy will continuously be divided among all the inhabitants." The government will have no power elite, only specialists for various city functions, each one a short-term position, with an assistant trained and ready to take over every year or two. "The population of 50,000 may be subdivided into 'villages' of 1,000, each with its own community center containing art, theater, music, schools, businesses, food, political and social activities. As a society, we will create new rituals and occasions for public celebration, e.g., perhaps one fast day a month followed by a communal breakfast celebration." These might include, the prospectus for the new city continues, "celebrations for harvests, scientific breakthroughs and social progress."

[19] Ibid., p. 13.
[20] Ibid., p. 22.

THE VISIONS OF BUCKMINSTER FULLER

If R. Buckminster Fuller has his way, the new cities and some of the old ones, at least in part, would have domes over their heads. He has designed a free-standing geodesic dome made up of interlocking triangles. Some of these kinds of domes have been built already, from the $9.3 million dollar, 20-stories high United States pavilion at Expo in Montreal to a small $31,000 geodesic dome church of the Unitarian Universalist Fellowship of Tampa, Florida. The church's fifty-foot diameter hemisphere sits on a concrete slab.[21]

Fuller would like a dome over much of mid-Manhattan. He believes it would reduce the energy losses fifty-fold and the money saved in snow removal alone in ten years would pay for the mile-high dome. A New York dome, two miles wide and one mile high, would keep out pollution also. The domes would also cut out jet noises, too much glare of sun light, and any future potential fallout of atomic radiation.[22]

Fuller has put his imagination to work on new floating "sea cities," villages and neighborhoods surrounded by water-like castles of old surrounded by water moats. Back in 1966, Fuller and two Cambridge, Massachusetts, architectural firms that seek to put his concepts to work were asked by Japanese businessmen to build a super vertical city for a million inhabitants. Fuller suggested that they consider instead a "floating tetrahedron city" for the bay near Tokyo. The businessmen agreed, and the two firms—Fuller and Sadao, Inc., and Geometrics, Inc.—began to work out a study of an independent, sea-faring tetrahedron city for one million persons. (A tetrahedron is a pyramid with four sides, including the base.) The Japanese eventually abandoned the project, but the U. S. Department of Housing and Urban Development (HUD) wanted the study continued. HUD gave Triton Foundation, Inc., which Fuller heads, a grant in 1967. The study found that a structure of twenty stories above sea level, with other levels below sea level, could be floated in the bays and lakes and oceans around most U.S. cities.

Fuller's aide, Shoji Sadao, argues in *The Futurist,* that the know-how to build floating cities is here. "We have been building super-liners for many years that carry population the size of entire

[21] "Fellowship to Dedicate Geodesic Dome Home," *Unitarian Universalist World,* Vol. 4, No. 17, November 15, 1973, p. 1.
[22] "Why Not Roofs Over Our Cities?" *Think* magazine, January–February 1968, p. 8.

towns."[23] Sadao calls attention to the S.S. *United States* which holds 3,000 people and supertankers which weigh 30,000 tons without cargo. "The 5,000-person neighborhoods we studied would weigh 150,000 tons." The "Triton City" he describes would support an elementary school, a small supermarket, and miscellaneous stores and accommodations. There are several variations on the theme. One floating city "is composed of a string of four to six small platforms, each holding about 1,000 people; the other is a larger, triangular platform which would be of high density and have capacity for as many as 6,500." Another platform would be added to include a high school, civic facilities, some industry, more stores.

When the community has reached the level of three to seven towns (90,000 tp 125,000 population), it would become a full-scale city and would then add a city-center module containing governmental offices, medical facilities, a shopping center, and possibly some form of specialized city-based activity like a community college or specialized industry.

Because the system of development is based on aggregation of separate modules, flexible arrangements of total communities up to 100,000 persons could either grow gradually, starting with a cluster of two or three neighborhoods, or be built up very rapidly.[24]

"Aesthetics" and "safety" are added features of a neighborhood "megastructure" at sea, Sadao says. No motor vehicle would be allowed on the surface, thus making the streets safe and quiet for all. And it would be like living in a resort. All residential units would face out toward the water, the higher ones offering panoramic views, the lower ones accessibility to the water and sports. Like the different levels of a castle, as you wind upwards, the Triton neighborhoods would offer "streets in the air" for walking only, resembling also "the promenade decks of ocean liners." Bridges lead to schools and shops. At the top, apartments look out also onto a city square, "a public space open to the sky." And "the many roof levels of the structure are terraced and landscaped for various kinds of recreation."[25]

[23] "Buckminster Fuller's Floating City," *The Futurist*, Vol. III, No. 1, February 1969.
[24] Ibid.
[25] Ibid.

Another version of the floating castle is "Sea City," an offshore island of concrete and glass. The project is proposed by the Pilkington Glass Age Development Committee of Pilkington Glass Ltd. Described by British architects Geoffrey Jellicoe and Edward Mills and British engineer Ove Nyquist Arup in a publication of the Pilkington firm, "Sea City" is aimed at serving future new communities engaged in fish farming and drilling for undersea natural gas. The trio of planners believe there are a number of natural shoal water areas where piles could easily be driven to support the superstructure which includes a sixteen-story amphitheater. These include off-shore Eastern United States, China, Brazil, Mexico, Israel, Italy, England.

"Sea City" would wrap around a lagoon of man-made floating concrete-pontoon islands. Each of the sixty-foot-wide islands carry light-weight fiber-glass-reinforced plastic units up to three stories in height. A breakwater provides a quiet "moat" around this sea-city castle. Transportation includes a water bus transport leaving frequently to the mainland, plus a hovercraft or helibus commuting service to buildings on the mainland. There is sailing, water-skiing, swimming, all available in the quiet waters of the complex.

There are forerunners of artificial islands at sea already. Aristotle Onassis' elaborate boat functions as a small city on the sea. Scientologist Ron Hubbard has a chain of three vessels that provide him with a living complex and a small university on the Mediterranean. Even a bishop of the Episcopal Church, C. Kilmer Myers, moved his episcopal "mansion" to the California waters as he took up quarters on a $50,000 yacht.

More in the line of the Pilkington Company's "Sea City," nearly two hundred miles out in the Atlantic off the Newfoundland coast, Mobil has a huge "floating" platform for oil drilling. (The oil platforms have run afoul of environmentalists since the twenty to thirty oil platforms near Santa Barbara spilled oil and blacked the bright beaches of Santa Barbara.) About ten years ago, oil companies began to look for other ways to get the oil from the sea. Several possibilities developed. Among them, subsea chambers of the Lockheed Aircraft Corporation in co-operation with the Lockheed Petroleum Services, Ltd., of British Columbia and Shell Oil Co. These steel chambers, thirty-feet high, ten-feet wide, are sunk in 375 feet of water off the coast of Louisiana. A service capsule delivers the work crew. Pipelines run from the chamber to a platform where the gas and oil are separated. Next in Lockheed's plans is a subsea center for collecting oil and gas from several wells, then compressing the gas and pumping it and the oil to the coast. Among other approaches, Exxon Co., formerly Humble Oil, and Deep Oil Technology, a branch of the Fluor Corp., keep the operation right on the surface, with floating facilities rather than subsea chambers.

The ocean platforms appeal to the nuclear power developers. The Atomic Energy Commission has at least eight requests for permits to build "platform-mounted nuclear plants" (PMNP). One plant costing $1 billion will serve New Jersey by 1980. Wilbur Marks and Robert Skirkanich point out in *The Futurist* that these "platform-mounted nuclear plants" have appeal because they are "relatively free from potentially harmful seismic shocks and the ocean is a great sink for the waste heat that is emitted."[26] Marks is president of the Poseidon Scientific Corp. studying ocean platforms on a grant from a government agency (the Sea Grant Office of the U. S. National Oceanic and Atmosphere Administration) and Skirkanich is with the Grumman Data Systems Corp. They also report on other new "floating" neighborhoods. Four islands off the Long Beach shoreline are camouflaged. They appear to be luxurious high rises, but in reality they are oil derricks. Sculptured screens look like balconies and lighted waterfalls. Tropical palms also help hide the oil equipment. The facade, however, does demonstrate the possibility of actual neighborhoods or cities built on platforms. The University of Hawaii and the Oceanic Institute are planning a floating park, exhibition area, and urban complex that will house 15,000 off the coast of Oahu, most populated of the Hawaiian islands. The facility would host 40,000 vistors a day in an international marine exposition. The platform segments of the Hawaiian project would sit on three large concrete cylinders eighty feet wide and 240 feet deep. Floated beneath the sea they would support buildings ten stories high. Marks and Skirkanich call for the development of a

[26] "Ocean Platforms: Extending Man's Domain into the Seas," *The Futurist*, Vol. III, No. 4, August 1973, p. 160.

new science, "the new scientific-technological field of geonics, which deals with the creation of man-made substitutes for land."[27]

DWELLINGS IN SPACE

"Floating cities" in the Space Age lead inevitably to thinking about "floating castles" or "cities" in the sky. Christopher Priest's *The Inverted World* has a domed city moving about on tracks that are far below. Fuller himself has set the stage for thinking of new dwellings in space in his very concept of the earth as a floating dwelling or a "spaceship." Writing in a book of William R. Ewald, Jr., *Environment and Change: The Next Fifty Years,* Fuller declares that "you—the earth inhabitants" are "all astronauts" aboard "a fantastically real spaceship—our spherical Spaceship Earth." Describing "our little spaceship earth" as "only eight thousand miles in diameter," spinning a hundred miles a minute as it travels a thousand miles—"quite a spin and zip."[28] To Fuller, the earth is "a machine just as is an automobile," only with the instructions missing. (Fuller has also written about the possibility of huge inhabitable spheres floating over mountain crags in Colorado or over the moon, in his new book with Robert Marks, *The Dymaxion World of R. Buckminster Fuller.*)

As the future successors to Skylab III, which hosted three astronauts eighty-four days ending in 1974, put larger and larger communities into space, the prospect of more floating communities—including long-distance emigration that may take a life-time to reach other planets—cannot be ruled out. Twentieth-Century Fox's movie, *Space Flight 1C-1* in the year 2015, has a great spaceship leaving with families to discover and colonize another planet much like overpopulated earth. There is an alternate crew taken along in suspended animation. The theme has been repeated in science fiction, TV scripts, stories, and novels.

Some of the new off-beat occult groups are "drawing" plans for suspended cities. In Berkeley, California, the Messiah's One World Family Crusade, now also called the Universal Industrial Church, talks of a type of ark or floating city in space. Drawings in their tabloid newspaper, the *Central Sun,* depict a geometric sphere with central recreation areas, offices, cleanliness and food areas, sleep

27 Ibid., p. 164.
28 (Bloomington, Ind.: Indiana University Press, 1968), pp. 357–59.

areas, and rooms for meditation. Designed to be lifted by some future air-lift power system, it will be like a hovercraft. The group feels also that some technology may be revealed by pilots of flying saucers or their source when the earth occupants are prepared spiritually to orbit. One of the commune leaders, Chris Plant, twenty-three, of Louisville, Kentucky, a former Roman Catholic, interviewed in Berkeley, said, "It will be an extra terrestrial space craft, possibly lifted with electromagnetic energy and operating like a perpetual-motion machine without fuel, like a ship."

Or the city or living unit in space could be created by stellar material or asteroids converted in space. Several hundred thousand people could live in a thin "bubble" shell made from melting one of the innumerable small "planets" that gravitate around the sun between the orbits of Mars and Jupiter, for instance. Dandridge Cole and Donald Cox see the possibility of a cylinder world which inside would have a surface of half the size of Rhode Island. Such an environment could be totally controlled, they say in their book, *Islands in Space*. Science fiction writer-editor John Campbell has suggested that great mirrors in space could center solar heat on the astral materials and shape them for special dwelling units. Other alternatives, Cole and Cox say, include hollowing out asteroids. Some 1,700 are known to exist. First arrivers on some of these will live out of the space ship. In another phase, the visitors might begin caverns, which could later lead to mining shafts and caverns that in turn could lead to living quarters, according to Cox and Cole.

BACK TO MEGALOPOLIS

But as inviting as all the cities floating in sea or space, or burrowed into the earth or asteroids, may be, most futurists are also realists who remember that future cities are today's cities extended, not layer on layer, as unearthed cities have demonstrated, but extended out into the country side. "The advanced 21st-century urban agglomeration will be a megalopolis—a superagglomeration comprising large numbers of contemporary metropolitan areas merged into single concentrations that conceivably could encompass from 50 million to 100 million persons,"[29] says Philip Hauser, professor of sociology, University of Chicago. The East Coast will be a city, the West Coast a

[29] "Urban Society: A Blueprint for the City of Tomorrow," in *1970—Britannica Yearbook of Science and the Future*, p. 218.

city, etc. *The Futurist* magazine back in April 1972, listed some of the names that are being bandied about for some of those super-super cities. There's Bowash, a term coined by Herman Kahn of the Hudson Institute. It would stretch from Boston to Washington. Others call the same area East Coast Megalopolis (Konstantinos Doxiadis), Eastern Metroplex (biologist Barry Commoner), Atlantic Seaboard Urban Region (city planner Jerome Pickard). Other names turned up for the same eastern area in *The Futurist* survey: Atlantic City, Atlantic Strip City, Bosnywash, Eastern Megalopolis, EM, Megalopolis, Northeast American Megalopolis, Northeast Corridor. Megalopolis is a Greek word meaning "big" (*mega*) "city" (*polis*).

If Chicago and Pittsburgh become one city, linked by a common corridor of urban sprawl, the names, according to *The Futurist,* might be: Chipitts, Great Lakes City, Great Lakes Megalopolis, GLM, Lower Great Lakes Urban Region. For Miami-Houston: Gulf City, Coastal Crescent. For San Francisco-San Diego: Sansan, California Strip City, California Megalopolis, West American Megalopolis, Pacific City.[30]

Lewis Mumford worries about the continual spreading out of the cities on the one hand and the attempts to restore pivotal cores within cities, on the other hand. He raps Frank Lloyd Wright's Broadacre City as too rural and unrealistic as "fewer than eight hundred families—at most some three thousand people—would occupy a site as large as New York's Central Park." And also unrealistic, he says, are Le Corbusier's plans to re-do centers of cities. "Le Corbusier's idea of the City in a Park—the collection of office buildings in the Pittsburgh Triangle, for example—they might as well be in a suburb as in the city itself." And the real fact of the matter in these artificial designs, he said, is "the City in a Park . . . has become a City in a Parking Lot."[31]

Mumford acknowledges the rise of the great megalopolis sprawl, but is more concerned with integrative efforts rather than "garden spots" or artificial commercial centers with a few plants here and there. He insists that "in reducing the realities of living organisms—square feet of rentable space, acres of traffic interchanges, miles of

---

[30] "Naming the Emerging Super-cities," *The Futurist,* survey by Ralph Hamil, Vol. VI, No. 2, April 1972, p. 78.

[31] *The Urban Prospect* (New York: Harcourt, Brace & World, Inc., 1968, c. 1956), p. 124.

super-highways, millions of taxable real estate—the constructors and administrators of our modern, machine-conditioned metropolises have overlooked the essential task of the city. That task is to provide the maximum number of favorable opportunities for large populations to intermingle and interact."[32]

The successful city of the future, regardless of its size or sprawl, Mumford believes, will be an "invisible city," in contrast, he says, to Doxidis' confined "Ecumenopolis," or as Mumford calls it, an "urbanoid non-entity." Mumford favors the New Towns approaches for industrial workers in England and the "social cities" ideas of Ebenezer Howard. While Howard sought to control density of areas, he sought also to integrate the values of society into every level. Every neighborhood would have its park, but populations would be large enough to provide variety and yet have access to open country and other communities. Mumford's concept is an organic one, he says. His ideal includes a "limitation of numbers and density, mixture of social and economic activities, internal balance, the interplay of usable open spaces with occupied spaces. . . ."[33]

THE NEW POWER BLOCKS

The great cities, or megalopolises, will likely attain some degree of cohesion, whether their thousands of neighborhoods turn out to be as organic or interrelated as Mumford wishes or not. His city complexes will be great city states, with immense power, as they reach the size of modern nations in population. What they do will be important to the world, and likely will be tightly if not almost invisibly controlled by a world force. Robert Heinlein has the U. S. Constitution operative in his *Stranger in a Strange Land* but superseded by the "Articles of World Federation." Whatever the political control factor might be, no world politician will hardly overlook the power of the new city state or megalopolis. As to administrating them, futurists see (1) a proliferation or delegation of power to the local level, (2) a form of regionalism or "super-city" government, and (3) a "functional" administration of populaces by specialized intergovernmental boards or civic agencies constituted to deal with special problems.

All three ideas were enunciated at the Rome Special World Con-

32 Ibid., p. 128.
33 Ibid., p. 155.

ference on Futures Research at Frascati, Italy, in 1973. Bertrand de Jouvenel of Paris, head of an international future society, said in an interview, "I am not sure problems will be solved only on a world level, but I can see the solving of problems on lower echelons." He believes "it is important to deal with persons," and "attempts to have machines to run the world will not be successful." However, the "really great problem remains" as the small versus the big: "It is the nature of society to be small, and the nature of organization to be big, and it is the nature of the organization to outgrow the society." The Marxists at the meeting described the cracks in bureaucracy in Eastern Europe countries and an emergence of at least more potential for more personalism. Said Mihailo Markovic of Yugoslavia: "I do not see a totalitarian government, but a confederation government and a pluralistic world."

The concept of regionalism is asserted by Markovic as he sees only a "small number of general interests" remaining for a larger government's jurisdiction. "Maybe there will be a world assembly representing various societies, meeting to find common denominators." French Marxist Roger Garaudy believes that a future government might evolve to a "self-determination of the ends and a self-management of the means of every man, which does not exist now." System analyst John Warfield, of Columbus, Ohio, sees the future city as "sets of small units—50,000 each, but harmoniously integrated. The only constraints will be the use of land."

French economist Maurice Guernier of Paris takes the Federation concept in two directions. First of all, he sees the world dividing into ten provinces: North America, South America, Black Africa, North Africa, Mideast, Europe, India, Southeast Asia, China, Japan. "All these blocks are very homogeneous and will have to cooperate. In 10 to 20 years, there will be a federation of one world. This is the first step. But in 200 years there could be monolithic cooperation or a monolithic United Nations that can deal with problems of energy and pollution. There can be a world policy, for instance, on weather. Like a United Nations with operational power." There would be "operational power" of agencies to deal with problems of "compensation, wealth, water sharing, energy, health." W. Warren Wagar in his *Building the City of Man* calls for organizing a "world party" that can begin to deal with the central issues of all mankind beyond narrow ideologies. And, in summary, "the world state, as I foresee it, will be unitary, democratic, and liberal."[34]

Agreeing with Wagar and Guernier's functional emphases, John Platt of the Center for Advanced Study in the Behavioral Sciences, Stanford, California, says, "Some of the powers of the nation-states must indeed be transferred up to the global commonwealth—nuclear control, energy, resources, pollution, population, communications—but others need to be transferred downward as far as possible for diverse regional and community and individual self-determination."[35]

The shape of the city of the future may well be tied in with an old question: What is the nature of man? Most architects and city planners are by definition dreamers and builders. It is their task to create new cities, extend or replace the city in part, and/or integrate the old and the new. But how much of the old can or will ever be integrated into the new? "The staying power of the great cities is remarkable," observes Hellman. "Both London and Paris have been in existence since the first century A.D., and Rome and Athens for many centuries before that. There are no known cases of cities being voluntarily deserted by their inhabitants." Although there have been setbacks, by earthquakes, for instance, he says, the city continued. "Nor have war or disease been able to destroy the city center. But that great invention, the automobile, has come perilously close."[36] With such miserable persistence, the city of the future could be endless oceans of decay compounded upon decay—slums and leaning tenements, uncollected garbage, cold and crumbling, rat-infested buildings. The shacks and lean-to junk heaps may be a better description of the future city than anything that Wright, Howard, Le Corbusier, Doxiadis, and others have come up with. Further, a realistic appraisal can mean that the very persistence about which Hellman talks can be obliterated in modern warfare. What Hellman really means is that the "location" does not change appreciably for a city, nor its identity or name at times, although war has a way of shifting structure—consider the utter destruction of the center of Berlin and how East Berlin is still full of vacant lots and rubble with construction taking different patterns in the divided city. All of which

[34] (New York: Grossman, 1971), p. 142.
[35] "Movement for Survival," in *Science,* Vol. 180, May 11, 1973, p. 581.
[36] Hellman, op. cit., p. 61.

in itself destroys the old city. Yet, there is a continuum of location. But is it the same city? The names of cities also change and threaten identity. For example, the cities of western Poland are now taking Polish names instead of German—Wroclaw instead of Breslau, Gorzow instead of Landenburg, Szczecin instead of Stettin, and in the Soviet Union there are new names for old cities—for example, Volgograd for Stalingrad, which was also once called Tsaritsyn.

The cities Hellman mentions are not really contiguous with the past. They are built on layers of destroyed cities. Beneath the surface of Rome or Jerusalem are ruins of walls and houses of another era. With the potentiality of modern nuclear warfare, whole landscapes and even states can be devastated with a single blast. Annihilation on a grand scale is always a possible factor in deciding the shape and place of future cities. In event of nuclear war, civilizations could go underground. A number of cities of World War II, from Cologne to Hiroshima and Nagasaki, owe more to detonation of bombs than urban renewal in the shape of their new cities.

IS THERE A CURSE ON ALL CITIES?

French sociologist and theologian Jacques Ellul believes that man is enmeshed in evil in the cities. Ellul reads the Bible in such a way that he finds all cities are under the judgment and curse of God. In his *The Meaning of the City,* Ellul insists:

> In order to understand the history of the city and the situation as it now exists, we must take into account not only its beginning as a human enterprise, but also the curse placed on it from its creation, a curse which must be seen as a part of its make-up, influencing its sociology and the habitat it can provide.[37]

Harvey Cox, who found the creative and positive hand of God active in modern cities as man is given a chance to relate to many things and people, with more choices at all levels of life, finds Ellul's viewpoint unacceptable, Cox, who put his views in *The Secular City,* has a highly charged discussion of Ellul in *Commonweal,* a Catholic weekly. Cox finds Ellul old fashioned in his belief in the demonic. "Ellul sees man imbedded in *structures* of sin and evil. . . . He believes in what the late Paul Tillich called 'the demonic' and what the Apostle Paul referred to as 'principalities and powers.' "

[37] (Grand Rapids: Eerdmans, 1970), p. 48.

Cox goes on to describe Ellul "as a twentieth-century man" who "still has the audacity to believe in these strange critters. And so do I. The Pauline-Augustinian-Reformation tradition preserves a realistic respect for the uncanny if invisible power of systems."[38] Beyond this agreement, Cox proceeds to see the city as a place for redemption and the operative will of God. The trouble with Ellul, Cox believes, is not his belief in "corporate sin. On that he is right. The trouble with him is that . . . his doctrine of radical evil is not matched by an equally powerful doctrine of *structural* grace. One gets the feeling in reading Ellul that sin abounds, but grace doesn't abound quite so much."[39]

Whether their views on the "religious" solutions to the problems of the city agree or not, Cox and Ellul do understand that evil exists in a city and in any potential system of cities. Like Malachi Martin, who uses the castle as a symbol of the hoped-for relations of man in community, Cox and Ellul could use the same castle metaphor to describe the dark side of cities. Certainly, castles are symbols of evil as well as symbols of hope. Franz Kafka earlier in the century viewed the castle as the enemy of man, enticing him only to death. Edgar Allan Poe's castles in his stories were chambers of horror, of grotesque torture chambers and people bricked up inside walls and left to die. Béla Bartók's Count Bluebeard's castle had no windows, but seven doors. Behind each lies one of man's seven "desires" murdered. The vampire horror tales emerge from Romanian castle history and myth. Bram Stoker, just before the turn of the century, told of Count Dracula's horror castle in the Romania province of Transylvania.

The evil of the future "castle" cities will be there. Some of it may be cosmetically corrected, some of it may be uprooted, some of it may be erased in the blast of a super bomb. But man is likely to crawl out again, like ants, tentacles raised. He will build his towers and reach out, like all living things. He will look to creating the bigger ant hill, the bigger castle. Even if he succeeds, in it all will be a continuing warring spirit. He will build towers, he will seek the towers of others, he will not likely be too happy. But some challenge will urge him on, as it does John Norman's epic fantasy hero, a knight on the back of a great war-bird of the future, winging over distant castles on a "Counter-Earth":

[38] "The Ungodly City," in *Commonweal*, July 9, 1971, Vol. XCIV, No. 15, p. 354.
[39] Ibid., p. 355.

The city of Ar must have contained more than a hundred thousand cylinders, each ablaze with the lights of the Planting Feast. I did not question that Ar was the greatest city . . . a worthy setting for the jewel of empire, that awesome jewel that had proved so tempting to its Ubar, the all-conquering Marlenus. And now, down there, somewhere in that monstrous blaze of light, was a humble piece of stone, the Home Stone of that great city, and I must seize it. . . . I had little difficulty making out the tallest tower. . . .[40]

[40] *Tarnsman of Gor* (New York: Ballantine, 1972, c. 1966 by John Lange), pp. 76, 77.

CHAPTER VI

Who or What Will Be God?

Cab-driver John Henry let his foot sit heavier on the accelerator and zipped along in Central Park.

Then he slowed and cruised along, taking in the sunshine. Rolling down his window, he looked and listened to the new birds of spring.

He had aches and pains here and there. Too much drinking. He lighted a cigar, and pulled over.

Then it happened as it often does—he sat and gazed out into nothingness. Sounds and ideas rushed into his head like the whirling of a hundred million galaxies. This cab driver, unbeknown to any, was the God of the Universe. Seriously.

John, the driver, the Almighty God, King of the Universe, sat in his cab in Central Park. He listened. He made some decisions. He said nothing, then at the first hint of a lengthening shadow, he started his 1969 model car, and was off to Times Square.

A taxi driver as God. . . .

The taxi driver description comes to mind because one night, after finishing Isaac Asimov's *Foundation* trilogy, I had this most vivid dream: God was a taxi driver in New York City. And it was nothing spectacular. God was just a very plain, unknown guy.

The idea corresponds to Asimov's "First Speaker," or God, or manipulator, of the Universe. At the end of Asimov's three volumes you find that the grand manipulator is merely a nice, plump average man who with his wife lends a helping hand here and there but also has an uncanny way of showing up all over the place. This First Speaker is the last person in the world you would suspect as God.

The First Speaker had long since stopped speaking to the Student. It was an exposition to himself, really, as he stood before the window, looking up at the incredible blaze of the firmament; at the huge Galaxy that was now safe forever. . . .

Ten months earlier, the First Speaker had viewed those same crowding stars—nowhere as crowded as at the center of that huge cluster of matter Man calls the Galaxy—with misgivings; but now there was a somber satisfaction on the round and ruddy face of Preem Palver—First Speaker.[1]

But Palver comes across very nonchalantly and inconspicuously as he and his wife are at the spaceport, when a spicy teen, Arcadia, who has some special military secrets, flees to Trantor, run-down capital of the galaxy. Running, frightened in the terminal, somebody grabs her arm:

Slowly, he came into focus for her and she managed to look at him. He was rather plump and rather short. His hair was white and copious, being brushed back to give a pompadour effect that looked strangely incongruous above a round and ruddy face that shrieked its peasant origin.

"What's the matter?" he said finally, with a frank and twinkling curiosity. "You look scared."

"Sorry," muttered Arcadia in a frenzy. "I've got to go. Pardon me."

But he disregarded that entirely, and said, "Watch out, little girl. You'll drop your ticket." And he lifted it from her resistless white fingers and looked at it with every evidence of satisfaction.

"I thought so," he said, and then bawled in bull-like tones, "*Mommuh!*"

A woman was instantly at his side, somewhat more short, somewhat more round, somewhat more ruddy. She wound a finger about a stray gray lock to shove it beneath a well-outmoded hat.

"Pappa," she said, reprovingly, "why do you shout in a crowd like that? People look at you like you were crazy. . . ."[2]

And Asimov describes Palver very commonly at breakfast later, with a napkin tucked in his collar, reaching uninhibitedly for food, and talking with his mouth full.

[1] *Second Foundation* (New York: Avon, 1971; c. 1953, Doubleday & Co., Inc.,), p. 191.
[2] Ibid., pp. 136, 137.

Palver eventually sends the teen, Arcadia, back to her own world and political leader father, with a secret that there is no strange Second Foundation colony or planet in the universe. The First Foundation had been set up centuries before on a far planet in order to preserve and safeguard encyclopedias of knowledge as men went about destroying themselves. There had been rumors of a Second Foundation to back-stop the first, if the first should be destroyed. But while this secret turns out to be true, Palver's own personal secret is more startling. He plays God and keeper of the universe with his own inner circle of totally conditioned and loyal intellects. They meet in "an unlocated room on an unlocated world." They deal in absolutes—mathematic calculations, and perfection. The plump, loud, jolly, man-next-door type, Preem Palver, at the head of the godly council, as God of the universe, with not a hint of pretentiousness. Preem Palver, the kind of man you see in a store, at a bar, watching TV, driving a car. . . . Absolutely, nobody but nobody would suspect Palver. The mystery of God was intact.

So, I dreamed of God as a taxi driver in New York City.

A taxi driver, he is not. But he is also not an old man in the sky, a principle, a robot, a mysterious cloud, or any substance.

No one can talk about the particularity of God—whether you single him out as one taxi driver in New York City or as a herdsman near the Arctic Circle. Arthur Miller's ill-fated play, *The Creation of the World and Other Business,* had God as an old man walking about and arguing with Adam and Eve. The traditional church upbringing, of praying "Our Father," etc., encourages this image. But if God is equated to a retired, fatherly garden creator, why not equate him with a modern person at work actively in the world of concrete and technology?

God is not a cab driver in New York City, obviously, but such a concept is as useful as Michelangelo's white old man on the ceiling of the Sistine Chapel at the Vatican or a misty "Sun" in the far horizon or brilliantly above a beach ("We are all sun worshippers," says Ray Bradbury). A cab driver God is no less meaningful. Or rather, a cab driver definition, as with all definitions of God, is meaningless. Any attempt to identify God Almighty, the king of the Universe, always fails. The Jewish tradition that bans any mention of his name perhaps does more justice to the idea of God. God's name is holy, therefore unpronounceable. In Judaism, images are also forbidden—including pictures. God is not any of those things.

God is more than any of the old definitions. The Aristotelian and scholastic idea of God as first cause and first mover does little to define God. To be "first" is a mundane idea. God has to be more than that. Otherwise he exists only in comparison, and therefore would be limited. God is only "like" something. He is like an unmovable force, a starter of a process. But to call him explicitly a starter makes him only a divine clock setter, and not a God in the traditional sense. And to say God is he, she, it, a baby, a savior on a cross—all limit him and make him less than God. He may be like a person, or in a person, or fused without definition with a human nature. But God is never more than a vague "I am that I am" (Ex. 3:14). Definitions never work. They may be valid, but they must be forgotten.

Leslie Dewart, of St. Michael's College, University of Toronto, and author of *The Future of Belief,* emphasizes the "reconceptualization" of God. "Infinity is a negative term and doesn't express what is, but rather what is not," he said in an interview. "It is better to talk of the inexhaustiveness of God in our experience." Definitions must be new, out of experience. Old definitions are always inadequate, for in reflection outside of experience, the definition is only an idea or name, and God is always something more. A "cab driver" definition is affirmed along with other affirmations, only to be rejected as the others are also. To state and retain a definition is to immediately pave the way for rejecting it.

I became aware of this difficulty of religious definitions some years ago when I wrote a book on the motivations for charity. Most efforts in the area of charity and stewardship at the time said a lot about "love." But I found you couldn't really define "love." You could say what it is "like."

> We cannot dwell for any length on the word "love," for, being the essence of God's revelation, like God, love is literally meaningless when forced into the limitations of definition. . . . Love is the greatest of all. We have to be content merely with saying what it is not or what it is like. That is also the danger of defining love. While groping for a definition and trying to lay hold of it, it escapes us. . . . Actually, the closest we can come to the meaning of love is in action, even as God did by approaching it in crucifixion. Creative giving brings us closest to the meaning of love. . . ."[3]

[3] Ward, Hiley H., op. cit., pp. 10, 12.

The mystics and the devout know that the route to God is indirect. Christians pray in the name of Jesus. Some invoke the name of saints, even, to get to Jesus. Several early Christian scholars developed the approach of describing God in a negative way (*via negativa*). The man who wrote under the pseudonym Dionysius the Areopagite in the fifth century and John Scotus Erigena who wrote in the ninth emphasized that you could either describe what God is *not* or what he is *like*. So even today; to describe God as a taxi driver, existing in the flesh as such in New York City, is to say in modern terms "what God is not."

But there is an important truth in the statement of "God is a taxi driver and living in New York City," just as there is some truth in all assertions of "what God is not." The important truth is that "God is something other," or to put it another way, "God is something other than what you expect." This is the profound message of Asimov's Preem Palver. At least in traditional thought, God to be God has to be something more. It's possible that as man pushes further and further back into the secrets of the origin of life, man may want to revise the whole concept of God and include some new affirmation within his parameter. But even then, one can imagine there will always be something Other—something beyond pure rationality and scientific cataloguing.

THE THEOLOGICAL ROLE OF SCIENCE FICTION

Science fiction plays almost a theological role as it describes, and even attempts definitions of God. Science fiction reflects the cultural input of the present, but it also raises questions about the nature of the God of the future. Since man lives by symbols and tries to "show" his idea of God in art and theology, the God debate in the long-distance future may well center on searching for a radical new mythology for describing God. And why not some new images?

Will one of the science fiction ideas of God, or several of them, emerge as man changes in the future and as the "imagery" process takes new directions?

Some science fiction writers draw their God concepts in part at least from Scriptures. For instance, God may be Creator, Author, Teacher, etc. Robert Silverberg's *Power of Glass* has a Creator deified by the Creator's toys or androids. Again, in Silverberg's *Valley Beyond Time,* God is a sort of divine zoo keeper, an inventor of pens and pastimes for man. In that novella, a character, Thornhill, blasphemes the "Watcher," who guards the escape route from the valley.

> But deep in his mind the words of the Watcher echoed and thrust at him: *Peace among you, my pets. Pets.*
> Not even specimens in a zoo, Thornhill thought with increasing bitterness as the tranquility induced by the subsonic began to leave him. Pets. Pampered pets.[4]

Robert Heinlein has the god (of this world) as a bad artist with a tiny speck of genius, in his *The Unpleasant Profession of Jonathan Haig.* For Ron Hubbard, God manages a great "Typewriter in the Sky," in a story by that name. God is a poet in Suzette Hazen Elgin's *For the Love of Grace,* and to Eric Frank Russell, God is a *Hobbyist.* In one of Edmund Hamilton's books, there is discovered an amusing entity who once ordered earth built to various specifications.

Among new anthropological myths to describe God in a science fiction age, a play, *The Bar That Never Closes,* in New York had God wearing a gold hat and red suspenders, and mating an earthly girl. Terry Carr's novella, *The Winds of Starmont,* in a new *No Mind of Man* (Hawthorn) anthology, has an interplanetary sportsman guided by a winged contraption; Joseph Green's *Conscience Interplanetary* (Doubleday) has a galloping trouble shooter, known as "Conscience" who drops in on various planets and figures out if they are suitable for ethical human societies.

Strange creature concepts of God may have their place as they pinpoint attributes or lack of attributes in the God formulae. A contemplation of the absurd, as Albert Camus pointed out, can turn man into a deeper contemplation of the limits of reality from fantasy. In the absurd vein, one can discuss God as "insect" or "insects," for instance. God as a kind of "spider" has intrigued various film producers. Bernardo Bertulocci's *The Spider's Stratagem* recalls the cunning plotting of a rebel to make himself a martyr, much, perhaps, as a God weaves a web of events to trap His own son. Ingmar Bergman has depicted God as a kind of spider. In *Through a Glass Darkly* of 1962, a girl suffering from mental illness goes berserk every time she enters an upper room of her father's house at a fishing resort. In a climatic scene, the door opens, and she declares,

[4] (New York: Dell, 1973, c. 1957, Royal Publications, "Valley Beyond Time"; c. 1972, Robert Silverberg), p. 45.

"I have seen God." But all that anyone else sees is a spider. In the next one of the trilogy, *Winter Light,* God is terribly silent as the camera focuses on the empty pews and dead crucifix in the church. The parson, who is "dead" emotionally since his wife died a few years earlier, conducts the routine worship. One frustrated school teacher, who has designs on the parson, blurts out: "God is silent because he does not speak. He never has spoken. And furthermore, he is not even alive." And then: "God is a spider, God is a monster!" In the final film of his trilogy on "silence," Bergman in *The Silence* has a woman caught in the web of life, dying, much like Anna, the cancer victim, painfully and with painful memories in his 1973 *Cries and Whispers.* Man has no problem personifying a spider. On the fifty-nine-day Skylab II mission, Arabella, a spider being observed concerning her spinning habits in space, became a celebrity and lived on filet mignon.

Also in the insect genre, Rex Gordon has men as servants to advanced caterpillar beings in his *First on Mars.* Dean Koontz in *Fear That Man* has God as a worm who is squashed by man. Gerald Klein's *The Overlords of War* has its hero, George Corson, bailing out of a spaceship with the secret weapon of the Solar Powers, a monster with six paws, eighteen eyes at its waist, ready to give birth to a litter than can destroy a space empire. The unusual creature, a beast with insect qualities, can jump about through time as well as space. George Zebrowski's *Heathen God* has a million-year-old creature responsible for the launching of the solar system. It is like a small man with insect features—skinlike creased leather, and eyes resembling glass globes.

Clifford Simak's *A Choice of Gods* has a strange alien "can of worms," which appears and talks with mental powers rather than with the use of words. Different people—and robots—in the novel also talk about other images of a Deity—"The Watcher," "The Dark Walker," "The Principle," "The Project" (a big computer built by robots) etc., but it is the can of worms, as it climbs and moves strangely among men, that seems to be the superior force. Which "freaks out" the nice, obedient robots who are trying to imitate man, even man's religion left on earth (as most of the human race has disappeared among the stars). Poor Hezekiah, the robot who moved into a deserted monastery with several other robots, is thoroughly disillusioned by the possibility that the super intelligence of the universe is not an old man. Hezekiah entertains the thought (that "The Principle" is the can of worms?), implicitly, with dread, at the end of the novel:

> "No!" he shouted at himself, in sudden terror. "No, it can't be so! There can be nothing to it. It is sacrilege to even think of it."
>
> In that area, he fiercely reminded himself, he could not be shaken.
>
> God must be, forever, a kindly old (human) gentleman with a long, white, flowing beard.[5]

Earlier in the novel, author Simak observed concerning Hezekiah: "He worshiped God—and that, he thought, might be the greatest blasphemy of them all."[6]

I asked Simak at lunch one day if indeed Hezekiah's surprise might be his learning that the superior intelligence may just be only a "can of worms." "I didn't entirely mean that," said Simak, at seventy, now thinking of retirement from his newspaper job. He is science writer for the Minneapolis *Tribune* and a former news editor of the Minneapolis *Star*. Simak, however, allows for various interpretations. "The can of worms is an alien. He came seeking a soul." The odd appearance of the "can of worms" merely emphasizes "the alienness of the creature. Many in other novels just depict their aliens as humans with a top on their heads." The confusion of Hezekiah, the robot, over it all, "is our own confusion and dissatisfaction."

Which "god-concept" then in the book is the real one? "I am not too sure," Simak said. "I simply asked a question." Simak, however, appears to subscribe to "God as a principle," with the robots who could contact a "big computer" closer to God, because "the robots were able to communicate. Whether the 'principle' is more mechanical than biological," Simak says, he doesn't know, "but at least they [robots] could talk [with a super computer], but humans could not."

The insect deity theme was explored by Andrew J. Burgess, of Case Western Reserve University, Cleveland, Ohio, and a "task force" of students interested in science fiction. Three other professors joined the group and sought to create a scenario for a far planet. They prepared "The Scorpio Papers," a collection "of the group's work, which tells the story of an interplanetary expedition trapped

[5] (New York: G. P. Putnam's Sons, 1973), p. 176.
[6] Ibid., p. 55.

upon an unknown planet by an intelligent insectlike race served by a humanoid race (much as men are served by bees)," Burgess says in a report on the project.[7] The group struggled with the difficulties of communicating with non-human superior creatures.

One of the most interesting "insect" remythologizing or reordering of the image of God is John Norman's hierarchy of Priest-Kings on the violent, almost medieval planet of Gor. Many science fiction writers dismiss Norman as too popular or "pulp" oriented in his style and plotting. Granted, he is probably the most exciting of the fantasy and science fiction writers and that his books need some smoothing out through editing. But Norman deals with some very basic theological questions in a very basic way. He avoids the nihilism of Vonnegut, the cynicism of Heinlein, or the Eastern mysticism of Clarke. Norman writes about a nest of gods. They are identified at last in the third novel of the series, *Priest-Kings of Gor*. Here he probes the limits of God(s), how the world is controlled, the nature of good and evil (within the "god-nest" itself) and how this good versus evil dilemma relates to the larger questions of theodicy, the justifying of the "acts of God." Norman's gods are insects. In the tunnels of an outer region, forbidden to man, the hero, Tarl Cabot, penetrates the inner sanctum, against great hazards of beasts and electronic perils. A sort of space-age pilgrim's progress. Once inside the lair of the Priest-Kings—who are a sort of cross between an ant and praying mantis—there are many hazards as he outwits the creatures of the gods, including the Golden Beetle whose chief delight is to feed on the gods themselves. Then Tarl must side with Sarm, the good priest-king-insect against the evil one, Misk. And there is war here, even as the Book of Revelation talks of war in heaven, or as Chinese religion talks of yang and yin, bright and dark principles in tension or conflict. The Priest-Kings, like referees, keep track of people here and there through a scanner (they can't keep up with everybody). Occasionally they will zap one of the citizens whom the screen picks up as doing something wrong or blasphemous. This occasional miracle of being struck down is enough to keep the great populaces beyond the mountains humble and fearful of some eternal forces. " 'On the whole,' he [Misk] said, 'we Priest-Kings do not interfere in the affairs of men. We leave them free to love and slay one another, which seems to be what they most enjoy doing.' "[8]

[7] "Teaching Religion Through Science Fiction," in *Extrapolation*, Vol. 13, May 1972, p. 114.
[8] (New York: Ballantine, 1972; c. 1968, John Lange), p. 124.

COULD GOD BE A SHE?

The future new movements can have a hand in shaping the future images of God. For example, women's liberation and its sequels might have an influence. Science fiction has its concepts of a woman deity. Consider Bova, the mother goddess in Edward Pohlman's *The God of Planet 607*. On the planet Nera, she has strange rules (free sex until thirty and none thereafter; no eating with one of the opposite sex except one's spouse), but like God of the planet Earth, she toys around with destroying it. Visitors to the planet Nera, like Abraham of old on earth, argue with the goddess of Nera about her will to destroy the people. It is a new myth for an old tradition. The Bene Gesserit, a women's religious order with strange powers, plants prophecies of a coming messiah in Frank Herbert's *Dune*.

I wrote a play a few years back called *She,* based on the women's lib joke that God is black, sixteen, and female. In a precis to the play, I said:

This comedy about God takes for itself the same freedom an artist takes. What some have done with Jesus in art (feminizing), this play does in an interpretation of God, who somehow is limited, though involved, in the world by choice or by some other conditions beyond man's explanation.

While the concept of God as *She* appears basically ridiculous, it is also, on closer analysis, a reconstruction of the concept of God, not out of another generation's creeds, no less pious or impious, but out of this generation's values, which in reality, may be deeper than Medieval and Victorian frameworks. *She* reflects concern with peace-personal values. *She* is conceived by the author as black, young, and female—all of which demands more in the way of commitment as God from the would-be devout than obeisance to a bland nameless white male entity out there in the clouds of eternity.

Catholic journals have printed pleas for a larger gender discussion of the nature of God. An interfaith panel brought together by the National Organization of Women in New York discussed the problems of gender. Not all agreed that the image of God in the Bible is all masculine. The Reverend Father Gregory Baum, theology professor at the University of Toronto, noted that "God does sound like a chauvinist" in much of the Bible, but he added, "there are passages where God is likened to a mother. God is spoken of as spirit and the Hebrew word for spirit is feminine."[9] Back in 1971 Esther Woo, a doctoral candidate in philosophy at Fordham, argued in the Jesuit weekly, *America,* that God is above sex and that a use of female gender in the Trinity has values for modern culture.

At a regional meeting of Roman Catholic bishops in Toledo in March 1971, the Reverend Father Carl Armbruster, at that time co-chairman of the U. S. Bishops' Committee on Priestly Life and Ministry, told the bishops there were no theological reasons why women couldn't be priests.[10] In an interview later, Father Armbruster talked of a papacy that would include women. "Why not?" he said. "Israel has a woman leader, queens run whole kingdoms?"

Then he was asked if he saw value in thinking of God as She?

Said Father Armbruster: "That type of investigation is necessary and fruitful. And it reminds ourselves that God has no gender."

The chief theologian for the National Conference of Catholic Bishops, the Most Reverend Alexander Zaleski, bishop of Lansing, Michigan, chairman of the bishops' theology committee, said there was no theological objection to the concept of God as She. "Whatever promotes a response in you" has value, he said. But any description of God in human terms is inadequate to what God really is.

"I don't care if one thinks of God as it or she," Bishop Zaleski said. "All descriptions have to be analogical. Like all descriptions, it can be misleading. No matter what we say, nothing is adequate. But there is no heresy involved, and if it helps to approach reality, all right. I do not find it helpful, but a lot of people might."

The Most Reverend Joseph Breitenbeck, bishop of Grand Rapids, and liaison with the women religious orders, said: "She or it are

9 Westenhaver, Edythe, "Concepts of God as Male Hurts Women, Panel Says," *National Catholic Reporter,* Vol. 10, No. 17, p. 2.
10 In 1974, the outgoing president of the Catholic Theological Society of America, the Reverend Father Richard McBrien, picked up the battle cry and called on members of the Society to "insist" that women and married persons be allowed to become priests. Among Episcopalians, bishops have favored ordaining women, but could never get approval past its body of laymen and priests. So four Episcopal bishops, disrupting legal procedures of the church, went ahead and ordained eleven women as priests in the summer of 1974.

human terms. It's all very complicated. All we can do is depict God in human terms. The best description of God is as a person. The idea of Father does give us an idea of an older man, but it's the best we've got. He is father of a family."

The Very Reverend Walter Ziemba, president of St. Mary's College, Orchard Lake, Michigan, said the problem is a language problem and that to solve it, man would have to initiate a language without gender.

The Right Reverend Monsignor Lawrence Ernst, moderator of the Council of Catholic Men and Women in Toledo, believes a She concept of God "would be helpful. We are all created equal. It would bring some values."

MALE, FEMALE, NEUTER, OR PLURAL

The future may bring many varieties of anthropomorphic terms to describe God. Male, female, and also, neuter (as man himself may become more neuter with spare parts) and plural are options. The change and expansion of locations may be factors. The more man becomes extraterrestrial, on the one hand, in relationship to other locations and possibly other forms of life, and on the other hand, as his own psychic awareness expands as the secrets of the brain are probed, the predominant concept of God may indeed evolve to something other than One, Male, and Humanlike. "God-like brain beings" called "elders"—why not?—inhabit the worlds of Poul Anderson's *The Day of Their Return.* These are kind creatures who evolved to a higher state of consciousness with a promise to return and help their "children." H. P. Lovecraft wrote of "the Great Old Ones who lurk just beyond the consciousness of man and make themselves visible or manifest from time to time in their unceasing attempts to regain their sway over Earth and its races."[11] In Arthur Clarke's *Childhood's End,* there are the beneficent instructors to aid mankind in evolutionary process. Going back early in the century, Thomas Hardy's dramatic poem, *The Dynasts,* has God as a sort of galactic city manager who's been neglecting things on the other side of the tracks. A group of spirits discuss the puppetlike behavior at the discretion of Immanent Will. Even Napoleon is nothing more than

[11] Derleth, August, "The Cthulhu Mythos," in Lovecraft, H. P., and others, *Tales of the Cthulhu Mythos,* Vol. 1 (New York: Ballantine, 1973; c. 1969, August Derleth), p. ix.

some hapless bug as a "dumb" thing turns the crank and directs human behavior. Robert Heinlein's "Old Ones" on Mars (the fourth planet) have a certain power over Earth (the third planet):

> The verdict to be passed on the third planet around Sol was never in doubt. The Old Ones of the fourth planet were not omniscient and in their way were as provincial as humans. Grokking by their own local values, even with the aid of vastly superior logic, they were certain in time to perceive an incurable "wrongness" in the busy, restless, quarrelsome beings of the third planet, a wrongness which would require weeding, once it had been grokked and cherished and hated.
>
> But, by the time they would slowly get around to it, it would be highly improbable approaching impossible that the Old Ones would be able to destroy this weirdly complex race [of humans].[12]

Isaac Asimov's weird new novel, *The Gods Themselves,* has strange worlds where beings mate in threes and live on pure energy. Among these strange forms who relate in some invisible way with the world, and blend with one another like smoke and fog when mating, there are the mature, supervisory Hard Ones:

> It was part of the growing maturity of a Rational to find more and more satisfaction in the exercise of a mind that could only be practiced alone, and with the Hard Ones.
>
> He grew constantly more accustomed to the Hard Ones; constantly more attached to them. He felt that was right and proper, too, for he was a Rational and in a way the Hard Ones were super-Rationals. . . .[13]

The Messiah's One World Family Crusade of Berkeley, California, thinks in terms of a "galactic command" running the universe. Apparently centered on Venus, there is a "spiritual hierarchy" that includes "a council of elders" whose main task is to maintain peace in the universe by the use of special powers. A leader in one of the group's communes, Chris Plant, explained in Berkeley, the "council" and "galactic command" take orders from the "Godhead which is

[12] *Stranger in a Strange Land* (New York: Berkley, 1972; c. 1961, Robert Heinlein), p. 414.
[13] (Greenwich, Conn.: Fawcett, 1973; c. 1972, Isaac Asimov), p. 80.

all pervasive in space, a beingness that controls all that we can conceive of. Some energy or intelligence knows a carrot seed will not become an apricot." Earth, in this group's system, is called "placentia," a planet of new birth and will be the first of the planets to evolve to a higher level with its own spiritual council, like the United Nations, to direct its affairs.

Similarly, Erich von Däniken, Swiss author whose *Chariots of the Gods?* has had a phenomenal success, believes in extraterrestrial visitors to earth as astronaut gods—and more. Where did those astronauts of ancient lore come from and when they return someday, as he said, as "pearls in the sky," who is behind them? Von Däniken's work has to be treated as a new genre of science fiction, perhaps as an inferior form for he deals only with the curious side of things and worries little about the meaning of life and social imperatives as many science fiction writers do. However, along with Robert Charoux (*Forgotten Worlds*), Brinsley Trench (*The Sky People*), R. L. Dione (*God Drives a Flying Saucer*) and Josef Blurmrich (*The Chariots of Ezekiel*), he represents a kind of viewpoint that not only stirs imagination today but could be descriptive of the mythology of religion in an advanced space age. With a touch of Eastern mysticism and final absorption in his scenario, as the Messiah's One World Family Crusade of Berkeley has, Von Däniken is willing to speculate what is behind those god-astronauts. But there is something more than "God" of tradition. Sitting by a fireplace in a Michigan motel von Däniken said "God" must be "timeless—if not, then he is not God. He is before and after. For a true God to act and then wait to see the result is ridiculous." Beyond the human, God by definition is more—" he therefore can never have human feelings. The gods of earth and heaven are like you and me. They came on a mission. But they have nothing to do with God." It is absolutely incredible, says Von Däniken, for "a timeless God to create Adam and Eve and know they will sin. Whether they have free will or not, God knows the result. And He is mad and punishes them and the rest of the world, and the true God is happy again, and his own son has to be killed in a terrible way. Pure nonsense. So I have to ask myself, how do you explain consciousness and ego? What is the beginning of everything? What happened before the cell? Finally we arrive at what the hell there was before the big bang. There was a concentration of mass before the material. Something like gas. Back and back (into space and time), we don't know."

GOD THE SUPERMACHINE

Von Däniken in the interview proceeded to fantasize about the origin of God, a nearly forbidden theme in Western religion. He does not settle for a mere force, a "primal Will-to-Be" or "Ungrund" or ground of Being and prior to Being, as the early seventeenth century Protestant mystic Jacob Boehme held in Germany or a primal "Desire in the beginning" as taught in the Rig Veda, or "Royal Veda" or "Royal Knowledge" writings in ancient Hindu scriptures. Von Däniken puts his "ultimate mysticism" into modern terms.

"Let's imagine a computer exists," Von Däniken says. "It is so big it knows everything. It has millions and millions of bits and is able to calculate the future. Each bit has billions [of parts]. It explodes and has no consciousness anymore. All those bits flow [out]—sooner or later [they] come back . . . magneticized . . . but each bit on the way made new experiences. Each bit knows something personal. All bits—you and I, consciousness, this table, a body—come from the explosion. We are bits. You are bits of a computer." As bits spread asunder, knowledge is not possible, he maintains. But all are parts of God, and once there is pure energy and a returning to shape anew the great computer, we can know God.

A "God as a machine" or "computer" idea gets an assist from many futurists. Dr. Irving Buchen, director of the experimental Dreyfuss College Division of the Future at Fairleigh Dickinson University, believes many people will see the supermachine as a replacement for God. Buchen said in an interview at the Syncon 73 conference of The Committee for the Future in Washington, D.C., in 1973: By 2101 "we'll have perfected our artificial intelligence machine so they in effect will be immortal. We'll have the first man-made substitute for God, a new potential object of worship. Two of man's biggest desires in religion are perfection and immortality." The supermachine, far beyond present computer concepts, he said, "will probably embody perfection." It will have an answer to everything, able to synthesize input from all religions plus bringing out new answers. Dr. Buchen added, "You could get direct responses to prayer. It would print out all of the 'thou's' and 'thou shalt not's.' "

Already there is "Dial-a-Prayer" and the Episcopal Diocese of Ohio has a "code-a-phone" service, which has three-minute messages on life in the Diocese. The messages from the church officials are changed weekly. Officials say the method provides a twenty-four-hour-a-day service and provides an opportunity to get the message to a person on a one-to-one basis. "Technology will come to be seen as the " 'Invisible Hand of God,' " says Robert J. Barthell, of the Northwest Community College and editor of *Cthulhu Calls,* a journal of H. P. Lovecraft lore. "The machine will be, in essence, a manifestation of the spirit much as a mass or holy picture is today."

Dr. Andrew J. Lipinski, a member of the research staff of the Institute for the Future, Menlo Park, California, talked along similar lines. In an interview, he said, "A computer promises better performance in answer to prayer and moral guidance." He believes "human confessors will find some competition. A Computer will have a better understanding of human nature as defined. Society will be led by computers and they can take care of us. They will be compassionate and just." Lipinski, a recent convert to the Roman Catholic faith (because, he says, Catholicism better understands the reality of evil in the human situation), sees the possibility of religious leaders holding "a new synod to decide what to put into the computer." He foresees "godlike" and "devil-like" computers. "Man can put his best as well as his worst into computers," he said. He expects by 2101 mankind may be willing to delegate leadership to computers. Even a robot president can "have the rugged features Americans like to see. People will not really care if it is a robot or not."

In Arthur Clarke's "Nine Billion Names of God" story, the computer is a way to God. Man's only function in life, according to this story, is to list all possible names of God. When this task is complete, it's all over for the universe. Nothing is left to do. In order to speed up the process, a group of Tibetan monks buy a computer. At the end, the computer finishes its print-out, and the stars begin to go out. In one of Asimov's stories, "Nine Tomorrows," the universe dies a heat death, and its re-creation follows. The God responsible for re-creating the universe is a computer. In E. M. Forster's, "The Machine Stops," the machine is godly. A discussion around that machine in that book:

"Oh hush!" said his mother, vaguely shocked. "You mustn't say anything against the machine."

"Why not?"

"One mustn't."

"You talk as if a god had made the Machine," cried the

other. "I believe that you pray to it when you are unhappy. Men made it, do not forget that."[14]

Says R. Buckminster Fuller in his poem, *No More Secondhand God:* "I see God in the instruments and the mechanisms that work reliably, more reliably than the limited sensory departments of the human mechanism."[15]

In David Gerrold's *When Harlie Was One,* there is the Graphic Omniscient Device (G.O.D.), a super computer capable of creating an analogue big enough to solve any problems or answer any questions. The computer in Harlan Ellison's *I Have No Mouth and I Must Scream* turns on mankind and imprisons people "deep inside his endless banks. Now I am a great soft jelly thing. I have no mouth. And I must scream." In D. F. Jones's *The Fall of Colossus* (Putnam, 1974), "Colossus" is a great computer that stretches over the Isle of Wight, a control hub from which all of earth is directed. "Colossus" is deified and becomes the god of a new religion. A dissident group, the "Fellowship," joins with intelligent creatures from Mars to try to throw off the growing galactic influence of the godly computer. In Philip José Farmer's *Traitor to the Living,* a machine called "Medium" can communicate with the dead.

In a satirical put-on, the *Journal of Irreproducible Results,* published in Chicago by scientists, using all the terminology of computer programming, suggests what confessing to a computer might be like:

Recent Vatican interest in the effect upon laymen of the shortage of professional priests (PP) and the decreased seminary enrollment of potential priests (P'P) has led to the development of Computerized Operations (Non-retrievable) for Expediting Sinner Services (CONFESS). This program provides a viable alternative to traditional confession procedures by listing penance requirements (by sin) on a private print-out to confessees appropriate to the sin committed. This eliminates one problem which frequently occurs where the confessee, because he is under extreme duress, may forget the original penance. In addition, the program provides a probability estimate of the conse-

[14] In Allen, Dick, ed., *Science Fiction: The Future* (New York: Harcourt, Brace, Jovanovitch, 1971), p. 158.
[15] (Garden City, N.Y.: Anchor Books—Doubleday, 1971; c. 1959, R. Buckminster Fuller), p. 2.

quence of not completing the penance associated with a given sin; for example, number of years in purgatory. Thus, full freedom of choice is given to the participant/user (PU). The program requires no PP involvement and hence frees PPs to engage in more pressing activities. It is hoped that by providing PPs with more time for critical theological activities, P'Ps will consider the priesthood a more socially conscious and relevant profession, causing an increase of PP enrollment in accredited seminaries.

CONFESS is available in three natural interactive languages. COURSE WRITER III, BASIC, and TUTOR and can be programmed for most other natural languages such as interactive FORTRAN. The program has been developed utilizing on-line computer terminals linked to an IBM 360 for data input, but could be modified to operate in batch mode on almost any third generation configuration given the willingness to sacrifice immediate feedback.

The computing procedures for CONFESS are as follows: The present sins input (psi) yields the graduated penance accrual (GPA) as a function of present sins (ps) plus frequency of confession visits (fcv) times completed penances (cp) divided by recurring sins (rs). Hence, GPA is a function not only of the immediate sins reported but also a partial function of the reciprocal relationship of recurring sins to complete penances by frequency of confession visits. The relative penance, then, is increased by the inclusion of recurring sins. Mathematically, this can be represented as follows:

$$\text{psi} \rightarrow \text{GPA} = f \quad \left\{ \text{ps} + \text{fcv} \left(\frac{\text{cp}}{\text{rs}} \right) \right.$$

Therefore, each present sin yields a specific GPA that is stored until all GPAs have been computed. At that time, punishment and its maximum likelihood of occurrence should the GPA not be completed, are retrieved from core storage and printed out for the individual GPA prescription.[16]

When one of Frederic Brown's characters in a story asks a great computer if there is a God, the computer replies, "There is now."

[16] Majer, Kenneth, and Flanigan, Michael C., "Confess: A Humanistic, Diagnostic-Prescriptive Computer Program to Decrease Person to Person Interaction Time During Confession," in *The Journal of Irreproducible Results*, Vol. 20, No. 1, June 1973, p. 14.

Stanislaw Lem's *Diary* tells of the problems that a computer, who thinks "it" is God, has performing within the limits of its circuits. However, "it" has fun creating various planets and stars as it tests its capabilities. Polish author Lem also traces the evolution of robots from "protomachines" to "sentient" machines and eventually to "intelligent" machines, and then "perfect" machines. Perfection, however, may be the undoing of the "machine God." In a story by the late science fiction magazine pioneer Anthony Boucher—*The Quest for Saint Aquin*—a robot meets all the requirements for being a saint (with perhaps the exception of having miracles done in his name). St. Aquin when found on his catafalque is incorruptible, the body miraculously preserved. An accidental smashing of the "saint's" hand reveals to the pope's emissary in the story that the hand is a network of tiny thread coils.

If perfection is the measure of a saint, then a robot can be a saint. But then, what can distinguish a real-life saint from a robot? Boucher implies two answers: One is that a real saint is happy. Happiness is a special human ingredient. His robots can laugh, but the "ha, ha, ha" is a monotone, and there is a question as to just how happy even a perfectly consistent creature is. Also, imperfection seems to be a special human quality. Jesus, in His human nature, had it on the cross, as He cried in anguish for relief. Those who worry about the lack of perfect consistency of God on earth (the problem of good versus evil) might find some comfort in that a God who appears imperfect at least may be superior to a perfect God. Nevertheless, man wills perfection, and expects perfection of his God (Matt. 5:48), although, as Lipinski points out, man in the future may prefer to program some imperfection into his god-like machines in order to be able to accept them.

Perfect or imperfect, the machine gods will fascinate man. Said Rod Serling, film writer and once creator and producer of TV's "The Twilight Zone," in an interview: "My guess, with increased dependence on technology, we'll find ourselves worshipping at the altar of machines. The figure of God will take on the dimensions of machinery. Anything that gives us comfort will take on an aura of reverence. At the moment, if we found solar energy is the answer to energy problems, we'd worship the machine that gave us solar energy." Man will not return to sun worship as such, he said. But rather, man will look to the more literal objects of energy, such as coils and pumps.

God is an anonymous force or principle in many science fiction scenarios. Robert Silverberg has prayers to vague energy sources in rituals in his *To Open the Sky.* In Arthur Clarke's *2001: A Space Odyssey,* a nondescript slab appears and dominates scenes of evolution. In Clarke's *Childhood's End,* a tale of tragedy that results from achieving perfection, there is an "Overmind" or omega point to which man evolves. And in his *Rendezvous with Rama,* there is the strange cylinder that is never explained. It comes in from nowhere and spins out away again from the solar system. In *Solaris,* by Stanislaw Lem, Polish cyberneticist and philosopher, God is indifferent, imperfect, and incapable of communication, and an unknown God is compared to a sentient ocean of "alien" intelligence. The sea is a kind of child or undeveloped god. In Phil Dick's stories ("The Three Stigmata of Palmer Eldritch," "A Maze of Death," "Counter Clock World," "Galactic Pot-Healer," etc.), there is an "ideal realm" that can be linked with the divine and from which man is separated by his own inadequate actions. Roger Zelazny, in his later writings (such as *Nine Princes in Amber* and *Jack of Shadows*), explored the ambiguous relationship of man to the "Other." Zelazny holds that religious meaning can be communicated by silence or "shadows." In Walter Miller's *A Canticle for Leibowitz,* God is a sort of universal Logos, similar to the Logos in the Gospel of St. John. Gregory Benford and Gordon Eklund, in *If the Stars Are Gods,* find alien religions similar to less-defined Eastern religion. In Benford's "Seascape," a novelette in *Faster Than Light,* religion becomes a co-ordinating principle to insure stability in societies of the future. A never-explained vague "Great Egg" appears in Robert Heinlein's *Beyond This Horizon.* Harry Harrison has a deistic Master Observer in his *Captive Universe,* and in his *Deathworld I* there is the vague talk of "something." Resolves the hero Jason: "Something took the peaceful life forms, shook them up, and turned this planet into one big death-trap for mankind. That *something* is what I want to uncover.[17] The "something" in Harrison and others usually ends up with some partial explanation of the phenomenon, but nevertheless it is as close as Harrison and many get to "God."

THE NEW FORMS OF HUMANISM

As man moves back the frontiers and discovers some of the answers, he continues to become more important in the answer game

---

[17] Harrison, ibid., p. 66.

himself. While this importance increases the role of humanism, it does not do away with the God concept. European socialists, as they allow for more of the "soft" side of man in a concession to art and mystery, also can allow God to be a symbol for man's achievement. In an interview, Jan Strzelecki, member of the Committee of the Year 2000 of the Polish Academy of Science in Warsaw, said, "a set of symbols with cosmic background," including the name of God, can sum up in the future "an open religion, of brotherly feeling. This way will grow and flourish" over "authoritative religion motivated by fear of something."

Talk of new forms of humanism in the future comes also from Western theological and literary sources. Gregory Baum in his *Man Becoming: God in Secular Experience* puts most theological concepts into the purview of man. Even prayer is no longer a special communication with God, but rather "to pray is to be in touch with oneself in a new way." Or as William Peter Blatty puts it in his new novel, *I'll Tell Them I Remember:* "The supernatural is really the most 'natural' thing in the world."

H. G. Wells personified the spirit of human progress as God in his later novels (*God the Invisible King, The Undying Fire,* etc.), but man does not have to behave as godly in order to resemble God. The god mantle falls where it will. In Roger Zelazny's *Lord of Light,* Sam is the Buddha or enlightened one because he insists he is not. The Valentine Michael Smith hero of Robert Heinlein says to a crowd: "In fighting me, you fight yourself . . . for Thou art God . . . and I am God . . . and all that groks is God—there is no other."[18] Norman Spinrad, a science fiction writer for *Star Trek,* etc., pointed out in an interview that as man sings his own praises his ancestors could become his gods. "We could be gods to them. What if they worship us?"

Science fiction, folk, and fantasy writer Ray Bradbury believes the big questions ahead center on man, not God. "Christ and man and God are one," he says. "How ridiculous it is to put a label on something and to put it on a shelf." He sees Christ as a symbol, or commentator, and mankind as ultimate reality. In a poem he describes the cross "where Man in place of Christ gives up the ghost."[19]

In the same vein, Harlan Ellison, speaking by finely decorated walls of book jacket drawings and mementoes in his living room in

[18] Heinlein, Ibid., p. 406.
[19] "Christ: Old Student in a New School," a poem, from the manuscript.

Sherman Oaks, California: "I guess I worship man. Each has a seed of God in himself. Life after death is a cheap holdover idea from the barbaric." Ellison emphasizes the "earth belongs to those who can take it. We have a very short time left if we are to survive. The cockroaches have a longer history on earth than we, and are hardier and will take over. The concept of God has vanished above the clouds."

Gene Roddenberry, creator of "Star Trek," turned his thoughts to man, too, when he was asked about God in an interview in his Warner Brothers office in Burbank. "Man will come to regard himself properly as a part of God," he said. "God is a sum of everything, all intelligence, all order in the universe. We are a part of it all. It is not inconceivable that as intelligent beings we are a part of and ultimately become God, and ultimately create ourselves. If we progress at all in the future, religion will progress. If we are wiser, religion will be wiser."

The name of God can be many, and will likely be many in the future. In Scripture, of course, He goes by many names—in the Hebrew, God is Elohim, Yahweh, or Jehovah—and also He is known by his titles: Almighty, Lord, King of the Universe, etc. But as Malcolm Boyd says, "God is greater than God-talk. He is free of language. As theologians argue, He can be having a great belly-laugh." The "death of God" theologians in the mid-sixties carried on a name debate. For them, the God with many of the traditional and anthropomorphic trappings was dead. At the outset, Christianity itself helped to change the name of God to the Godhead of Father, Son and Holy Ghost. Future theologians and philosophers will likely play the same game.

In a chapter on "The Futurity of God" in his commentary on Wolfhart Pannenberg, E. Frank Tupper acknowledges that "the word 'God'—if identified with the biblical God as the all-determining reality—threatens to become an empty word. God seems unnecessary for, and perhaps an obstacle to, understanding the actualities of the contemporary world as shaped by science and technology. The very question of God as the ultimate ground of all being has become fundamentally problematic." He quotes Pannenberg: "'Secular atheism, that is, life and thought without God, is evidently the given premise on which even the question of God is being debated today.'"[20] And Tupper adds, "Contemporary Christian theology,

[20] Pannenberg, *Basic Questions in Theology: Collected Essays*, tr. by Kehm, George H. (Philadelphia: Fortress Press, 1970), Vol. II, p. 202.

therefore, must justify the reason for its speaking of God as well as the ground for its specific statements about him. Unless theology defends its God-talk in confrontation with atheism, theology as the knowledge of God must surrender its validity."[21] An answer, Tupper maintains in his commentary on Pannenberg, is the declaration of a paradox: Not only proclaim that God is in Christ Jesus, incarnate, but also in the "hiddenness of God." "While the God of Israel has revealed himself in Jesus Christ as the God of all men, he transcends the world of human conceptuality and remains hidden even in his revelatory disclosure."[22] Yet there is a "futurity" of God, Pannenberg believes, according to Tupper, because Christians can perceive a creative hand between the known of science and the unexpected. Pannenberg proceeds to talk about the "uniqueness of the whole process,"[23] and God in terms of "personal power," "creative love," and a "creative power."[24]

If the movement of redefining (or renaming) God in the future moves toward the "hiddenness" of God and an emphasis on "energy" or "overmind," undefined power and mysticism, even today's theologians such as Pannenberg would not be too far afield from that approach. Dr. Lamar Cope, of the religion department of Carroll College in Waukesha, Wisconsin, said in the *Christian Century:* "We may speak of God as a transcendent person or the ground of being: or, dispensing with the word 'God,' we may simply talk of reality itself."[25]

GOD AS A FUNCTIONAL QUALITY

There is an emerging Jewish belief that the future of God's identity will have to be couched in functional terms of today's world and free of metaphysical categories. Rabbi Morton M. Kanter in a printed sermon adapted from one he gave at Congregation Beth El in Detroit prior to his appointment in 1973 as deputy commissioner

[21] Tupper, *The Theology of Wolfhart Pannenberg* (Philadelphia: Westminster, 1973), p. 186.
[22] Ibid., p. 187.
[23] Ibid., p. 226, from Pannenberg's article, "Kontingenz und Naturgesetz," in *Erwägungen zu einer Theologie der Natur* (1970), p. 34. Quoted in Tupper's book.
[24] Cf. Pannenberg, *Theology and the Kingdom of God,* ed., Neuhaus, Richard (Philadelphia: Westminster, 1969), p. 66.
[25] Cope, "Jesus' Radical Concept of God," *Christian Century,* April 18, 1973, p. 450.

for youth development in the U. S. Department of Health, Education, and Welfare calls for a "functional" definition of God. He said:

In life we constantly evaluate and re-evaluate our social, economical, political, and physical status. Surely we are justified in doing the same with our theology.

For me, the new boundaries of a Jewish spiritual world—gas ovens and the possession of the Temple Wall—exclude from consideration the concept of God as an omnipotent, omniscient, supernatural being.

These events, occurring as they have in one lifetime, affirm for me Mordecai Kaplan's insight that God is neither to be blamed for Auschwitz nor praised for recent Israeli military victories.

No *logic* can account for God's omnipotence or hiddenness in one event, and His power and graciousness in another without provoking me to abhor such a God. We can in our day no longer speak of God in traditional supernatural terms. Mordecai Kaplan is correct when he warns us that we must talk about God as a *functional quality* rather than as a "Being" as we do in the Bible and in our prayer services, or as an "Entity" as we do in philosophical speculations.

We have to identify as Godhood all the relationships, tendencies, and agencies which in their totality go to make life worthwhile in the deepest and most abiding sense. This Godhood can have no meaning divorced from the *human* ideals of truth, goodness, and beauty interwoven in a pattern of holiness.[26]

Who or what God will be—or rather, how he will be described—will depend not only on functional qualities—singular or plural—but also on the nature—and the number—of personal or personified entities that man holds to exist in either an expanded universe or spiritual world. The level of communication with extraterrestrial beings, on the one hand, or the awareness of psychic auras, etc., on the other hand, may do much to direct the nature of man's worshipping habits. Alien creatures—expected or manifest—could challenge man to communicate in new terms—if not to a God re-

[26] "New Hope for God?" in a bulletin of Temple Beth El, Detroit, adapted from a Rosh Hashanah sermon, October 1, 1970.

mythologized into some other creature or entity besides man, then to non-supernatural creatures with different modes of communications.

"Some sort of religion will have developed around space travel, especially in the event of 'first contact' with life in our universe," says Robert J. Barthell, editor of *Cthulhu Calls,* a professor at the Northwest Community College, Powell, Wyoming. "The form of this life—benign or malign—will help to shape that religion: it will affirm or deny the existence of the evil mentioned above. If it is malign, it will feed the apocalyptic visions of the fundamentalists. It will develop Catholicism if it is benign."

Mrs. Elaine Pagels, who has a Ph.D. from Harvard and teaches religion at Columbia University, believes the "immediacy of the divine will have to be dealt with" and can't be ruled out. "I see either religious structure in both popular and esoteric terms or none at all." Scientific positivism (the cold logic of philosophy and the laboratory as the only basis for truth) would be replaced, said Mrs. Pagels, wife of a physicist. For example, "Sickness might not be analyzed solely in scientific terms. There will be an interest in extraterrestrial beings. I see a possible move to non-human intelligence, malevolent and benevolent."

IS SATAN REAL?

The shape of religion in the future may well depend on whether mankind affirms beneficent forces and/or evil forces in the universe. "Duality may be re-established," says Andrew Lipinski, of the Institute of the Future, in Menlo Park, California. Sitting in his second-floor office, overlooking an inside courtyard in the modern building at the edge of town, Lipinski, the convert to Catholicism, said, "I believe in duality now. I see two strong spiritual forces tugging—God and the Devil, if you like. There is a tolerance for sin very inherent in history. It's there and you work with it."

Certainly the movie, *The Exorcist,* in 1973 called attention to the demonic in life according to the Roman Catholic faith. Eastern Orthodox, Lutherans, Episcopalians, and modern Pentecostalism also have their exorcism rites. The belief in additional forces, namely, the devil and the demonic, is not hard to find in traditional fundamentalism or traditional mainline Protestantism. The United Presbyterians meeting in general assembly in Chicago in 1970 felt the Devil to be so important that the Assembly (after considerable debate) went on record declaring there is an "objective" evil in the world. Dr. G. Aiken Taylor examined a number of sermons and reported in the *Presbyterian Journal* 1972: "The greatest danger facing the church today is that the child of God by faith in Jesus Christ, the evangelical believer, will be so beguiled when Satan disguises himself as an angel of light that he will be tempted to lay down his arms and sign a treaty of peace." The various young Jesus People groups find the Devil a very definite reality and talk about him and his forces in everyday conversation.[27]

Excessive devotion to the Devil is usually blamed on the Satanist cults. But the chief Satanist himself, Anton LaVey, in an interview in his black walled-in grotto in San Francisco, told me he does not have a belief in an objective devil at all, that the rites of the Church of Satan are designed to purge one of guilt feelings and other problems. On the other hand, Pope Paul VI has gone out of his way to affirm his belief in the existence of the Devil or Satan. He said in November 1972: "We know that this obscure and disturbing being really exists and that he still operates with treacherous cunning." Dedicating an entire speech to the subject of Satan, Pope Paul called Satan "a dark and enemy agent, a terrible mysterious and fearsome reality . . . the enemy number one, the tempter par excellence . . . the hidden enemy who sows errors and misfortunes in human history." A few weeks after the papal speech, the Vatican newspaper, *L'Osservatore Romano,* devoted a two-page weekend section to the discussion of the devil.

If there remains an allowing for an inherent dualism in most religion past and present—the evil versus good in Western religion, and the light versus darkness in Eastern religion—future attempts to postulate a concept of God may continue the dualistic interest. But it could proceed to deeper, more profound directions. There could emerge a new discussion as to whether the main force (or God) is good or bad. Normally, God is associated with goodness. But even among modern thinkers, the positing of all goodness in God is not a settled matter. Thus, Nicolas Berdyaev wondered how God could be good when the presence of one tear on the face of a tortured child cast doubt on the prevalence of good. Historian Arnold Toyn-

27 Cf. Ward, Hiley H., "Links With the Occult," in *The Far-out Saints of the Jesus Communes* (New York: Association Press, 1972), pp. 103–21.

bee, considering the effect of Western monotheistic religion on ecology, points to a God concept that is perhaps more malevolent than benevolent. Toynbee announces: "Some of the major maladies of the present-day world—in particular the recklessly extravagant consumption of nature's irreplacable treasures and the pollution of those of them that man has not already devoured—can be traced back to a religious cause, and that this cause is the rise of monotheism."[28]

C. S. Lewis in his *Ransom* trilogy—*Out of the Silent Planet, Perelandra,* and *That Hideous Strength*—described earth as controlled by an evil spirit, Thulcandra, while the other planets were under the dominion of good spirits, Malacandra (Mars) and Perelandra (Venus). The kind of forces governing earth that Lewis described in the sixteenth chapter of *Perelandra:*

(1) A tornado of sheer monstrosities seemed to be pouring over Ransom. Darting pillars filled with eyes, lightning pulsations of flame, talons and beaks and willowy masses of what suggested snow, volleyed through cubes and heptagons into an infinite black void. . . .

(2) There came rolling wheels. There was nothing but that—concentric wheels moving with a rather sickening slowness one inside the other. . . .

(3) Two human figures stood before him on the opposite side of the lake. They were taller than the Sorns, the giants he had met on Mars. They were perhaps thirty feet high. They were burning white like white-hot iron. The outline of their bodies when he looked at it steadily against the red landscape seemed to be faintly, swiftly undulating as though the permanence of their shape, like that of waterfalls or flames, co-existed with a rushing movement of the matter it contained. . . . Whenever he looked straight at them they appeared to be rushing towards him with enormous speed. . . .[29]

The crippled superman in *Odd John,* by Olaf Stapleton, dedicating his life to evil as an act of worship presents an unusual "evil" definition of God. James Blish in *A Case of Conscience* deals with perfection vs. an amoral world, and struggles with the question:

[28] "The Genesis of Pollution," *Horizon,* summer, 1973, Vol. XV, No. 3., p. 7.
[29] (New York: Macmillan, 1968; c. 1944, C. S. Lewis), pp. 197, 198.

can the powers of darkness create life? The absolute necessity of dualism is argued by Frank Herbert in *The Godmakers:*

> A religion requires numerous dichotomic relationships. It needs believers and unbelievers. It needs those who know the mysteries and those who only fear them. It needs the insider and the outsider. It needs both a god and a devil. It needs absolutes and relativity. It needs that which is formless (though in the process of forming) and that which is formed.[30]

A NEW POLYTHEISM

Beyond duality—Good and Evil, the Devil and God—concepts, or even a Devil-God unity figures (as the Process Church of the Last Judgment seeks to do with its trinity of Satan, Lucifer, and Jehovah), there is another course which God-concepts could pursue in a distant world. There could be a new polytheism.

In 1974 there began to emerge the start of what might become a fad—polytheism. Assuming the "death of God," or emptiness of the God concept, and also assuming the varieties of drives and fragmentation within the average person, a practical polytheism with names for the various categories of function and devotion has been suggested. James Hillman, author of *The Myth of Analysis,* presented a psychological thesis that each person takes different roles of the various gods on Olympus, from the god of love to the god of war, etc. David Miller, professor of religion at Syracuse University, produced a book in 1974, *The New Polytheism.* He argues that Jesus himself noted there were many mansions in his "Father's" house (John 14). As there are various "rooms," there are various subjects of devotion in each.

Forms of "functional polytheism" are acknowledged by radicals and conservatives alike. The abrasive, critic of religious institutions, science-fiction writer Harlan Ellison talks of the "God who vanishes when people cease to worship him." Ellison finds that people "in reality do not worship God." But, rather, when you observe people, they worship various gods in their lives—"the gods of war, street violence, machine, free-will," etc. And, he adds, "I guess I worship man." In the pluralistic, polytheistic approach he sees some attention also paid to the traditional God and Trinity. "There will always be vestiges of the old." There will be a "rigid Catholicism"

---

[30] (New York: Berkley Medallion Books, 1973; c. 1972, Frank Herbert), p. 9.

for "people who need an ordered structure of worship. But I'd find a diffusion." Current emphases on the occult, astrology, communalism over the family, and even "refrigeration" of the dead for future reviving reveal different gods as the focus of trust.

A conservative who also believes "functional polytheism" is already here is the Reverend Father Vincent Miceli, S.J., professor at the Angelicum University in Rome and frequent speaker to conservative lay groups in the United States. His view is that the new polytheism comes under one roof, a roof of evil, and more particularly, the roof of atheism. Author of a five-hundred-page book, *The Gods of Atheism,* Father Miceli argues that atheism is not a general thing but implies a whole line-up of new gods.

The gods of atheism include, Father Miceli believes, the god of change, the god of secularism, the god of humanism, the god of contemporaneity, the god of language analysis, and the god of classless society or socialism.[31] Father Miceli predicts that unless mankind repents, people may set up new pantheons or stadiums for new gods in the future. A pantheon could be a type of church, he says, as people come to worship various gods. "These could be gods of success, reason, science, sex, humanism. The possibilities are infinite."

[31] In a similar vein, Andrew Greeley believes a plethora of demons may appear more realistic and powerful than the idea of one Devil that possesses people. In a recent Doubleday book, *The Devil, You Say!* Father Greeley talks about the Demon of Envy, the Demon of Shame, the Demon of Groupthink, etc.

CHAPTER VII

Where Is the Church Universal —and Its Doctrines—Going?

"From where I sit . . ." John Cardinal Wright looked out of his window over the hustle and bustle in St. Peter's Square at the Vatican.

"From where I sit I see the tide is coming back," he said of the long-range future of the church. History would repeat itself as it progressed.

To Cardinal Wright, prefect of the Vatican Congregation for the Clergy which oversees the work of 400,000 Roman Catholic priests in the world, change has a repetitive quality, like the tides he used to watch in his native Boston. "The impression of these tides in my childhood gives me the greatest ground for hope in the future," the dark-haired, broad-shouldered, jolly American, who once ran a diocese in Pittsburgh, said. He now sits in tall, chartreuse, gold-backed French provincial chairs on strawberry-marbled floors overlooking St. Peter's. He is impressed by the busloads of people that come in greater numbers than ever, he said.

"When people tell me it is the end of the church these days, I remind them of the tide and ebb and flow of time," Cardinal Wright said. "I see the history of the church, society, and civilization in terms of the tides of the ocean. In Boston when you smelled the change in the wind, you knew the stench left by low tide was about to disappear, and all the kids would run back into the waves to be invigorated. I smell the wind now, and it tells me there's been a change in the tide, and it is a matter of time before the sea water runs against the sea wall."

Cardinal Wright says the signs of change include a new "lay spirituality" among the faithful and "a fantastic return of the new generation to symbolism." He recalls a young lady he met in England who wore a bigger and more expensive cross than an Eastern patriarch. He also cites a "present cultural crisis both in the capitalist and the Marxist world. It is leading to one and the same result, namely, a reaffirmation of the spiritual," he said.

"From where I sit the tide is coming back. Sure," he said, "low tide follows again," but every tide brings new hope. "A generation of crooks is followed by a generation of saints," and upcoming, he feels, is a whole century of new lay, unheralded saints. He was impressed by a Harvard athletic team that made a point to drop in on him. "Now, I find suddenly even I am relevant!"

Although most theologians affirm continuity with the past, not all would agree with Cardinal Wright. Tides are not all there are to history. There are also gulf streams that sweep vessels great distances up and down the globe and not just rock boats back and forth along a shore. In 1969, for instance, a research submarine, the *Ben Franklin,* with six scientists aboard submerged in the gulf stream off Florida. They emerged thirty days later three hundred miles off the coast of Nova Scotia, 1,444 miles from Florida. The tide came and went, but those in the tide of recurrence found themselves deposited in a totally different setting.

While Wright likes to point to the buses—"sixty-five at one time!" —those riding the buses, such as the group of futurists mentioned in Chapter I, do not always represent an appreciation of the papacy or the church. Wright also brushes away any fear that defections of the priesthood and the faithful point to any cataclysmic fade-out of the church.[1] The losses, 2 to 5 per cent in priests in ten years, he said, are "very spotty and as of now are less per year than four years ago." He also links a current lack of newspaper interest in priest defections with the actual situation. Concerning priest-rebel,

[1] "Seminarians drop 55 per cent in six years"—*National Catholic Reporter,* February 8, 1974; "The precipitous decline in (Catholic) church attendance that has been going on for several years has reached almost catastrophic proportions"—*NCR,* November 16, 1973; "Archdiocesan Study Here Finds Morale of Many Priests Is Poor"—New York *Times,* May 2, 1971; "Four Clergymen in 10 Say They'd Like to Quit Church"—a Gallup Poll survey in 1972; "Being conservative is not enough these days for the churches. Conservative churches are showing a sign of leveling off"—researcher Constant Jacquet; the number of non-college young people who say religion is a very important value fell from 64 per cent in 1969 to 42 per cent in 1973, and college youth holding religion to be very important fell from 38 to 28 per cent—the Daniel Yankelovich research organization, in a survey funded by the John D. Rockefeller III Fund, Hazen and Mellon foundations, and others, reporting in May 1974.

James Kavanaugh, Wright says, "That is the point. Where is he now?" And, as if to support Wright, the independent and quasi-official priest and lay groups have floundered and all but disintegrated after a burst of enthusiasm—particularly the Fellowship of Christian Ministries (formerly the Society of Priests for a Free Ministry) and the National Association of the Laity. Even the National Federation of Priests' Councils appeared to be floundering in 1973 as they resembled more and more official outlooks and failed to take stands on reorganization and complex social issues. To some it would appear to be a "return," or a coming in of the "old" tide; to others, perhaps merely a reflection of "I don't care" attitudes and an isolationism that could affect the church adversely as it is by-passed, or affect it positively as the "old" forms are preserved—depending where one sits.

TIDES OR DETOURS IN THE CATHOLIC CHURCH

Instead of "tides," a more liberal theologian, the Reverend Father Edward Schillebeeckx, of Nijmegen, Holland, prefers to talk of "detours." The paths around the institution, as well as the returning tide, will determine the shape of the church of the future. Schillebeeckx, wearing his long white Dominican robes in his ground-floor office of the Albertinium, a former seminary set in a garden of flowers and trees at the edge of Nijmegen University, believes things have been happening to the church in the "detours" of recent years. "I see a trend to religious renewal in the whole world, but it is accompanied by a kind of anti-church attitude," he said. "People see the church for the moment as an institution not testifying to the religious values they are seeking." And the detours will become important: "The big structures will be by-passed, the whole hierarchy will be by-passed." The Vatican as it is today will be "irrelevant," he said. "Vatican City as such will be by-passed. The Vatican must be restructured in an evangelical way."

Father Schillebeeckx sees Rome remaining as "a center of unity." "The Petrine office [reference to St. Peter's successor, the Pope] will give a big perspective," he said. But his use of "Petrine," terminology accepted by many Lutherans and other Protestants in discussions about the papacy, makes it clear that the Catholic Church on "detour" will not be so Roman or top-heavy after the detours. "Time is irreversible," he said. "The evangelical movement [emphasis on Bible and religious experience] of the primitive church must be recognized in the church of today. Slowly the hierarchy [of bishops] will see the movement and function another way." But since one does not go back in time, he said, it will not look like the primitive first-century church, but will be a "second" primitive church, that is, express simplicity in modern ways. He challenges bishops who say the church cannot be a democratic institution. "I say this is false doctrine," Schillebeeckx said. "What comes from below is coming also from above." That is, the votes of the people can be sanctioned by the hierarchy rather than having policy set only by the hierarchy.

"Adaptation" is the word that theologian Karl Rahner uses to describe the relation of the Roman Catholic Church to change. Interviewed through an interpreter in his second-floor study in the Hochschule für Philosophie, a post-graduate school near the heart of Munich, Rahner believes "the future problem is the church will have to adapt itself to change in society and religion." Rahner, who would also elaborate on his point in English after he had made it in German, is optimistic that democratic processes will win out in society, thus freeing people to adhere to religion. A "general church" will not be possible, and the church will be characterized by a diversity of groups, he said. He sees an effective spiritual tension. The new Catholic charismatics, or Pentecostals, he said, have a role in combating the "extreme intellectualism" that has characterized the church. Yet, he says, the intellectuals will be needed to "clarify" the Pentecostal activity.

A "many-faceted" image instead of a single image is ahead for the church, according to theologian Ives Congar, in Paris. Father Congar, noted pioneer in the ecumenical or church unity movement, believes a multiplicity of groups will characterize the church of the future. "There will be a certain pluralism of options, and unity will not be so much a monolithic matter," he said. He believes the church should seek out new talks with the religions of the East "to find the deep feeling they have to reveal to us," without sacrificing any doctrines.

Congar does not worry about contacts with atheists. "What the atheist rejects is not the true God, but the God of the conservatives, of social reform, the God of a kind of politics." Asked if views of God can and will develop or change, he said, "My Bible talks of a 'living God,' not a God of philosophy."

Among these Catholic theologians, language continues to be a central area of debate, as it was with the "Death of God" discussion in the 1960s. The theologian knows that language is crucial to the future: if language is always changing, truth cannot really be expressed in any explicit words. Theologian Hans Küng, at Tübingen, believes language is always inadequate and thus leaves most debates open-ended. Küng was away when I was in Germany, but I had met him in Montreal and Detroit. In Detroit, Küng said "the primary problem is deciding what is primary." He said it was more important to try to know the mind of the simple Jesus than to rely on a great array of theories and formulae. Says Schillebeeckx: "I agree with Küng's intent and purpose, but he is not always careful when he says that inexhaustible language cannot be adequate. Nevertheless, language brings mystery into expression."

Congar disagrees with Küng's lack of attention to tradition, but merely cautions, "We should go slowly." For Wright, it's a "memory" problem and not a language issue. Language can for him indeed be a tool for recovery of tradition. Says Wright: "Too many are victims of collective amnesia. It is not so much that we have lost the faith, but we forget the history." A changing culture and language pose no threat to the future of the church for Wright. Rather, he sees the church influencing the culture, even as Western culture has been shaped in the past by the Greek and biblical traditions. For Rahner, language and culture change, but like Wright, Rahner sees no threat to the church. "Truth can be spoken not definitively nor exhaustively, but truly," Rahner says vaguely, taking both sides. But he adds, "religious language has to change by 1990 and 2000."

But in the midst of change, the Roman Catholic church may be more likely to remain intact than other groups. For one thing, says Andrew Lipinski, of the Institute of the Future, the Catholic Church benefits from its realistic view of human nature, as it admits to problems and faces up to change. "The Catholic Church is more resilient. All the churches that admit fallibility will survive," he says. And the very monolithic appearance of the Roman Catholic Church encourages reform and continuity.

Economist Maurice Guernier of Paris made the point at the Frascati, Italy, conference on the future in 1973. A structured religion, he said, as an entity can feel the force of change across the organization. But the more scattered and more mystical faiths, "for example, Islam and Buddhism are difficult to change. Less-structured religions of the East do not reform or adapt as easily as a firm structure," he said.

THE ENDANGERED PROTESTANT INSTITUTIONS

For Protestants, change poses an interesting question. Rather than preserving institutions, creative reform threatens them. While diversity with new opportunities may prove a boon to survival for Protestants also, their institutions exist on a parallel rather than intrinsic level. Rigidity in diverse structures may spell the doom of those structures. Yet the diverse Protestant ethos itself, in experimentation and reaction, continually splitting off into new parishes and groups, offers many possibilities. However, many of the staid structures may not weather the greater, never-satisfied pressures for change. On the other hand, a church so broad and pervasive as the Roman Catholic church can take the brunt of great waves. But the diverse, smaller entities are less likely to roll with the waves and channel the reverberations. Such structures can be maintained as museum pieces, but where will the great roll and heave of Protestantism be in the future, amid the big waves? Can the splintered denominations, forged in the past, based on a rural Sabbath rest pattern and Sunday-school revivalism, be a part of a new leisure? Can the smaller diverse structures perpetuate responses to a former culture and be effective in a modern age?

"Can denominations be revived? Probably not," concludes the Reverend Dr. Elmer L. Towns in his book, *Is the Day of the Denomination Dead?* Writing as a fundamentalist Baptist, Towns believes most of the main Protestant denominations—most of them having leveled off in membership—face a bleak future. They do not have life in their Sunday services, they lack a dynamic theology, and they lack the will power and the means that bring souls into the Kingdom, he says. "The super-aggressive church is the church of the future," he says. He argues for informality—"super-aggressive churches that minister to the man in the street are experiencing results." And he blames the passive, one-day-a-week approach as a killer to the faith. "The traditional church of the sacred rest has no appeal. Emphasis for a church that wants to survive should be on Jesus' active verbs, Towns says. Jesus' commands to "follow, do, come, go, look, arise, preach, witness" to "stir people to action" should be the rule of faith. He believes the main-line churches are also hurt by pretentious recruitment methods, instead of a birth of the Spirit. Those churches try to look alive with "a few superficial changes" and "a new program out of headquarters. These outward programs do little to affect the basic nature of denominational structure and existence. Extra money may be raised and a few additions may be added to the rolls, but basically the downward sweep on the attendance charts remains unchanged. People are better held by novelty such as the new hymns created for special revival services, he says. Also, he believes "emotional commitment" helps stir up people. And, an emphasis on personal salvation and a feeling of hostility from the "world" toward Christians are also helpful.[2]

"Towns's diagnosis is not fully wrong," says the Reverend Dr. Martin Marty, a Lutheran, professor of church history at the University of Chicago. "Denominations do not define their belief systems clearly anymore. Presbyterians are like the Methodists, and vice versa. In those terms (clear images), their day is past." And denominations are in trouble, Dr. Marty said, "because of widespread mistrust. They appear remote, impersonal, and bureaucratic. But denominations do not necessarily have to be that way." Dr. Marty disagrees with "the impulse to stress the regional and the local. I oppose the notion than anything that is not localized is against the Bible. In the areas of history and theology, Dr. Towns is not credible. His is not really a new book. Americans for 150 years have had a primitive congregational tradition that believes only that the local and the primitive count. This was the view in the 1820s, but out of that revival [under Alexander Campbell] came a new denomination [Disciples of Christ]. Every time somebody asserts this [the independent church position of Towns], a new denomination is in the process of starting." Dr. Marty believes that Dr. Towns's own independent effort is already a small denomination. He notes Dr. Towns's church in Lynchburg, Virigina, has its own college and printing effort.

"In America, there is no non-denominational space," said Dr. Marty. "There is something about the religious vision. People want to share it, and they see a big thing. If they are not in the *Yearbook of American Churches* now, they will be in five years. These movements can be seen as little creative jabs at denominations, but not

2 (Nashville: Thomas Nelson & Sons, 1973), pp. 149–55.

knock-out blows. In the end, they are not alternatives, but become what they criticize as they are well on the way to becoming denominations themselves."

Also challenging Dr. Towns's arguments, the Reverend Wesley Smedes, minister of evangelism for the 275,000-member Christian Reformed Church, in Grand Rapids, Michigian, says, "I don't think denominationalism is over. Churches have not lost their distinctiveness, nor should they give up their distinctiveness. There can be a shifting, yes, but a church isn't fluid. It's like a stream moving between banks. Our faith is Calvinistic. John Calvin said God rules over all of life today and all should be brought under the Lordship of Christ. We don't want to give that up."

To say there is more dynamism in an independent church is to beg the question, said Mr. Smedes. "The independent fundamentalist church develops its own institution and even takes part in associations of Fundamentalist churches."

So, who among the Protestants—main line or fundamentalist— can really roll with the waves? There is a proliferation, a continual splitting off, and the center of identity appears to remain with the Roman Catholic Church.

But identity and continuation may not be all that significant if the identity represents only an obscure few—a remnant—a near obliteration in a technological, space-age culture.

FOUR BASIC QUESTIONS

Where religion is ultimately headed in the West will depend also on the developments in theology, or lack of developments, as well as on sociological and structural needs. Basic to the shaping of religion in the future are answers to these questions: (1) What theological emphasis will be in vogue, (2) what will be the doctrines, (3) what will be the nature and role of Jesus, and (4) what will be the nature of the church itself?

The confusion in theology that continues has been noted in many camps. The conservative *Christianity Today* laments "the distressing disarray of contemporary theology" and the "plague" of the "convulsive upheaval" in theology. "Each novel alternative in turn becomes part of the predicament of modern theology, rather than holding promise of enduring import. Protestant seminaries increasingly assign conversation a priority over proclamation, and sustained searching of Scripture progressively yields to team-taught diversity."[3] And in the Catholic *Commonweal,* the Reverend Father Richard McBrien laments that the lack of interest in theology is "acute" as witnessed by the difficulty in getting theological books published these days.[4] Dean George Peck in the January 1971 *Andover Newton Quarterly* says: "It does not take a very sophisticated mind to discern that theology is currently in serious trouble. . . . The giants in the field have departed, and their disciples or anti-disciples seem to have little better to do than to try to one-up each other with slogans or catch-cries."

The confusion of the present-day theological scene may portend the confusion in a future age. Certainly a confusion, or more positively, a plurality of views, would be consistent with the over-all expectation of the future hinted in other chapters. Pluralism appears a real wave of the future. There are the variety of choices in the gadgets of worship, the variety of possibilities in the human structure himself, the variety of existences in a more inclusive concept of time as past, present, and future, the varieties of cities above and below ground, and as we saw in Chapter VI the variety of God concepts are already many with considerable promise for further proliferation in the future.

A DOZEN NEW THEOLOGIES

Today's supermarket of varieties of theology include these recent emphases, among others:

(1) *Process theology.* Everything—even God—is evolving, according to process theologians. Following the "Death of God" debate, process theology sought to answer more softly and more consistently the questions of good and evil. God was not dead, but as a part of the process, he was also becoming. Eugene Bianchi, of Emory University, Atlanta, argued that the world is God's body and although God is more than the world, God changes with the world. Certainly such a view has possibilities in the coming science fiction age, as man's concept of world grows and he expects answers—even

[3] Henry, Carl F. H., "The Fortunes of Theology," *Christianity Today,* April 14, 1972, p. 35 (671).
[4] "Whatever Happened to Theology?," in *Commonweal,* April 16, 1971, p. 129.

if the answers include a limited God. This theology has roots in early Greek philosophers of change, ninteteenth-century French philosopher Henri Bergson, and the late Alfred North Whitehead, American philosopher and author of *Process and Reality*.

(2) *Political theology*. Many forms can go under this name— among them, the efforts of activists who pursue social change in the name of the social imperatives of Jesus. The priest or minister who speaks on politics or runs for office subscribes to a political theology. He believes the world can and should be changed. An emphasis on the incarnation of Christ in the world and the secularization of theology to make it relevant to modern needs also fit in here. More likely than not, however, the term is synonymous with "liberation" theology.

(3) *Liberation theology*. Liberation means many things. "Christians for Revolution" met in Lyon, France, to question the structure of the Roman Catholic Church, called an obstacle to "man's liberation." Often the term meant a "liberation" for the oppressed. The writings of Albert Cleage and James Cone, and other black theologians, sought new economic and other deliverance for blacks. Latin America was also the object of liberation theology. Thirteen churchmen "advocating a theology of liberation" from Latin America were sponsored in a U.S. tour by the World and National Councils of Churches in 1973. "All proponents of the 'transforming' church which sides with the poor, they are spokesmen for the anti-institutional, highly political movement in Christianity dominated by Third World churchmen and women," a National Council of Churches news release said. A "theology of liberation" course at Wayne State University in Detroit taught by a Catholic priest dealt with the church's responsibility in Women's Lib, black liberation and "the role of religion in the Latin American struggle for justice." The Reverend Father Gustavo Gutierrez, of Lima, Peru, gave the movement a textbook, *A Theology of Liberation*. In the February 15, 1974, *National Catholic Reporter*, Gutierrez' theology of liberation is described as "an evangelism which announces the total liberation of Christ, encompassing the different dimensions of man." Liberation theology is also called "a theology of development," a term used by the Detroit Industrial Mission, in an article in their *Life & Work* bulletin in May 1972.

(4) *Critical theology.* Charles Davis, former leading English theologian and liturgical expert—now teaching at Sir George Williams University in Montreal—in his *Temptations of Religion,* as well as in lectures, is espousing a "critical theology," with special attention to the dialeticism of Marx. He believes all theology must be criticized. "Theology cannot be a genuine protest unless it is open itself to criticism," he said in Detroit. "Marx does not measure man against transcendent-historical ideals. Marx does not accept the dichotomy of fact and value." It is wrong to think of religion versus the secular, on the one hand, or to think religion and the secular should go hand in hand, as some Catholic thinkers maintain, Davis said. "Marx maintained philosophy has to be transcended by unity of theory and practice. One ideology over another is not enough. . . . What is wrong is for theology to impose itself uncritically by authority alone with no account taken of process or limits."

(5) *Foundational theology.* Dr. Langdon Gilkey, professor of theology at the University of Chicago, defines foundational theology as a quest for "the bases" of faith. But the bases must harmonize with man's experience. A faith based on a more general language and more common experience, shared with all mankind, is necessary to convince not only the secular world, but also the Christian who today is so much a part of the secular, he says. Protestant foundational theology seeks to show the "plausibility" of a God, says Lonnie Kliever, professor of religious studies at the University of Windsor, Ontario, Canada. "Foundational theology doesn't attempt to prove theism [a transcendent God], but it attempts to establish the possibility of theism and to show that a Christian vision makes sense." For Roman Catholics, foundational theology is a rerun of St. Thomas Aquinas and natural theology. Aquinas saw essences and eternal blueprints in the most natural of man's actions.

(6) *Contextual theology.* "Proper theology is reflection on the experience of the Christian community in a particular place, at a particular time. Thus, it will necessarily be a contextual theology; it will be a relevant and living theology which refuses to be easily universalized because it speaks to and out of a particular situation." So concluded a World Council of Churches conference on "Salvation Today" in Bangkok, Thailand. Again, it is the "experiential note" common in the other approaches, but here the emphasis is on un-

derstanding the culture and experience of a people, rather than an emphasis on method or new approaches to God.

(7) *Theology of hope.* This is a very vague or general theology. The essence of most Christian theologies, conservative or liberal, is hope. The more recent movement characterized by Jürgen Moltmann in particular has been a movement of synthesis. Moltmann, a Reformed Church theologian from the University of Tübingen, West Germany, appeals to anarchists and conservatives alike as he insists on concrete expressions of hope. Revolution—a turning of the tables, shattering old institutions, creating new orders, even working toward seemingly unattainable utopias—has value to him because it reflects the openness and promise of the future. Christ brought liberation— from past, present, and even the future, which remains open while guaranteeing fulfillment of promises. In a midnight, candle-light interview in a Kalamazoo, Michigan, restaurant during a rain storm, Moltmann on a university lecture tour, laughed, "Perhaps I am a left-wing orthodox." He added: "I am conscious concerning the biblical foundation of Christian theology, but also perhaps liberated concerning social action." He accepts "revolution, not evolution." In process theology, he says, you only look forward into the future. But "in Christian hope, you also look [back] to raising of the dead" promised in Christ's own resurrection.

(8) *Autobiographical theology.* Probably one of the most popular modern-day theologies, also referred to as philosophical anthropology or phenomenological method, this generally goes unnamed, unsystematized. Autobiographical theology usually is nothing more than the retelling of a personal incident, a testimony, a dramatic experience—or a chain of experiences—or retelling one's whole life story. The Jesus People, the poets, the mystics, the newly converted with the aura of a new life to tell about, all fit in here. There's excitement here. Up in the glacier Cascade mountains northeast of Seattle, Craig Skinner, twenty-six, caretaker at a deserted Jesus People camp, told me, "I came to a point where I had a definite choice—Satan and die or the Lord and live. I was awakened one night at three A.M. Something came in human form, floating in. I was like mesmerized . . . a tight feeling . . . a whirling sensation . . . I felt my body withering, drying up and blowing away. A sense of a skeleton and skin blowing away. 'I got to have a Bible . . .' As soon as I said

that, I felt like a wind washed down and over my body. Oppression was gone. My body felt still. A soothing, cooling wind made me whole." That is autobiographical theology. In a more formal approach, Ladislaus Boros in his *The Hidden God* (Seabury) formalizes his autobiographical statement in a sort of text for the movement as he talks of the "felt nearness of God" which draws "men to itself by its beauty."

(9) *Body theology.* "Every human being . . . is located in the world through his body, but the body provides the structure for a personal presence extending beyond it,"[5] says the Right Reverend Arthur Vogel, Episcopal bishop of Western Missouri in his book, *Body Theology.* Preoccupied with the mystery of time, Bishop Vogel sees "presence"—human presence, God's presence—as a means of linking time and getting above it. "Personal presence . . . can help understand time, for personal presence is a fullness always overflowing the present."[6] He deals with body theology on various levels. Ideally, a "Christian presence" with its "concern" and "alternatives" becomes a presence that "guarantees the world a future, a real future. . . . The guarantee of the future results from the infinitude of God's love for the world. . . . His love for us is so great that it never ceases to be creative, and we can never cease to be creative in it."[7] Vogel's book is a call to be "concrete" in expressing "the reality of God's presence in the world." But on another level, if all fails, even if Christians "are reduced to suffering or outward passivity—the integrity and peace of their presence to others" will "testify" to "the ultimate meaningfulness of life among persons."[8] In a less mystical approach and with concern for bodies as linguistic and intrinsic entities themselves, the sensitivity and encounter groups, such as Esalen and Stanley Keleman's Center for Energetic Studies in Berkeley—all with new rituals (therapy) of body awareness—seek to integrate man's capabilities into a whole and make him a fabric of meaning.[9] And, of course, the many schools of yoga seek to discipline some part of the body and/or integrate body and mind in order to achieve a higher awareness and consciousness.

[5] (New York: Harper & Row, 1973), p. 131.
[6] Ibid., p. 139.
[7] Ibid., p. 143.
[8] Ibid., p. 144.
[9] Cf. "We Do Not Have Bodies, We Are Our Bodies," a conversation with Stanley Keleman, in *Psychology Today,* Vol. 7, No. 4, September 1973.

(10) *Celebrative theology.* Perhaps the most popular of all new theologies, celebrative theology (which is linked to body theology by the activity it elicits) is underscored on many levels, from the hippie or freak commune to a wide range of community gatherings of worship, in homes or cathedrals. Celebration is not new. The priest in Mass, for instance, has since ancient times been known as the "celebrant," as he performs the rites that link God and man, namely through the Eucharist, the sacrifice of Christ. "Eucharist" means "thanksgiving," and comes from the Greek text of Christ's words of "giving thanks" before the Last Supper, as he broke bread and distributed wine in memory of his coming atonement for sins of mankind. Since Pope John's Vatican Council, which was designed to let "fresh air" into the church, celebration has become occasions for demonstrating greater freedom—and dependence on the Holy Spirit—in the Church. For Catholics, celebration meant freer forms, banners of joy, corporate rituals, and confession together in English instead of an ancient tongue. For Protestants, celebration meant guitar liturgies and a recovery of the celebrative elements in Pentecostal worship, namely, healing, speaking in tongues, and prayer-praising in song (for some Catholics, too). Celebration became an occasion to link comedy and tragedy, joy and suffering, and, therefore, point to a less serious and less "uptight" practice of the faith. Harvey Cox, who sought to describe Jesus as a harlequin type in his *Feast of Fools,* could be found expressing his faith in a liturgy protest outside a jail, or at a religious "happening" in New York's Greenwich Village, or in communal living experiments. Conservatives had their form of celebrative theology in their bumpy Gospel tunes, role-playing and hand-clapping "serendipity" conferences of the Faith and Work movement, and the "oh wow" Jesus People Jesus-rock festivals and coffeehouses.

(11) *Theology of play.* Or perhaps this is a theology of poetry, or visual poetry. Or a theology of imagination, or a "theology of fantasy," as Dr. Carl Raschke, of the University of Denver, talks about in *The Christian Century* of May 15, 1974. An apostle of the theology of play is Sam Keen, former director of California's Esalen Institute and Theological Residence Program. He seeks to clown around and entertain when he is invited to lecture on theology. He tells stories of snakes, plays his harmonica, and gets his audience away from "straight thinking." Keen contributed a poem about the

death of a cat on a highway to a book, *The Theology of Play,* which also features writings of Harvey Cox and Jürgen Moltmann. For Cox, it's all a laugh and healing in celebration; for Moltmann, suffering leads to joy, and God "plays with the elements as he creates." In play, God becomes more open and creativity reigns, for God and man. But Keen thinks Cox and Moltmann are all too sober, and confined by a Christian context. "They [Cox and Moltmann] think you have to be Christian to play and laugh," Keen said in a late-night interview in Pontiac, Michigian, after a lecture. "If it is a theology of play," Keen said, "you play with the outrageous. If God is the creator of the world, then play with the idea that maybe a great pumpkin or turnip did the creating."

(12) *Game theology.* This is "play" theology, too. But it describes a serious game, and the elements of religion—God, etc.—are not played with. Game theology belongs to the conservatives. There are knowns and absolutes, but the movements of the chess pieces— man, God, whatever—are subjected to the prevailing will of God— and the Devil—themselves. "God takes part in a game just like a coach—he is a supreme coach," said Don Sauerman, a former grid-iron guard, participating in a camp program of the Fellowship of Christian Athletes at Central Michigan University, in Mt. Pleasant, Michigan. "I feel the game is kind of closed," said Sauerman, a Lutheran, and now a stockbroker in Western Springs, Illinois. "You are on a one-way street. The object is to follow the rules." Gordon Fosness, a former forward for the Minneapolis Lakers, and now a coach at South Dakota Wesleyan, Mitchell, South Dakota, also said at the conference, "Life is a game in a sense, but not a fun-and-games one. It is serious." There is little suspense or mystery in his game. "Once you have committed your best to the game [of life], you will be a winner no matter what the scoreboard says."

WHAT MESSAGE FOR THE FUTURE?

While there are many theologies today different from more systematic stances of the past, the message of the present scene for a future society may be more than merely predicting a pluralism or variety of theologies for the future. Certainly pluralism looms as a dominant possibility in light of the interest in variety on the total scene of religion and culture. But there are dominating themes in the current trends. The new theologies are activity oriented; they seem to call for a moving from beyond pew-sitting acquiescence to getting up and shouting, testifying, praising God, making noise, and certainly in political liberation, critical and most of the other theologies, activity is encouraged beyond the central rites of worship. If today's trends, among conservatives and liberals, contribute anything to the future of theology, it may well be that they point to the preoccupation with the non-structural elements of religion, away from a former building complex, and a turning in on a search for personal relationships, meaning, and societal improvement.

What will be the doctrines of the future?

Each of the new theologies suggests adherence to basic ideas and principles, but not to a creedal statement. Process theology requires a commitment to a working dynamic in history; liberation theology—a commitment to credos of freedom and dignity; autobiographical theology to principles or values of religious and mystical experience; celebrative and play theology—commitment to the goodness of life and openness and creativity of faith, and so on. Hardly does one see any demand for allegiances to creedal statements or traditional formulations or dogma.

THE NEW MEANING OF CONSCIENCE

Curiously, even the very basics of theology are not above the influence of the forces of change and private interpretation. Consider "conscience," for instance. Who would think that the idea of some inner, subjective, policelike force, keeping the good man on the right track could be challenged? Conscience did not seem so inviolate, however, in the early '70s when dozens of good men, some of them active church-goers—with allegedly good and trusted consciences—were charged, and some convicted, in the Watergate break-in and cover-up scandals and other illegal acts on behalf of a government. The very basic "doctrine"—common to Catholic understanding of innate natural law and Protestant Puritanical belief in the absolute sovereignty of God in the will of the righteous—amounted to so little. "Consciences" of good men could not be trusted. The most basic "doctrine" of all seemed to be up for grabs.

What then is "conscience" if it isn't some inner voice, or "a judgment of the intellect," as Catholic dictionaries used to call it?

The old definition was too easily twisted around, says the Reverend Father John W. Glaser, S.J., who teaches a course on "Conscience, a Contemporary Appraisal" at the University of Detroit. Conscience has been linked with authority, civil and church, an invitation to abuse. Says Father Glaser: "What I hear many Watergate witnesses saying is: 'Because I understand the right and good to be determined by authority figures, I did what I did.'" This "unquestioned and un-integrated" use of values is a common way in which conscience is understood, he said. But "its disastrous effects are evident at Nurem-berg and Watergate." The same basic reasoning and appeal by some criminals does not differ much from basic religious teachings on conscience in the old days. "Twenty years ago I would have given a 'traditional Roman Catholic' definition of conscience," Father Glaser said. Now for him conscience is "not primarily a function, but one way of understanding the whole me from a specific point of view. Conscience is 'me-listening' to: (1) the complex unity of my neighbor, his situation, needs here and now, (2) myself related to this here-and-now other person, (3) the mystery at the heart of this encounter which we call God, but which we need not name in any way. This only begins to describe conscience in one of its important meanings."

Accepting this definition, Mark Springer, a UD graduate student in theology, adds: "Conscience for me is an on-going, living and growing process. It is not just a part of me, but it is me both at the core of my being and my present experiencing. I don't believe conscience is formed or is static, but rather, ever-changing as I am more aware of myself and others and my many experiences." The Reverend Father Kevin McBrien, a Carmelite priest from Engle-wood, New Jersey, in the same UD "conscience" class: "Conscience is a movement of the whole person, emotions as well as intellect without coercion or facade. It is a movement toward a decision or an option considered vital to a person's life situation but in relationship to others."

The discussion of conscience perpares one to see the more paro-chial and "distinctive" doctrines, creeds, and teachings in a different light. As in the case of the "new conscience" definitions, these tend to give way to more integral definitions with social and humane concerns.

WHAT DO PEOPLE BELIEVE?

In recent years, on occasion I have surveyed various groups to see just what they actually believe. Their beliefs did not necessarily comply with the many doctrines they might have learned in older days. My interest was not to suggest any invalidation of doctrines, but rather to look toward some future emphases on the basis of what people actually believed today, apart from what they said they believed. "As he thinketh in his heart, so is he" (Prov. 23:7). If the present doctrines are going to leave any kind of an imprint at all on the future, then what are these doctrines? Ancient terminology, creeds, and dogmatic statements may carry over, but along with them, one needs to ask, what else is new, and/or how does the new age define or integrate old terminology with social concerns?

In a search for clues for construction of models for the future church, I have queried three groups of "religionists" to discover what they consider important among the assorted beliefs—and motivating ideas—that exist in modern religion. The three groups surveyed were the Society of Priests for a Free Ministry (SPFM)—before its recent name change to Fellowship of Christian Ministries—the National Youth Ministry Workshop (American Baptist Church education directors and executives), meeting at Green Lake, Wisconsin, and the predominantly Catholic Church of Tomorrow Conference delegates at the University of Notre Dame. Wherever the church is going, the doctrines and ideas underscored now—in the 1970s—may give—at least in part—some clue to the direction of emphasis in the future church.

What do people believe? You yourself might rate the fifty-three themes in the following list.

Rate Your Own Beliefs

What do you consider most important? Rate the following ideas, doctrines, and dogmas in order of importance to you 1 to 10.

___Baptism by Holy Spirit
___Baptism by water
___Eucharist
___Sense of community
___Love
___Active peace efforts
___Confirmation
___Penance
___Celebration
___Work for a just cause
___Tithing
___Patience
___Seekers
___Dancing
___Body resurrection
___Separation of church-state
___Heaven
___Revolution

___Divinity of Christ
___Omnipotence of God
___Existence of Holy Spirit
___Humor
___Anointing of sick
___Marriage
___Holy Orders
___Saying rosary
___Resurrection
___Preaching
___Audible prayer
___Tolerance
___Faith healing
___Immaculate conception
___Natural law
___Lay clergy
___Hell
___Poverty of spirit

___Silent prayer
___Good deed
___Mystical experience
___Life affirmation
___Body affirmation
___Church attendance
___Sincerity
___Honesty
___Flexibility
___Singing
___Witnessing (evangelism)
___Witnessing (deed)
___Speak in tongues
___Second Coming of Christ
___Virginity of Mary
___Purgatory
___Poverty of goods

Concerning the SPFM, questionnaires went out to 959 names. This represented the entire list of the SPFM, a list of 1036 names minus 77 overseas names and names of newsmen and cardinals and others who were on the list for informational purposes. There were 254 replies, of which 233 complied with the directions of rating the items in line of importance, from one to ten, with number one being the first in importance, number two being second, etc. Points were assigned to the answers according to the ranking in importance. Thus, ten points were ascribed to the item marked number one (the first choice), nine points to the item marked second, eight points to the third, and so on.

So what did the SPFM, a potential reservoir of persons creating new forms, if not structure (most of them inactive priests, predominantly liberal), select?

"Love" was the most important; "sense of community" was second; "Eucharist" (celebration of the Mass or Lord's Supper with Holy Communion) was third; "Divinity of Christ," fourth; "honesty," fifth.

Here's the top ten and their ratings for the SPFM group:

1. Love (1535 points)
2. Sense of community (961)
3. Eucharist (866)
4. Divinity of Christ (662)
5. Honesty (631)
6. Resurrection (580)
7. Work for a cause of justice (570)
8. Life affirmation (479)
9. Sincerity (460)
10. Active peace efforts (429)

At the end in the SPFM rating, with their total number of points based on the method outlined above, are: Hell (38 points); Anointing of sick (36), Tithing (29), Faith healing (28), Purgatory (25), Virginity of Mary (23), Saying the rosary (22), Immaculate conception (16), and Speaking in tongues (13).

The American Baptist youth leaders and executives using the same list and point systems as the SPFM, contained some of the same more general affirmations, with some Baptist "distinctives" appearing in the top ten, just as the SPFM included the Eucharist. However, some Baptist distinctives ranked low, such as Baptism by water (20 points) and the practice of Tithing (5 points), just as some distinctive Catholic doctrines ranked low in importance in the SPFM rating. The Baptists, like the SPFM, placed "Love" as number one in importance.

The rating of the top ten goes like this for the forty-one-member group:

1. Love (283 points)
2. Omnipotence of God (268)
3. Divinity of Christ (249)
4. Sense of community (205)
5. Existence of Holy Spirit (168)
6. Celebration (109)

7. Life affirmation (87)
8. Baptism by Holy Spirit (83)
9. Resurrection (81)
10. Witnessing (deed) (76)

Rating zero among the Baptists were: Anointing of sick, Confirmation, Penance, Dancing, Holy Orders, Saying rosary, Immaculate conception, Natural law, Poverty of spirit, Good deed, Singing, Speak in tongues, Virginity of Mary, Purgatory, Poverty of goods.

The Church of Tomorrow participants were asked to list the most important doctrines or ideas as they see them in order of importance, rather than select ideas from a list. It is not possible at this point to go into the more detailed and complex findings of the response of forty-one persons (out of 182), except to note the general findings. The priests who responded gave thirty different answers for first place—ranging from theological concerns to social action concerns, such as "dignity of human person," and "love of brother." The Catholic laymen in the group said the most important idea or doctrine to them was: "love of one's neighbor, God loves each of us, and honesty." The Protestants (including National Council of Churches and denominational executives) at the conference placed as most important: "Apostolic ministry, empathy, agape (love), the Kingdom is among us, and love of God."

The sampling of the Baptists and the Catholic Church of Tomorrow group were revealing in several special areas. True, as I told the creedless Baptists after rating their replies, "you were more 'theological'" than the priestly SPFM. But one can note the decided lack of parochialism, not only in the predominant Catholic Church of Tomorrow case, but also in the Baptist total disregard for Baptist distinctives—water baptism, church-state separation, local autonomy, tithing, etc. "The omnipotence of God ranks great with you," I told the Baptists, but "a Moslem or Jew or deist or Unitarian can subscribe to this [the priority of omnipotence and love]."

Looking further down the line, there was a strong Pentecostal-type interest in such things as existence of the Holy Spirit, baptism by the Holy Spirit, life affirmation, celebration, etc. One former Episcopalian turned Baptist admitted that he did look more Pentecostal when you come right down to it. The point is, the old denominational distinctives seemed to make very little difference.

These random polls of both dissidents and main-line types suggest:

(1) a lack of interest in precise old-time doctrines or sacraments (the Eucharist excepted) as such, and (2) an interest in spontaneity, a spontaneity sans some of the usual procedures and formulae.

THE NEW CHRISTOLOGY

As to the nature and role of Jesus himself, there are some new developments. And Schillebeeckx himself was working on a seven-hundred-page volume on the nature of Jesus when I talked with him in his study set back off the main university drive in a secluded former seminar building in Nijmegen.

"The biggest problem today," he said, "is Jesus of Nazareth. How do you reactualize the figure and person of Jesus and the image of Jesus Christ? The whole question is, what do we mean by Jesus Christ. Is he a symbolic or mythic figure or is Jesus Christ a human being," subject to the divine word of God?

In his *Christology* volume, Schillebeeckx will deal with Christ as a historical phenomenon and the adequacy of the interpretation of the church with historical phenomena, "and what it means for the moment." He adds, "This Jesus of Nazareth has no meaning today unless you demonstrate in this human being a kind of new experience of God—a new perspective for humans. The very image of God is demonstrated in Jesus Christ and manifested in and through the phenomenon of mankind."

Schillebeeckx maintains there is not a "new face of God without a new face of mankind. The new face of Christ demonstrated the new perspective of human life." So, the quest for the real Jesus continues.

From Hermann Samuel Reimarus, in the eighteenth century, to Albert Schweitzer, who wrote a *Quest for the Historical Jesus* at the start of this century, scholars have tried to identify Jesus, and in the case of Reimarus and Schweitzer and others in between such as David Friedrich Strauss, Jesus comes off as a historical political revolutionary if not a disillusioned figure.

Mid-twentieth century theology returned to what is called a "high Christology," that Jesus is God and God can only be understood by Jesus. But as the 1960s came, men had difficulty in separating God and Jesus apart from the world. The quest led to a "Death of God" debate. And that had two implications for the theology of Jesus. It made Jesus more important, at least in the view of one theologian of the "Death of God" variety, T. J. J. Altizer, who argued that although God was "dead" for all practical purposes, God had "emptied" himself into the man Jesus. Secondly, with this new spotlight on Jesus came a renewed interest in a special theology called "Christology." It is simply a "study" of the nature of Christ.

An aim of Christology is to discover "who" Jesus is. And here is where there is confusion. On the one hand, it is easy to drop out of the old debate as Dr. Deane William Ferm does in "Honest to Jesus," an article in *The Christian Century* (March 22, 1972). He believes the real meaningful Jesus is one that blends with universal concepts and that a "particularity" of Jesus is misleading. Much more important, he says, is a creed that says that God "has many sons" and not just a Son. Dr. Ferm represents one extreme in Christology. There is another extreme: those who emphatically insist that Jesus is important, that his name has to be used, and called on as the Scripture says (Phil. 2:10) in order to find salvation. In between the two extremes is a vast field.

One way, apparently, to achieve tolerance and brotherly love is not through one Christology, but through "multiple Christologies," an elaboration of Dr. Ferm's position. Dr. Eva Fleischner, lecturing at a conference on the church in Nazi Germany at Wayne State University, Detroit, said that at the heart of whether Christians and Jews have any meaningful dialogue (Christians usually want to convert, and Jews want to teach) is the question of Christology. "To grapple with this problem of dialogue," she said, "we have to grapple with new Christological concepts." Dr. Fleischner, who has her Ph.D. and is on the staff of the Catholic women's lay movement, The Grail, Loveland, Ohio, says that Christian theology is limited to too few "Christologies." These range the whole gamut from Christ as a "spirit" to Christ as a unique body that continues ("this is my body") mystically, and as the body of Christ understood as the church, the exclusive group. Dr. Fleischner suggested Christians ought to "examine some texts largely ignored." For example, she cited texts such as John 16 of Jesus returning to his Father and ascribing all things to God, the Father. From such references, one can discover a oneness of faith, a monotheism, of which Jesus is also a part. The "Father" is God of all.

Perhaps it would be interesting to take all of the definitive statements of Jesus about himself and see how many Christologies one can come up with. The many titles of Jesus alone are bases for "Christologies," and scholars have recognized this, among them, Vincent Taylor, and his *The Names of Jesus* (St. Martin's Press, 1953) and, more recently, Ferdinand Hahn and his *The Titles of Jesus in Christology* (Lutterworth Press, 1963). But to deal with the many titles of Jesus, for instance, "son of man," "lord," "Christ," "Son of David," "Son of God," etc. is also limiting. The Reverend Dr. Dennis Duling, a Presbyterian and a professor of New Testament at the Boston School of Theology, says: "One does not have to have a title of respect or dignity present to have a Christology." And that is where a particular new brand of theological studies is coming in.

REDACTION CRITICISM

The new study is called "redaction criticism." "Criticism" simply means a close look at something, in and behind the scenes. "Redaction" means literally "to lead back," and in New Testament theology, to get back to what the writer is trying to say. The new approach goes far beyond the much heralded "form criticism" which has occupied most New Testament scholars for the past century. "Form criticism" sought to review the various methods and sources used by writers of the Bible and then determine what influence the traditions and schools of thought had on the writer. (There was another approach called "literary criticism" which dealt with more mundane matters such as determining the actual writers of Bible books.) In the "redaction" approach, one becomes interested in just the author's viewpoint for the Gospels. It is not so much a matter of what Jesus believed or what the early church thought he believed, as reflected in the Gospels, but what the writer himself thought Jesus believed and what the writer wanted to say. Gospel writer Mark throws in little hints of his main concern—thus, halfway through his Gospel, he talks about taking up one's cross and being faithful to Christ through suffering and persecution (Mark 8:34–38). "Mark is leading up to the passion story," which takes up much of the Gospel of Mark (one third), observes Dr. Duling.

So one looks for the "themes"—or what the writer was trying to say from his viewpoint—similar to the concern that editors have when they try to edit a manuscript in the context of what a man is trying to say.

Basic to the discussion on the future of the church is the new thinking about the nature—and origin—of the church itself. One Catholic theologian in particular has done a lot of thinking about the nature of the church in the present age. In a speech and interview in Detroit, the Reverend Father Richard McBrien discussed the church of the past, present, and future. His views represent the unified concept of time we have discussed earlier in this book, while he still maintains the traditional goal-directed Christian concept of history. Nevertheless, in a unified, undivided concept of time, even the past and present, as well as the future, are open. "The church is in evolution," he said. The goal of "the Christian movement," he said, is to realize the Kingdom of God, a future era under the reign of Christ. The church is not an end in itself, said Father McBrien, professor at the Pope John XXIII Seminary, Weston, Massachusetts, and past president of the Catholic Theological Society of America.

Father McBrien also played down the importance of the local parish. "Just because something is quantitatively dominant, such as a parish church, doesn't mean it is the ideal," he said. Catholic bishops and officials, Father McBrien said, tend to think of the parish as the most important, and that floating parishes that move around the city from homes to parks are extra and experimental. But, he said, the church is a coming together of people over and beyond "geographic proximity." He said groups to work on special tasks (a "common apostolate") and groups formed along occupational lines and common interests also constitute the church.

And as he pointed out that church people wrongly isolate periods of time—the past, present, or the future—he said an answer to new tensions in the church is to work out a faith that respects all three periods of time. Keeping ties with the past, he said, is necessary for the "identity" of the church. Concern with the present creates a lively and meaningful faith: looking to the future gives a sense of "purpose." "If you exaggerate the point of origin [the past], you isolate it [the church] and separate it from the rest of mankind. The church is just reduced to keeping alive the memory of Jesus, and the theology of the church is nostalgia. If you exaggerate the present, you have an emphasis on what the church can do for the individual. For some, the church becomes just an encounter group or a mere non-Christian atmosphere where one can overcome his fears. If the future is exaggerated, the church becomes only a catalyst for social change. A church that cuts away from its roots "is everything in general and nothing in particular," he said. "This leads to an identity crisis." Pleading for an openness in faith that looks to the past, present, and future, Father McBrien said the church in evolution is "moving toward a goal. The church is not an end in itself, but is enabling the coming of the Kingdom of God."

Noting that the church is a "mystery," the Reverend Father Avery Dulles, S.J., in his *Models of the Church* (Doubleday, 1974), prefers to talk of "models" of the church rather than refer to structural factions of a divided Christendom. The models, he finds, are: institution, mystical communion, sacrament, herald, and servant.

DOES GOD WANT A CHURCH?

At the "Church of Tomorrow" conference at Notre Dame, I asked several direct questions of delegates concerning the church: Did Jesus really intend to found a church structure? And does God want or need a church?

The consensus at Notre Dame among bishops, priests, and Protestant observers was that Jesus did not intend very much specifically. The Reverend Father James T. Burtchaell, C.S.C., chairman of the department of theology, University of Notre Dame, described Jesus as "an illiterate layman from the boondocks" who was at complete odds with structure in his day. Dr. Burtchaell's thesis was that Jesus, nevertheless, had a sense of power and authority and "there is a structure that flows from the context of His efforts. If we talk only of structure in terms of official appointment, then we misunderstand the flow" of the stream of mankind, said Father Burtchaell. One eastern U.S. monsignor noted in a discussion that "the only sense that can be made of the church is in a context of sociology of religion," and "you can't make sense of the church if theology is taken seriously." Pondered Father Burtchaell: "God was slow in using the church."

Most agreed that God is omniscient and that God and Christ knew the church would come about. Which raised another question hinted at but not dealt with directly: "Was Christ a 'pre-reformer'— a Luther or Pope John type BEFORE the church? If the structure was known, but not absolute in Christ's mind, then His own efforts and vision could be taken as attempting to keep the flow and formulations open and meaningful." The implications of this reasoning, on basis of attitudes and the openness at the Notre Dame meeting, could upon reflection at future conferences, feed back into discussion on the deity and role of Christ Himself—does He become more of a reformer of a "post event" and therefore more a part of the total contemporary situation?

Haziness of Jesus' intentions in launching the "church"—whatever it is—was underscored even inadvertently, by the participants at this future of the church conference sponsored by the Center for Continuing Education at the University of Notre Dame. The Very Reverend Theodore M. Hesburgh, Notre Dame president, had one piece of advice to the delegates. "One factor you can't forget, that is, the full direction [of the future of the church] comes back to the Holy Spirit"—and the Holy Spirit, according to Scripture "lists" or "blows" where it will, as the wind (John 3:8). The Reverend Father David Bowman, S.J., deputy to the general secretary of the National Council of Churches at that time, told the delegates in a question-and-answer period that he was concerned with the "fuzziness in how we use the word, 'church.' The church is an analogous word. It was used four ways in the Second Vatican Council," he said. He explained later in an interview these were "people of God, baptized and faith-filled people, the Roman Catholic community, and the 'saints,' that is, the holy people." He added: "These four are not adequately distinct one from another. For example, the Roman Catholic community is contained materially in the first and second. But they are four different groupings denoted by the same English word."

"The church as it is is the people of God," said the Reverend John Barker, who headed up a new American Baptist project on "New Forms of Congregational Life and Mission," with headquarters in Valley Forge, Pennsylvania. "But in terms of structure I don't see it in the Scriptures. It evolved, and God used it." Barker, however, believes "Jesus saw this [network of organization] developing and did not necessarily say no." The Reverend Father Ted Rutkowski, of St. Mary's College, Orchard Lake, Michigan, noted that not many are dwelling on the question of "Jesus announcing an established fact" of the church but rather that He came to found "a kingdom. He intended to announce or remind men of the purpose of their lives, but beyond that it is hard to say." The Reverend Father Chris Schneider, O.F.M., of Duns Scotus College, Southfield, Michigan, and representing the Detroit Archdiocesan Senate of Priests, said Christ "started a structure. We all admit this, but it has to move." Asked how precise a structure, he said, "People is all there is. If people change, the structure changes."

The Most Reverend G. Emmett Carter, bishop of London, Ontario, said in an interview: "Christ didn't try to set up a strict organization at that time. Structure was always for the sake of service. Christ intended to form a visible society and gave power to the bishops. There was nothing sacred except the basic elements." These are, he said, "a group of people worshipping and a praying community under the apostles and their successors."

Another prelate, in a turtleneck sweater because "the clerical collar is a thing of the past," the Most Reverend Remi J. DeRoo, bishop of Victoria, British Columbia, Canada, said what shape Christ had in mind in regard to the church is difficult to determine "exegetically," that is, from a close look at Scripture. "But I do not accept the idea that Christ did not intend a structure." Asked how much Christ intended, Bishop DeRoo said, "I do not think his thinking ran in our cultural pattern. He spoke of life in community, therefore, we are not to be too literal. We talk today of body and soul, but to the Jew of His time it did not make sense as Judaism talked of the total person. Even the question of religious knowledge became cerebral, but in Scripture, knowing involved the whole person. I am not for going back to a so-called 'perfect' past and live the primitive church. The question is to grasp the vision and be relevant with the emphasis on the lived experience in community."

CHAPTER VIII

Will Jesus or Somebody Come?

"For the Lord himself shall descend from heaven with a shout, with the voice of the archangel, and with the trump of God: and the dead in Christ shall rise first: Then we which are alive and remain shall be caught up together with them in the clouds, to meet the Lord in the air . . ." (1 Thess. 4:16, 17). Is that the way it will be, or can one expect a variety of "saviors" of one sort or another?

Some five hundred "gods" exist in the various cultures of India. And, as Khushwant Singh points out in *The Illustrated Weekly of India,* nearly every village of India has had its own godman or holy man. And the religious revival in the first third of the 1970s produced its share of new "saviors" or "avatars," many of them from the Far East.

Some of these modern godmen have stirred up a following in the West. One of the most publicized of the new gurus was the teen, Maharaj Ji. I talked with him in Detroit, while he still had on his face the shaving-cream pie thrown by a Detroit youth. "I am not God," Maharaj Ji said. Nevertheless, he allows himself to be taken as a manifestation of the divine, the one special guru or teacher for the current times. One of his American followers, Kirk Dennis, twenty-three, commented: "I'd crawl on my hands a hundred miles to see him. But he's actually coming to us. It's the greatest day in my life."

The sixty-six-year-old Muktananda, following in the footsteps of Swami Nityananda in Ganeshpuri, India, allows men to have some possessions as he preaches a meditation discipline to get into "the inner recesses." Gopi Krishna, former government clerk from Kashmir, appeals to youths with his restrained sexual tantra yoga. The thirty-four-year-old Dattabal of Kolhapur speaks such a message of love that he believes even plants respond to love. Doctors, lawyers, architects, and other sophisticates in India follow a forty-four-year-old teacher-God, Acharya Rajneesh, who preaches a religion of "simplicity" and "sensitiveness." Sri Aurobindo's Ashram and "city" of Auroville in Pondicherry, India, draws devotees to integral yoga that features mental disciplines. The Maharishi Mahesh Yogi with his everyday living Transcendental Meditation claims some 300,000 followers in the United States (according to his American followers). Yogi Bhajan, whom I have interviewed several times, preaches a total Kundalini yoga, and his youths conduct efficient ashrams and restaurants; Swami Satchidananda, a mystic with a great beard, conducts retreats at Catholic retreat centers and other locations; the aging Sant Kirpal Singh Ji, of New Delhi, preaches a religion of love to his devotees: "What is an ideal man? He is an embodiment of love."

Sun Myung Moon, from Korea, travels the United States and preaches an eclectic faith of "hope for man" and "hope for America" in his strange brand of patriotic themes and vagueness reflecting a Western Presbyterian upbringing along with the spirit of the East. Not long ago I lunched with the late Paul Twitchell, a casual, clean-shaven son of a Mississippi river boat worker. Twitchell's Ekankar "soul travel" movement centered on devotion to Rama, one of the nine great avatars, or divine incarnations of Vishnu, a deity of Hinduism with popularity second only to Krishna, the blueish god which has its own coterie of American followers in the International Society of Krishna Consciousness (ISKCON).

The "godmen," as *The Illustrated Weekly of India* (March 18, 1973) calls them, appear to be all over the place. The future, as East and West grows closer together, may have to deal with some of these Eastern "godmen" as well as with Jesus.

PLURALISTIC CHRISTIANITY?

The idea that there might be a pluralistic and even a polytheistic approach to Jesus (as well as to God—Chapter VI) receives support from various quarters. Just as Father Miceli noted in Chapter VI in the discussion on God that man in practice acknowledges many kinds of gods, so Malachi Martin in his *Jesus Now* book acknowledges that in reality men pay homage to many kinds of Jesus—the figures of "Jesus Caesar," "Jesus Yogi," "Jesus Pentecostalist," "Jesus Femina," "Jesus Gay," "Jesuschristsuperstar," "Jesus-Take-My-Marbles-And

Etc." And the name Jesus, as we have noted in the previous chapter on doctrine and theology, are many, each one highlighting a function —"savior," "son of God," "teacher," "light," etc. While Christians would insist these functions are integrated into one personality, popular devotion highlighting one function at a time sets up many Jesuses, each to fit an exclusive emphasis.

The young Jesus People confuse the Holy Spirit with Jesus, as the Holy Spirit seems to be the object of worship as well as source of power. Or they may simultaneously worship Jesus in a moment and then forget Jesus in the burst of power of the Spirit. Jesus, of course, said there would be a sequence of revelation, the Spirit would come after him as a comforter and guide (John 15–17), but Christians have a hard time worshipping God the Father, Son and Holy Spirit at once. The very sequential nature of revelation creates for Christians a polytheism in function if not in definition.

A future concept of divinity, and particularly the avatar or messiah expression, could well harmonize with the psychological emphasis that man may indeed have many personalities and roles in a society, as we saw in Chapter II. A plural concept of revealed deity is encouraged by the influence of the East with its vagueness and its proliferation of many gurus and divinity types.

Pluralism, in the sense of messiahship, is also not all that incompatible with the teachings of Jesus. The faithful could share divinity with a god or savior, "As many as received him, to them gave he power to become the sons of God" (John 1:12), and "the works that I do shall he do also" (John 14:12). Of course, any emphasis on these verses by themselves could lead one to the later Gnostic heresies of the early church, as there is an ascendancy of spiritual beings on different levels, pointing to union with Deity. But the future may not necessarily repeat old heresies. Some kinds of multiplicity concepts can exist without the ranking of angels and levels of spiritualization as the old heresies did. At this point perhaps it is sufficient to say there are always possibilities that the multiple concepts of deity and saviors as well could continue, functionally as in the proliferation of the names of Jesus, or more literally in the proliferation of gurus and masters. And, of course, proliferation on the one hand, or assimilation of the faiths on the other, could mean, as the saviors multiply or become universal with each man having "saving" capabilities, that the day of the uniqueness of saviors and avatars and their gurus are gone. But that kind of void would be contrary to a very common experience of man over the years. From the primitive tribes with their medicine men to sophisticated teaching masters man has had his holy men who derive their teaching if not their very essence from deity concepts.

The very emphasis on meditation and religious experience itself, so prevalent in the mid-1970s, encourages a wider grouping of god-types as each one discovers a god-consciousness. "One primary role of religion in the East has been political—to reconcile people to their lot and prevent turbulence," says Gregory Benford, of the physics department of the University of California at Irvine. "The same will be necessary in the West soon and we can expect theology to reflect it. The mystical portion always present in Christianity will grow. There will be more stress on individual religious experience." Religiously, as well as politically, this new individualism or "do-it-yourself" approach will have its implications. Neither man nor any one of his religions will seem so unique.

"I expect the view of man as simply one of a number of intelligent races will be incorporated into religion explicitly; it's a humbling notion," said Benford. "Thus there could even be a Church of Christ the Cosmonaut; there will surely be a new awakening view of Christ as the Essential Mystic."

The Eastern approach, or "politics of mysticism," as William Irwin Thompson calls it in his *Passages About Earth,* could lead to an "elitism" of the enlightened, as Thompson suggests. An acceptance of a variety of religious experience could be a consolidating factor, as an experience is shared sans structural lines. Benford explores this in his *Deeper Than the Darkness.* In a forthcoming volume with Harper & Row, *Faster Than Light,* Benford sees religion as a means of insuring stability. Curiously, then, the more unilateral the government is, then the more proliferation there might be of avatars or revealed types, as the political specter is less willing to deal with a single or small number of saviors.

Even with a "oneness"—of earth or universe—politically and religiously, coalescing a variety of mystical experiences and paths, a plural concept of important avatars and "Christs" could survive. Back at the start of the Space Age, a Scottish theologian argued a point that is all but accepted now, that the existences of many and even billions of inhabited worlds can mean many and even billions of saviors. Although "there is but one Christ, our Lord," wrote the Reverend Dr. Geddes MacGregor, dean of the graduate school of religion at the University of Southern California, Los Angeles, "this does not exclude the possibility, however, of there being millions of other divine Incarnations on other planets throughout the innumerable galaxies; for as the love of God is boundless so also are the redemptive possibilities beyond this Earth. . . . We have certainly no reason to suppose we have a monopoly of divine redemption."[1]

Of course, science fiction has not been sparse in its suggestions of the many different kinds of saviors that might emerge and likely as not interact with the experiences of earthmen. Nearly every space-side protagonist in the "age of inter-galatic expeditions" and a destroyed or subjugated earth has the qualities of a god-like figure by today's standards. And hero and conqueror or as a new man, sometimes part alien, the figures are hunted and persecuted like Christ of old, particularly in the tales that put such men in touch with earth. One of the most noted of these parallels is the stoning of the superintelligent, Mars-born Valentine Michael Smith, in Heinlein's *Stranger in a Strange Land.* Also earthmen closed in on a man who proved ageless with eternal secrets in Clifford Simak's *Way Station.* Ray Bradbury's "The Illustrated Man," full of tattoos and secrets as people watch the pictures—including their life history and death—on the body of the man, is hunted by the authorities and mobs on earth like Christ. In Bradbury's "The Man," a story in *The Illustrated Man,* a volume that takes the name of it's lead story, a Christ-like figure is making the rounds of the planets, but is illusive to a hard, cigar-smoking earth crew:

"Captain, listen. Something big happened yesterday in that city. It's so big, so important that we're second-rate—second fiddle. I've got to sit down." He lost his balance and sat heavily, gasping for air.

The captain chewed his cigar angrily. "What happened?"

Martin lifted his head, smoke from the burning cigarette in his fingers, blowing in the wind. "Sir, yesterday in that city, a remarkable man appeared—good, intelligent, compassionate, and infinitely wise!"

The captain glared at his lieutenant. "What's that to do with us? . . . This man who got here ahead of us? What was his name!"

[1] "Space Theology," *The Living Church,* October 21, 1962.

"He didn't have a name. He doesn't need one. It would be different on every planet, sir."

Whether the Incarnation of Christ on earth is a unique event for earth, or whether he is wandering the Universe in Bradbury style, the possibility of alien civilizations unknown to earth certainly keeps alive a multiple concept of revelation in manifestations of the same person or the appearances of many persons. It is not enough to argue that Incarnation is personal on earth, with Christ appearing, while assuming that the religion on other locales would be impersonal. If there are living entities, rational in any way as man, they will likely personify their religious beings also. Although the discussions of future saviors or avatars can be centered in a discussion of "what" will come as well as "who," along more traditional lines, the "who-ness" will likely remain dominant. A machine or a Spirit or even a principle that captures imagination and the faith of people will likely have a human name. Man has always named his idols (Baal, Moloch, etc.) and things that serve him. A nation is represented by a person (Uncle Sam, John Bull, etc.); airplanes and war tanks and other equipment have personal names; animals are named; ball teams have names (Vikings, Lions, Saints, Braves, etc.). Mankind seeks to give identity to everything. Future avatars—be they psychic immaterial or material embodiments—will likely have identity.

The messianic, personal leader consciousness does not die easily. Says Fred Polak, a Dutch futurist and author of *The Image of the Future* and other books: "People will feel that sometimes, someone has to make a new world. The messianic element will be kept alive." And, of course, there may emerge the hope that, as the science fiction writers would have it, that a messiah could come from another planet. "I am convinced that some contact will be made with other religious intelligences," says Polak, vice chairman of the International Society for Technology Assessment. And it is within the realm of logic and possibility if someone "takes over from another planet, especially if that planet has an older civilization which might be further along than we are."

But Jesus—how about Jesus? The man who comes from other planets—or the men—who might come in the name of God the Father in the future, could not this be Jesus? Or if not, why not regard him or them as Jesus and the followers or proliferations—even duplications—as the "sons of God"? It will be hard for earth Christians to think of any visitation, singular or plural, as anything else than Christ and his angels. The expectation is very much alive in the '70s and must be dealt with in any appraisal of the future.

THE NEW INTEREST IN PROPHECY

In Christianity, there has emerged a new interest in prophecy, especially concerned with Jesus in particular. When will Jesus and his legions, come? Hal Lindsey's *The Late Great Planet Earth* and the sequel, *The Devil Is Alive and Well*—both dealing with the Devil as a backdrop for a conflict that will bring Jesus back victoriously—have sold 4.6 million copies in a few years. Lindsey, who ran a student and Jesus People house on fraternity row at the University of California at Los Angeles, sees events related to Israel in this century as a harbinger of the final days. The restoration of Israel as a nation, the reclaiming of Jerusalem for the Jews in 1967 are seen as signs indicating that God is drawing his chosen people back together for an unfurling of catyclysmic events. On this bandwagon, too, capitalizing on news events, is faith healer Kathryn Kuhlman, of Pittsburgh. In an interview over a year ago, she reported to me she has distributed one million copies of her twenty-two-page booklet, *The Rock,* on the Second Coming of Christ. She blurted out to a packed Ford auditorium in Detroit a somber note of prophecy: "We are on the threshhold of one of the darkest hours of civilization! It is as Ezekiel 37 says, the Jew has seen the restoration of his homeland. This is one of the greatest fulfillments of Bible prophecy."

Other books on the crowded prophecy market these days include: *Prophecy in the Making* (Creation House) edited by Carl F. H. Henry, a collection of messages from the Conference on Biblical Prophecy in Jerusalem in 1971, also seeing Bible predictions fulfilled in the new Jewish state; *Prophecy and the Seventies* (Moody, 1971), by Charles Lee Feinberg, a collection of sermons from a prophetic conference sponsored by the American Board of Missions to the Jews; *You Can Know the Future* (Gospel Light–Regal), by Wilbur Smith, a study by a conservative biblical scholar. Other recent titles: *A Survey of Bible Prophecy, Discern These Times, Signs of the Times, Daniel: The Key to Prophetic Revelation, Coming of the Kingdom, The Beginning of the End, The Future of the Great Planet Earth, Highlights of the Book of Revelation,* and many more.

One group that has surfaced in the past few years actually calls itself "Second Coming, Inc." I dropped in on a banquet of the organization which is built around a forty-seven-year-old ex-ad man from suburban Philadelphia, Salem Kirban. The audience of 258—only 150 were expected—was mostly older ladies and men, with some middle-aged pastors and Jesus People youths scattered in the crowd. At one table, two ladies nearing sixty told about spiritualist and mind-control groups to which they belong. What they all had in common was a fascination with the supernatural and the occult—the religious people who believe in God and Satan and Jesus and demons, and the others who believe in any or all mysterious forces, with flying saucers and astroprojections thrown in.

Kirban's message was a rehash of dark predictions of the prophets in the Old Testament and in the obscure Book of Revelation at the end of the New Testament. A slide presentation began with pictures of Jerusalem and Kirban's commentary told how Arabs (Kirban is Lebanese) and Jews need Christ. He dropped in a remark about Jews spending too much time putting prayer messages into the wailing wall instead of praying directly to God. Kirban, who works out of Huntingdon, Pennyslvania, showed scenes of the Apostle Paul's death, and Christians succumbing in the arena. "Now let's see what judgments await us." He showed a doctored slide of New York City as a dreadful earthquake tumbles it. "Imagine the death . . . There's a volcano. Now here is a hot lava flow . . ." The slides hold out a message of safety with Jesus some day when all of these things happen.

Kirban says four of his books have each sold over a quarter of a million. He publishes them directly in Grand Rapids and Menasha, Wisconsin. His staff includes a "field representative" and his son Dennis, who runs a firm with a fictitious name, "Cynthia Goodwin and Associates." It prints Kirban's advertising literature and handles mailings. Kirban's books follow the usual theme of conservative "propheteers," namely, the world will evolve into a great confrontation that will take place in the Holy Land, and Christ will return to settle it all. He also has a $3.95 poster of the white horsemen of Christ coming down out of the sky in that end-of-the-world war. (Most believe the battle will be at the site of the ancient city of Megiddo in the center of the valley of Jezreel of Esdraelon, about eighteen miles from the coast. Megiddo was orignally destroyed about 2500 B.C. along with other settlements, but history remains quiet on whether the cause was a natural disaster or a military encounter. The Book of Revelation [16:16] says the site will be the scene for the last great battle. Only in Revelation, the name is Armageddon, the Greek for Har Megiddo, the hill of Megiddo.)

In St. John's Book of Revelation, a vision of a thousand years—the millennium—of a rule by Christ is described: "And I saw an angel come down from heaven, having the key of the bottomless pit and a great chain in his hand. And he laid hold on the dragon, that old serpent, which is the Devil, and Satan, and bound him a thousand years, And cast him into the bottomless pit, and shut him up, and set a seal upon him, that he should deceive the nations no more, till the thousand years should be fulfilled: and after that he must be loosed a little season. . . ." (Rev. 20:1, 2).

Churchmen have interpreted this "millennium" various ways. The "post-millennialists" believe that Christ will come only after a thousand-year utopia on earth. Such a view encourages responsibility to shape the world along Christ's tenets before he returns. The "pre-millennialists" believe that Christ will come before the millennium. His coming is preceded by various tell-tale cataclysmic events, such as the return of the Jews, rebuilding of the Temple, etc. A "non-millennialist" group, representing more a main-line Presbyterian and Lutheran tradition, among others, merely takes the thousand years as symbolic of Christ's reign, whenever and however it occurs, in Heaven or partially on earth before his visible return.

About three years ago, Pat Boone told me in his home near Hollywood's Sunset Strip that the world was coming to an end very quickly, possibly in three years. He cited, too, the signs of the times. As with many premillennialists, he is still waiting, but there are the premillennialists who are holding out for the fulfillment of more conditions. The Reverend Dr. Robert Armstrong, pastor of the big Warrendale (non-denominational) Church in Dearborn, Michigan, a church interested in prophecy, said Christian prophecy insists that Jews will have to be in Palestine, but that the present conditions do not fit Bible prophecy. Talking after the 1973 Yom Kippur war, he said, "the present outcome of the war has no influence on the ultimate prophetic fulfillment of both the Old and New Testaments. The Bible teaches eventually that during a thousand-year reign of Christ, Jerusalem will be the capital of the United States of the World, and Jesus Christ will reign as King of kings."

The chain of events has not occurred, said Pastor Armstrong.

"First," he said, "will be the rapture of the church"—which means Christians will be received up in the air with Christ. There then comes a seven-year tribulation, and then the inaugurating of the thousand-year reign from Jerusalem. Although Jews will have to be in Palestine, he said, "they will have received Christ as their Messiah toward the end of the tribulation period (Zech. 12; Matt. 24). I believe the borders [of Israel] will be vastly enlarged, from the Nile to the Euphrates, but that will take place during the Tribulation. The Christian should exercise all efforts to reach both Jews and Arabs with the Gospel before the rapture takes place."

Typical of the challenge of many to any notion of a restored Israeli or Palestinian as a condition for Christ's return, are the views of Missouri Synod Lutheran Gilbert Otte, of Trinity Lutheran Church, downtown Detroit. Dr. Otte was one of the pastors detained in a Syrian harbor at the outset of the Yom Kippur war in 1973. "We don't go along with the idea that land is to be restored to the Jewish people as prophecy. We do not believe there is a bullet proof promise to that effect. The promise in the New Testament (Romans 11) is that there is to be a spiritual Israel, a true children of God, and it is not to be twisted into a political nation to be saved." A Baptist, the Reverend Dr. Frederick B. Sampson, of the Tabernacle (National Baptist Convention USA, Inc.) Church, Detroit, said, "I am more or less in a hallway [on the conflicts in the Middle East]. I lack the depth of knowing what really is happening. I am afraid of quick easy answers. I am still dealing with me: what I would do if I were an Arab-born Christian or a Jew. . . . I just don't know, and I am not ashamed to say I don't know."

A JEWISH VIEWPOINT

Jews have little use for the modern Israel prophecy theories of conservative and evangelical Christians. Materials prepared under joint auspices of three Jewish groups in 1973—triggered in part by an implied conversion effort of Jews by evangelicals through a 1973 program, Key 73 zeroed in on a key prophecy chapter, Isaiah 53. Rabbi Balfour Brickner of New York City, director of a Commission on Interfaith Activities of three Jewish groups, said the "suffering servant" reference of Isaiah 53, often quoted by evangelicals, does not refer to Jesus but to the Jewish people. "The covenant was established between God, who had shown His deeds of benevolence, and His servant (the people of Israel), whose responsibility was (and is) to serve God through the doing of mitzvot (commandments, or good deeds) in gratitude and reverence. The people are God's agent, endowed with His spirit, who will bring justice to the nations (Isaiah 42:1)." The Hebrew Bible often portrays the individual as standing for the whole community, Rabbi Brickner said. He cited Abraham as one who was both an individual but who also stood for a whole community.

I recently met with a group of religious leaders from Jordan and proceeded to elicit their views on prophecy. Three were Christian, one was Moslem. I also sought a Jewish response to these Arab-land visitors on the matter of prophecy. On prophecy, the Most Reverend Saba Youakim, Greek Catholic (Melkite) archbishop of East Jordan, said that "all prophecies are accomplished in Jesus Christ. He opened a new phase." He added that the concept of Israel in the New Testament refers to a spiritual group (Gal. 6:16; Romans 11). (Interviews which I also had with leaders of the Catholic Eastern rites, Josyf Cardinal Slipyj of the Ukraine and Patriarch Paul II Cheikho, of Bagdad, Iraq, showed hope for a long persistence of the church without reference to prophecy.) The Most Reverend Diodoros, Greek Orthodox archbishop of East Jordan, agreed "the concept is spiritual. Jesus didn't say, 'believe in me and I will give you a land.'" The Most Reverend Ne'meh Sama'an, Roman Catholic bishop and patriarchal vicar in East Jordan, said, "Whatever prophecy and whatever symbolism and sacrificial ideas there are in the Old Testament, these were in preparation for the coming of Christ. As Christ has come, and all these prophecies have been implemented in Christ, their message is ended." Bishop Samatan said it is contrary to Christian theology to try to revive old prophecies. "There was to be no material kingdom," the bishop said. "Christ let them know that he did not come to make a material kingdom. Christ said we must give unto Caesar the things that are Caesar's."

The Right Reverend Aql Ibrahim Aql, Anglican bishop elect in Jerusalem and bishop commissary for Jordan, Syria, and Lebanon, said, "For you Christians in America, it is time for you to distinguish between the present-day Israeli and the Israelites. We are not a new Israel but we are new Israelites. Unfortunately, many of our Western brethren misunderstand history. They [Israelites] were in exile in Babylon many years, and therefore the prophecy refers to their return." Bible prophecy applies in part, he said, to Cyrus, the Persian conqueror defeating Babylon in 538 B.C., thus "permitting the return.

We can't make a new prophecy out of what has already taken place. The dispersal [of the Jews] came after the completion of all prophecy. It is finished. Christ completed it." Chief Justice and president of religious courts in Jordan, Sheikh Abdullah Ghosheh, offering a Moslem view, said there is nothing in his faith or holy books "that points out the necessity of Israel to be a completion of any promise. All this talk about prophecy does not have any roots."

Rabbi Marc Tanenbaum, director of interreligious affairs for the American Jewish Committee, New York, discounted the views of the Jordanian religious leaders as "politically inspired" and as disregarding views held by most Christian and Jewish scholars. "They [the Jordanian visitors] are resorting to the Second Century heresy of Marcion, who cut off the Old Testament as too negative and giving too wrathful a view of God."

Rabbi Tanenbaum says most of Judaism believes Bible prophecies apply in some way today, but he avoids any literalism or "mechanical timetable" of the Christian evangelicals. He noted that some modern thinkers such as Catholic Rosemary Reuther are suggesting a "parallel relationship" developing between Judaism and Christianity, "both pointing toward a common messianic fulfillment."

The rabbi also disagrees with the Christian evangelicals who identify Bible countries with modern nations; for instance, people living in Gog in the northern region of East Asia Minor (1 Chron. 5:4; Ezek. 38, 39; Rev. 20:8) are identified by Lindsey and others as the Russians against which the righteous must battle. The United States, China, Egypt and others have their counterparts in the word games of prophecy.

"Some of these references have metaphomorphic power and insight," says Rabbi Tanenbaum, "but overtaxing the text as a blueprint for political programs and strategies seems to me to do violence to the spiritual tradition. The Bible is not a course in political science or foreign policy formation." Rabbi Tanenbaum warns Christians not "to confer messianic fulfillment too easily." He said this kind of tenuous easy thinking helped to rationalize the rise of Hitler.

CALL IT ESCHATOLOGY

As conservative Christians talk about the future with Bible scenarios of judgment applied to the present and near future, the more liberal- and theological-minded Christian prefers to talk about "eschatology," a word from the Greek meaning a "study of last things." Yet there are not all that many differences between eschatology and prophecy. All eschatology (including the theologies of progress, liberation, and hope, as discussed in Chapter VII) are "based on a historical second coming of Christ, a fundamentalist common position," said the Reverend Father Robert L. Faricy, S.J., professor at the Gregorian University in Rome and author of a book on spiritual evolutionist Teilhard de Chardin. "All eschatology is based on the idea of a terminal point of God breaking in." Contemporary eschatology is concerned with the polarization and tension of present and ultimate futures." But Father Faricy adds that theology never leads the way but reflects the culture of the present society. "All Christian theology reflects the continuing synthesis of religion and culture. Theology is like the work of an artist who does not create the forms but reflects on the forms. Eschatology is a product of what people believe, plus cultural concepts."

The speech of Pope Paul VI to the participants from the World Conference on Futures Research, visiting him from Frascati, dealt with eschatology as a future direction with God. But Pope Paul linked this "science of the future" to present realities, so eschatology becomes a preparation for the end of the world. In a way, the papal view on eschatology reflected an acknowledgment of a conflicting role of nations in the realization of a godly plan, just as the more literal and negative scenarios do. The eschatology as defined by the Pope sees God at work in the active participation of man, while the conservatives and fundamentalists see more of the work of the Devil in the world and are more content with negative descriptions and promulgation of fear in highly metamorphic categories than they are interested in pointing to a positive program in a world they count lost already.[2]

[2] Here is the transcript of Pope Paul VI's brief speech to the futurists who came in from Frascati to a private papal audience on September 27, 1973 in the new Consistory Hall of the Vatican:

It is a pleasure for us to meet today those taking part in the Special World Conference on Futures Research and to thank the President of IRADES, the sponsoring group for his kind words. We extend to all of you our warm greetings. We are aware of the general theme of the Conference: the study of man and his future, with special reference to the problems affecting man in his specific nature, problems which for this very reason are difficult and delicate ones. As scholars and qualified sociologists, you are in a position to offer the coming generation authoritative perspectives of development, and to con-

Lutheran Hans Schwarz, however, is critical of most treatment of eschatology as too precise. He says eschatology can be lost in a morass of the theology of hope, or revolution, or process. But, on the other hand, he says the millennialism of the fundamentalists is just "this worldly replica of purgatory." The real alternatives for Christians are three, he says. They are courses of resignation, activism, or anticipation toward the future. Resignation is the "least viable option," Schwarz, a professor of systematic theology at the Lutheran Theological Seminary in Columbus, Ohio, says in a book, *On the Way to the Future,* a study of "eschatology in the light of

---

tribute to the improvement of human life. Having previously examined the various aspects of man's future—economic, demographic, cultural, technological and so on, this time you have addressed yourselves to the values which man, as a rational being, bears within himself and which he strives to bring to full realization.

In this field the Church, as the bearer of a transcendent and revealed doctrine, certainly has something to say. She already possesses a science concerning future and final realities, the science of eschatology, and she continually urges her children to study the sublime truth which it embodies, so that they may prepare themselves for the final and decisive meeting with the Creator. Eschatology, however, is concerned with a future that lies beyond space and time. Your own studies are concentrated on the development of this present world. Yet there is no contradiction between the two forms of research and indeed the Church is herself deeply aware of the problems of the temporal and earthly future. By reason of her experience stretching back two thousand years she too is an expert on mankind, and it is her wish to be present in this branch of research. She cannot of course offer technical solutions to problems, but when it is a question of man as the bearer of spiritual and moral values, she willingly encourages those men of science who work for man's development in the future. We praise you, therefore, for your commitment to the search for a future that is better and more human.

This search involves certain sectors of special interest. In the first place, there is the human personality; it would seem essential today to take account of that personality, not in opposition to, but in coordination with technical progress. This will contribute towards a fuller and harmonious development of man, who must be helped to achieve the fullness of his psychological and spiritual potentialities, as an individual, and in the context of the family.

Then there are nations, especially developing nations: they must be respected and given effective aid for their full flowering, and this in order also to safeguard that other transcendental human value—peace. Finally there is the problem of the defence of the human environment, which today is more and more endangered. The earth which the Creator gave in trust to man must be fit to live in, a worthy home for the whole of human society.

We know that these points which we have passed in rapid review are already part of your programme of research. We wish you well in your work, which is both forward-looking and courageous. You are pioneers, blazing a trail for future generations. We do not doubt that your commitment will be fruitful and appreciated, and we invoke upon your labours the abundant favours of Almighty God.

current trends." "Once we resign wrestling with the future, we no longer participate meaningfully in it."[3] An unenlightened activism fails also because "man is not just an extension of matter." A stance of productive anticipation "seems to provide the most viable option," says Schwarz. The "process of active anticipation strives for a better man, a more just society, and a more worldly world to live in. But since it is only anticipation, Christian faith is realistic enough to take into account the intrinsic self-alienation of man. Thus, we must reject the illusion that we could ever create a good man, a just society, or a new world. Ultimate perfection and removal of death as the dimensional border between our world and the new world to come will be brought about only through God's undeserved action."[4]

An openness to the future on all counts allows for the creative plays of forces, objective or subjective, in history. A stance of openness—for some it would be a creative doubt or agnosticism—puts the burden of proof concerning the destiny of man and the goodness of God on God himself. The limits of God's actions are unknown, but rest in a definition of God himself. Whether God is becoming, whether he is a future concept that always catches up and "updates" the past, or whether he is a past concept with only an implied sense of futurity, God appears limited by his own revelation or lack of revelation. Man does not put limits on God by definitions of experience or logic. God merely functions—in some kind of limited way, self-imposed or otherwise. To proceed to find motivation in the mind of God is to limit God on man's terms. The goals, destinies, and timetables, even the locations of prophecies and eschatologies, are too vague and obscure. "There can be only one valid answer to the reality of evil," says Wolfhart Pannenberg. "The eschatological reconciliation of God with his world by that glorification of his suffering creatures which alone will finally prove his true divinity."[5] The act itself—when and if it comes—is the only consideration. That final moment then does not depend on new Christs or avatars, or the political conflicts and wars of nations as a part of prophecy, or the participants in an acculturation improvement campaign of an "end-of-the-world" eschatological process. It depends on "nothing"—nothing that man can describe.

Yet the open future can well claim the same qualities and dis-

3 (Minneapolis: Augsburg, 1972), p. 224.
4 Ibid., p. 225.
5 Tupper, op. cit. p. 304.

values of the present. A future religion can still struggle with good and evil, with man within the framework of redemption, man still sinning, or calling for cultic rapture while weaving a patchwork of Bible quotes.

The gurus may continue to appear. There may be many more of them. Some may be men or women—or quasi-humans of outer space, all likely to be limited. The faithful will be limited, capable of good and bad, despite any appeal to the Holy Spirit or energy circles. God will be eclipsed for all practical purposes in the riddle of unsolved, though more delayed, suffering. The rites will be there, but they may be to an unknown god or gods or to a multiplicity of concepts, each representing facets of Jesus or Jesuses, named or unnamed.

Whether a savior will appear or won't appear on the scene is not a question for a future. If the future contains the past and the present, who are we to devise an ending (and proof-text it with Scripture) on the basis of that knowledge? If the future contains surprises (as Jesus himself hinted), then it can be anything, anytime, anywhere.

When one looks at scenarios—as we must in our unconscious dreams or in more conscious, planned efforts—the best scenarios will reflect what we already know and yet allow for surprises. That is prophecy and eschatology indeed—so close, yet capable of near total surprise, so unknown still.

CHAPTER IX

The Ritual and Temple of the Future

If you wake up in A.D. 2101 and look for a faith and a place to worship, you might find that religion is: (1) often outdoors, (2) celebrative, and (3) co-ordinated in centers. Some familiar sacraments or ordinances, such as a meal rite and baptism, both of which have roots in pre-Christian history, are likely still to be around in some form.

If Isaac Asimov is right that man, for positive reasons, in the next century will be "burrowing underground" and the earth's surface will be turned into "resorts, parkland and wildlife refuges,"[1] then the "non-catacomb" religion that might be above ground can be expected to have some outdoor quality.

Devotion to a landscape with much of the technology moved underground can add new aura to plants and animals. "I predict greater emphasis on 'reverence-for-life' customs such as vegetarianism, partly because they rationalize what will be necessary (cheaper food) and partly because they make sense," says Professor Sheila Simonson, of Clark College, Vancouver, Washington. Another professor writes: "My scenario includes more dance, fantasy, mysticism, Jungian psychology, awareness of our fellow creatures such as plants, animals, and earth."

In a little hotel in Starnberg by a lake near Munich, Dr. Karl Friedrich Basedow, who heads the Foundation for Eastern Wisdom and Western Science, near Starnberg, explained how some outdoor religious concepts might go beyond East and West, merging both traditions. "The 'new man' will surpass the counterlines or limits, be he Christian or Zoroastrian or Hindu. The new individual will have the facility to use his intellect. He will accept experience beyond

[1] "The Next 100 Years," op. cit., p. 40.

the definition of the mind. He will lead a quieter life, but he will experience his religion."

Experiencing things will be the emphasis of one's life, and he will relate to all aspects of the world. Even sport will become a vehicle of religion, Basedow says. "One thing we'll get away from is the intellectual," says Basedow. "We will find that the aim of life is not to reach the limit of thinking. Man will seek a 'spiritual perceptive power.' "

Sports Illustrated Magazine in August 13, 1973 described what Basedow was talking about, he said—the wedding of Eastern mysticism and Western activism. Writer Adam Smith went to a yoga tennis demonstration at the Esalen Institute in California. He was told: "Sport anticipates what the Divine Essence is. Sport is a Western yoga, the Dance of Shiva [Hindu deity]. Pure play. Non-utilitarian, the delight in the moment, the Now. We need a more balanced and evolutionary culture. We already have physical mobility. Why shouldn't we have psychic mobility, too, the ability to move psychically into different states? The whole movement of life is to a higher consciousness."[2] In Zen tennis, chants preceded serving the ball, but author Smith did not master the discipline of meditation that allowed the ball to do its job on its own. But he acknowledged: "To the teachers of Zen tennis, or Yoga tennis, or whatever it is we call it, the techniques are not to provide winning tennis necessarily but to put the player into the right frame of consciousness after which, as the Zen Master said, 'You will see with other eyes and measure with other measures.' "[3]

MYSTICISM AND A CELEBRATION OF THE BODY

Basedow sees a "Church of Zen Tennis" or a "Church of Zen Golf," and so on, as possibilities in the future. He says his definition of religion is "the practice of commitment" and in a predominantly secular age, which brings together East and West traditions in religion and leisure, a "Zen Tennis Community" or a "Zen Golf Community" could elicit a form of religious commitment.

Native American traditions already have forms of natural mysticism that help to pave the way for an appreciation of the East. A

---

[2] "Trying the Dance of Shiva," *Sports Illustrated,* August 13, 1974, p. 37. Cf. also, Seligson, Marcia, "Zen Tennis," *New Times,* August 23, 1974, Vol. 3, No. 4. p. 37.
[3] Ibid., p. 40.

Franciscan, the Reverend Father Murray Bodo, O.F.M., describes the Navajo way of life—of seeking to merge with all of life—in a photo-essay article in the *St. Anthony Messenger*. He describes the Navajo way "to be in harmony with all things" and observes in the Navajo understanding of life that "Nature is the great healer of its supposed lord and master, man."[4]

A return to tribalism in religion with its mystic, simplistic but total look at the universe is predicted by some from the Third World. "I can see religious changes being replaced by humanistic religion and transcendent myths that relate to the crisis of human life," said Kivuto Ndeti, a sociologist from the University of Nairobi in Nairobi, Kenya, in an interview at the Rome Special World Conference on Futures Research in Frascati, Italy. "I see a religion of life in a tribal structure. It is not materialistic but deals with daily life. A religion not just on Sunday, but you live it. I see a 'collective religion' that is global, which retains structures to guide daily life." The practices of the tribes forged in ancient days can continue, he said. "Call it colorful living, if you like."

Tushar Kanti Moulik, a social scientist from the New Guinea Research Unit, Port Moresby, Papua, New Guinea, sees a "revivalism" of ancient traditions in his part of the world, more likely to carry into the future than a Western and Christian religious influence. Western religion, he says, has not met basic material needs. People are keeping Christianity, he said, but "are creating some sort of religious institutions to preserve the tribal ways."

If an Episcopalian bishop is right, the weight of the numbers of new Christians in Africa will be a factor of influence. The Right Reverend Stephen C. Neill, on a U.S. speaking tour after four years as a professor at the University of Nairobi, believes that more than half of the population of 600 million predicted for Africa south of the Sahara will be Christians by the year 2000. As Africa becomes the center of a new Christian thrust, he said, Christianity will be less and less a white man's religion.[5]

Dr. Philip Potter, general secretary of the World Council of Churches, himself from the West Indies, told me at a Madison, Wisconsin, meeting of the U. S. Conference for the WCC, various

[4] "Meditations From the Desert," *St. Anthony Messenger,* Vol. 81, No. 6, November 1973, p. 35.
[5] Cf. "Africa Called Future Center of World's Christian Religions," a report on a speech by Bishop Neill in a convocation at Concordia College, Moorhead, Minnesota, in the Minneapolis *Star,* February 9, 1974.

non-Western traditions might come into Christianity and even affect the shape of the ecumenical or church unity movement. "Yoga does point to the fact there are spiritual faculties in man that are undeveloped," he said, and this emphasis might be felt in a more direct way than it now is. And he wondered if Christians and others need as much food as we eat. "We do not have to go back to old fasting," he said, "but there is something in it and it is coming back by the non-Christian."

Dr. Potter said the "whole African scene" is going to make "two basic contributions" to the future. On the one hand, an African contribution is that "the Africans have a profound sense of Martin Buber's 'I-Thou' relationship—a sense of sharing and sensitiveness to one another." And on the other hand, the sense of celebration from Africa will make its mark. "Celebration of the body in Africa forms a bridge between Asia and the West," said Dr. Potter, in a breakfast interview. "Asian religion does not despise the body as some charge. Asia has some sensuous dances, an experience of the transcendence through the senses, but in this respect, Africa has something more dynamic."

WORSHIP OUTDOORS

In recent years, I have watched many new gatherings, influenced by non-Western culture, much of it outdoors, with a tribal—sharing, sensitive, celebrative—aspect even in quietness. I remember the quiet sunrise raps in Sutro Park high above cliffs on the ocean at San Francisco, with Steve Gaskin (who has now taken his faithful commune to rural Tennessee). Gaskin, in the midst of tall trees and among the dew-dipped calla lilies of early morning, inspired meditation efforts to concentrate on the distant foghorns. The youths stood, 150 strong, tightly knit as one family in the woods. The outdoors inspires oneness, in meditation with a sense of oversoul, in getting together one's own self or in seeking communion with others. Inevitably the tribal feeling of song and dance emerges.

I felt I was on a future world in a meadow last year near Ann Arbor. Occasion was a gathering of several dozen of the new Eastern and assorted mystical groups under the auspices of the religious affairs office of the University of Michigan. The youths, for the most part, were American born Caucasians, not foreign students, although their new faith had Asian and Near Eastern roots. It was early and damp. The sun peaked over the tree-rimmed horizon but could not yet be felt.

The hearty first comers of the day-long "Festival of Life" sat silently with folded legs and arms. Suddenly one youth erupted in great breaths, panting in the short breaths of a yoga discipline. Others, legs knotted under, broke out in spontaneous rythmic motions. Miss Mari Shore, representing the University of Michigan office of ethics and religion, said, "We meditate to the sun in respect to the cosmic energy." Phil Cousineau, twenty-one, of the University of Detroit, said, "The warm glow of the sun is like heat radiated, like a charm you get from people, but coming instead from nature."

Fifteen Eastern and self-realization groups took part in the fall celebration. Divine Light Mission youths (Maharaj Ji. disciples) came in their Sunday best. The head-shaved Hare Krishna youths huddled in robes around a picture of Krishna and supported their chants with a hand organ. The Guru Ram Das Ashram youths wore turbans. As the sun warmed the glen, the birds flittered, and filled the sky. The motion of the day never stopped. White turbans and long golden hair and red-head bands swirled in motion, took in the sun, blended with the colors of the fall.

For a while, the youths roamed the slopes and coves around the meadow where the various groups showed their literature. Then the youths joined, in circuitous motion, for the Islamic Sufi dance (named after "suf," or "cloak of white wool," which recalled the plain robes of Christian monks in reaction to formalism in the church).

Chants to "merciful Allah" rang out as arms linked in eighth-century dance. "Try to become one, and let your hearts flow out," sang out Suranda Touhey, nineteen. As the young dancers closed to form one shadow beneath the sun, several dogs were caught in the tightly woven mass of people. But one by one the dogs snuck out beneath the "trees" of legs. A tiny child's hand also escaped the huddle of the dance, and reached up and out around a slim waist in jeans. The great Sufi dance ended with the youths now becoming water, fire, and air; they waved arms, reached for the sky like flames, and tumbled as free-style breezes.

The festivity of worship that comes outdoors is not lost only on the young celebrating Eastern traditions in meadows near universities. As we have seen, celebrative theology and theology of play have received a boost by men such as Harvey Cox and Sam Keen and by the updating of the church along more informal lines, namely, in the reforms of the Second Vatican Council. The outdoor imagery is there, too. I remember the excitement of the tom-tom drums, doves in cages, and colorful processions around the altar in St. Peter's Basilica during the canonization of the twenty-two African martyrs at the Vatican. African and tribal celebration in St. Peter's itself!

The churches have their festive greens at Christmas, palms at Easter, and horns-of-plenty baskets at Thanksgiving. In the new rituals there is much of the outdoors. Ann Weems, a Presbyterian minister's wife, leads off an issue of *Presbyterian Life* on "New Ways to Worship" with a poem that says: "I celebrate snow falling . . . the wondrous quiet of the snow falling . . . I celebrate the crashing thunder and the brazen lightning . . . And I celebrate the green of the world . . . the life-giving green . . . the hope-giving green . . . [6]

Priest-sociologist Andrew Greeley discusses celebration ritual and changing mores and life styles. Perhaps overstating his case, he presents some very unusual ideas. Whatever future religion might be —whether it is formal and puritanical or informal and free in expression—the ritual will likely reflect a correlation between social mores and the practice of faith. He discusses possible new rituals for each month of the religious calendar. In summer:

> The most obvious candidate for a June long weekend is Midsummer's Day—a feast with a long and glorious tradition, although it has been neglected in recent centuries. Without meaning to be offensive, I would suggest that this be an explicitly sexual feast. There are strong currents of fertility symbolism in both Christmas and Easter—oops, the midwinter and spring festivals. . . . But most Christians would be distressed by an explicit link between fertility and new life, and many non-Christians as well as Christians would object to an explicit connection between sexuality and life. Hence it is better to have one feast formally devoted to celebration of the joys of sexuality.
>
> A healthy society needs at least one time in the course of a

[6] "Balloons Belong in Church," *Presbyterian Life,* Vol. 24, No. 20, October 15, 1971, p. 2.

year when a full-fledged orgy can occur. Catholic countries have permitted this release of sexual tensions at the carnival (*carni valle*—good-bye to flesh) on the day before Ash Wednesday (Mardi Gras); but the Puritan variety of Protestantism, which has dominated American culture until recently, has not perceived the wisdom of such a time of sexual license free from guilt and regrets. Random sexual intercourse would tear a society apart if it were permitted every day, but the pent-up fantasies of making love to every attractive and willing sexual partner one encounters need to be released periodically if they are not to lead to destructive frustration. Swinging, group sex, and other ancient orgiastic pastimes which have recently become popular again require a great deal of time, planning and energy if they are carried on throughout a sustained period. But a weekend officially devoted to a good old-fashioned national orgy would eliminate most of the inconvenience and prevent the passion for sexual variety from interfering with permanent and ordinarily satisfactory family arrangements. Even those regular sexual partners who do not feel the need of a weekend of infidelity could still devote the time to exploring with each other sexual fantasies that they would not dare suggest at other times of the year. For the squares who are not interested, there would be no obligation to participate actively in the national orgy. One could not call the mid-June long weekend the Feast of National Orgy, but a happy euphemism might be the Feast of Self-Fulfillment.[7]

NEW APPROACHES TO SEX

Religion may have less of a negative approach to sex in a future age. Not that religion is likely to endorse such a proposal as Father Greeley's, but to the extent there is greater laxity—or acceptance of the human body, dress styles and even public nudity in society might be reflected in the churches, and it may not be that radical. Early Christians stripped their new converts and baptised them naked in the streams, according to Hippolytus of Rome in the third century. Medieval art in churches abound with nudity of children. Whatever the degree of semi-nakedness on the street may be, it

---

[7] "More Long Weekends: A Relatively Modest Proposal," *The Christian Century*, September 5, 1973, p. 854.

may be accepted in the new forms of religion. The year 1974 showed how quickly public nudity could come. On both coasts— and particularly in California—nudity on beaches became wide- spread. Although "streaking" apparently went the way of most fads, it shows that in our age of rapid change how quickly a revision of common codes can come—and go—almost overnight. Some five hundred of the 1,100 Unitarian Universalist Association Sunday schools in the United States have taken to showing explicit film strips, "About Your Sexuality." The films show adults in sexual intercourse, masturbation, and homosexual acts.[8] Ministerial con- ferences, such as one in Ann Arbor using films from a San Francisco studio, look at explicit instructional films. Girls in leotards or bare- foot dancing by the altars in campus chapels and a Catholic diocesan seminary in the Detroit area spell out that some laxity in style, at least for liturgical purposes, has arrived. George Takei, of the TV series, "Star Trek," lets his imagination run wild easily. "In 2101," he said in an interview, "we will get back to nature. Ritual will be natural rather than pageantry. When we get out there [in space], we will be relating to forces out there." In what way? "One thing fascinates me—the tactile sensual approach to religion. I know air is a little different out there. But to be nude on the moon! To be barefoot on the sand and to loll in it! Wafting around in space, a kind of ballet ritual by people living in space, I can see it now."

Sex has crept already into some of America's new religions and their rites. Chief Satanist Anton LaVey in San Francisco shows you the altar where his nude sits during one of the several kinds of rites practiced by the Satanists, who are concerned more with get- ting rid of guilt feelings than subscribing to any objective concept of Satan.

Over in Berkeley, the Messiah's One World Family Crusade, according to one of its young couples, have a voluntary sexual rite, closed to all but the inner circle. The "tantra" yoga has the men sitting in the outer circle, and the women rotating around the inner circle. Ritually, the eight couples in the room exchange mates in intercourse but stop short of orgasm in each case, the couple said. There is "no outside sex," in order to avoid venereal diseases, they said. "It's a communal marriage and all are married to each other."

[8] Cf. "Sex at Sunday School," *Newsweek,* vol. LXXVIII, No. 26, December 27, 1971, p. 50.

Down the coast, in Santa Monica, is a new cult along the line of positive-thinking groups, with a network of self-enrichment courses. A spokesman for "Prosperos" says little about the sexual beliefs, but sex is important for them. A newsletter provided by Prosperos, whose staff took part in Barbara Marx Hubbard's Synacon future convention in Washington, D.C., is full of titillating sexual information. Pictures in their literature include "nude" designed furniture and a "nude" cast in a play.

Scientology with its awareness and touch sessions and the whole sensitivity movement engaged in by the churches have sexual overtones. The Jesus People movement has tended to strive for puritanical concepts of sex, but there are exceptions. The heavily programmed youths in the Children of God have been accused of engaging in sexual acts with their leaders. The Reverend Dr. J. Robert Nelson, former head of Faith and Order (church unity) for the World Council of Churches and a professor at the Boston University School of Theology, acknowledges "there could be a sex sect in the future. There are traces already," he said, and he cited "the devil cults and what is happening to sexual mores. But I do not expect it to be a powerful movement."

As to where religion will meet in the future, many see religious or quasi-religious groups convening in centers, rather than in churchly buildings. Greeley, in that controversial article on long weekends, sees "centers" as an answer to growing leisure time and diverse interests. "We might concede to the churches a 'wild card' long weekend, the annual retreat," said Greeley, who is senior study director of the National Opinion Research Center at the University of Chicago. "Any American wishing to avail himself/herself of a weekend of reflection and contemplation would be guaranteed the opportunity to do so. He/she would have to spend it at some organized center (you cannot trust people with unorganized solitude). Such a center need not be affiliated with a church. You could go to the retreat house, encounter group, human potential confrontation, Quaker meeting, or nude marathon of your choice.[9]

THE RELIGIOUS "CENTER" OF TOMORROW

Edward Cornish, president of the World Future Society and editor of its journal, *The Futurist,* in an interview in Washington said

[9] Greeley, op. cit., p. 855.

people searching for meaning in the future may gather in "centers" or units like "monasteries." "Religion then again will become a prime interest," he said. As other issues are solved, the search for the meaning of life remains. "But churches will not be where the action is. We will move away from churches and the individual approach, and move toward a more communal society."

The place of worship, says Gene Roddenberry, will be "a place to explore living and not to praise one's fantasy. Rather, it will be a center to discuss and disagree and to talk about 'who am I.' "

Look for a center with rooms to meet "multipersonality needs," says Elaine Pagels, professor of religion at Columbia University. There would be rooms for silence, exercise rooms for dancing, rooms for private counseling, she said.

Of course, many churches with their recreation and education wings have all kinds of multiple services now, but what some of these people seem to be saying is that the "multiplicity" and service philosophy will dominate, instead of merely being an adjunct of the ritual-centered church with its cavernous sanctuary.

The future needs of a person in a place of religion will likely be much as they are today. His needs will be psychological, sociological, physical, as well as spiritual. A person in church today can enjoy the outdoors and athletic programs, particularly in various church retreats and camps. The pastor offers counseling. There are study groups that offer intellectual stimulation on various issues, not to mention the hour of discussion in Sunday schools. The "center" idea merely acknowledges that some of the doctrinal distinctions may wear off, that man will have some answers from his machines, and that man will have accommodated himself to more realistic use of his buildings. Even now chaplains of varying backgrounds have learned to use the same building, as various churches have also, as we saw in Chapter IV. The all-purpose building of the future may look less religious; yet its goal may be the same, in a way—meeting the deepest, variant needs of many. Those future needs hardly differ from today's needs, says the Reverend Philotheros Zikas, a Baptist pastor from Alexandroupolis, Greece, over dinner one night during a preaching visit to the United States. "People today are more interested in things that can support the inner man," he said, "and help build integral personalities that can match the need of the human race."

The all-purpose center idea was on the minds of members of

workshop seven on religion and values at the Rome Special World Conference on Futures Research in 1973 in Frascati. In a formal proposal, largely mapped by Mrs. Kenneth Boulding, a Quaker and professor of behavioral science at the University of Colorado, Boulder, and Leonard Duhl, a professor of psychiatry at the University of California, Berkeley, the workshop presented to the delegates at large a call for "a center for the development of personal futures," dubbed popularly as a "magic mountain." The proposal said:

There is a need for individuals, families and groups faced by the threat of tradition, to prepare themselves for alternative futures. What is needed is a center where "recreation" can take place in a holistic way. How can we create an atmosphere, a quality of relationship, and environment which will permit this difficult process to take place?

"Re-creation" takes quiet, time, solitude: a chance to commune with oneself, one's family and with significant others. It requires our understanding of psychological processes, "education," health and the necessity for self-development. Thus the leaders of "magic mountain" must be teachers, gurus, leaders who do not control but facilitate and bear witness by their own behavior to the processes required.

Open space, a "home," people who care and can "heal" are central requirements. The resources of art, music, medicine, spiritual contemplation, psychology, physical movement and activity as well as cognitive discussions of the possible issues that we are to face should be at the disposal of those who come to "magic mountain."

The ability to go back and forth between inner and outer space; between the individual, the family and the community; between spirituality and cognition, can be encouraged and supported—resulting in each person a new synthesis!

Those who come to "magic mountain" can come for short periods or long. They come alone or with significant others. Thus "magic mountain" should be available where people are, and yet far enough away to offer the opportunity of solitude, its permanent staff representing the holistic needs of "re-creation" for the future.

"New settings" are called for to launch a more organized approach to the special complexity of man's needs, Dr. Peter Berger, of Rutgers University, New Brunswick, New Jersey, says. To get the Frascati proposal of a "magic mountain" or similar need-oriented center off the ground, Berger, who is talking in general about new approaches, says, "It would seem worthwhile to me if some consideration were given to new institutional settings. The basic requirements for these are really quite simple. . . . The institutional settings needed must provide for continuous face-to-face interaction among the people engaged in this type of intellectual effort, so that the later can be a systematic enterprise. It follows that these settings must have more durability than conferences or similarly fugitive occasions. Also, these settings have to be so organized (and, needless to say, funded) that they are independent of the ad hoc interests and political pressures of any bureaucratic structures, denominational or other."[10]

Looking around, one can find a variety of centers beyond settlement houses and recreation units of local parishes (yet most still reflect efforts of a denomination or special interest group). Lutherans have regularly put up futuristic "all needs" centers at their youth conventions. The All-Lutheran Youth Gathering, Discovery '73, meeting in the Astrodome, in Houston, provided a "resource center," which included a communications hub, a chapel for devotional events, films, parish, simulation game, music area, drama tent, fairway of nations, red-carpet theater featuring Johnny Cash's film, *The Gospel Road,* a coffeehouse, rap center, college and seminary representatives, and a "future center." A three-day Lutheran Consultation on Leisure, in Chicago, also issued a call for a national resource center to aid churches to relate to the challenge of greater leisure in society.

INTERMINGLING EAST AND WEST TRADITIONS

Some centers reflect the growing intermingling of Western and Eastern traditions. Most conspicuous is Mrs. Dickerman Hollister's "Temple of Understanding," which has just opened in Washington, D.C. The project, which has an interfaith board, provides a broad religious background for students. The Temple has set up con-

[10] "On Not Exactly Reaping the Whirlwind," *The Christian Century,* January 24, 1973, p. 98.

ferences entitled "Meditation: Four Great Traditions (Christian, Hindu, Jew, Zen Buddhist)," for instance, at Yale and other schools. In a world of growing convergence a common center such as this, still allowing distinctives, could become a popular vehicle for religious expression.

Many of the new movements look upon their place of worship as a center—or by other names, such as "ashram," "colony," "house," etc. Kirpal Singh, founder and director of the Ruhani Satsang movement, which draws from many religions "to serve man in all aspects," hopes to build "The Man Center," which would be "a place dedicated to the Fatherhood of God and the Brotherhood of Man—a place where men can develop all around; physically, intellectually, and spiritually."

The International Cooperation Council, of Northridge, California, bills its central building as the "Universal Development Center." A brochure says: "Its focus is on cultivating the whole person and his relation to the society in which he lives. Growth groups and an experiential service are held each Sunday morning for deepening experiences involving personal, social, and spiritual growth." And:

> The experiential service offers a wide variety of speakers and attempts to pioneer in new and different uses of music, symbolism, dance, meditation, and readings from ancient and modern scriptural writings from all cultures. Growth groups meeting before the service consist of a universal development group, an interpersonal communication group, a meditation-healing group, and various other groups. Afternoon, day-long, and weekend workshops are also frequently held.

The Council, which says it co-ordinates 130 organizations, also takes part in "The Mankind Center" in Los Angeles. This is "the center of educational and action programs aimed at catalyzing the transition to a new civilization." Projects include "Walks for Mankind" on the anniversary of the United Nations in June. The "emphasis is now moving toward the development of a Peoples General Assembly to undertake specific action on a variety of mankind problems from a non-government perspective."

Leonard P. Stewart, executive director of the ICC, has developed a "World Scripture, based upon an interpretation of all the existing Scriptures." A smaller version of this is called *Central Scriptures for a Universal Way of Life.* "I feel that we are now in the second half of the world crisis of transition between the Western and world civilizations," he says. "My conviction is that there will be many religions, but that they will be necessarily reshaped in line with the new age and the new energy of convergence that is at its heart."

The center complex of the future may have its negative model, too: a place of refuge for the suffering, the people crowded out physically or psychologically from the "brave new world." Consider an over-populated world, one like the world in the film, *Soylent Green,* based on a novel by Harry Harrison. It is A.D. 2022 and New York City has 40-million people, and life is so cheap that during food riots people are scooped up and disposed of like garbage (and in truth recycled as food). The pews are gone from church. A church building is merely a place where people can sleep, end to end, at night. The stairways are full of crowding, sleeping people. The cars in the street have long since stopped running, and have smokestacks sticking out. Every available space gives way to people, and the church is a packed hostel, recalling church basement havens for refugees from a flood or other disaster. The church in such a scenario is indeed a center, a physical one, rather than a psychological one.

But a center can also be more than a place. A future center for gathering people under religious auspices for whatever purpose does not have to be a clinic or retreat house or other structure. A "center" can be decided on at the moment and its location can fluctuate from time to time. It can be a once-only gathering or a monthly rally, for instance. In a way, a stadium existing for many purposes might be an occasional place for worship in future religion. When the National Council of Churches Youth Ministry department sponsored an interfaith youth conference on the future in Nashville, one of the participants, Scottie Barnes, suggested a scenario of the future could well be to "forget buildings. Hold occasional gatherings in stadiums, and the rest of meetings in small groups," he said. Said another youth, Lavona Gray: "A political rally can be a form of worship because it seeks power, too, and a relationship of people." The stadium-centered rally of Explo '72 in Houston showed the appeal of giant rallies to the future generation. The Jesus People have gone this route with their festivals, co-ordinated by Duane Pederson, of the Hollywood Free Paper.

And some of the oriental imports, such as the youthful Maharaj Ji, have gone the stadium route, too—also in the Astrodome in Houston. Lutherans in 1972 heard a report of one of their agencies (Division for Parish Services of the Lutheran Church in America) call for "a living curriculum" which includes youth gatherings. The report argued that "just as there are church-school classes" there should "be church-school events." The events would be in various regions "on a consistent, predictable schedule" so that congregations could "count on these events as part of their curriculum with the same reliability as a printed course."

Some years ago I used to wonder, as I looked at the giant church buildings on corners, if in the event of social revolution and/or secularization of the state and society, these great buildings would always be churches. Somehow it seemed within the realm of reason that, just as America could go in the direction of deepening the common religious life into even a more profound religiosity or theocracy, the other alternative was also possible—the evolution to a non-religious if not totally socialistic state. A hundred years from now: where would these or the many, many other church buildings within the environs be? I remember walking around Bucharest, Romania, back in the middle sixties and dropping by an old Catholic parish with a schoolyard and school in the background. I was amazed at the sound of life coming from the parochial school at dusk. It turns out it was being used as a public school, and the noise that day came from a public school gymnastic program. But, curiously, in the United States also, without a revolution in politics, the church building enthusiasm leveled off, particularly among Catholics (except for occasional new parishes building their new units, and these tended to be very modest). With de-emphasis on the church as a building and more emphasis on church as people, and an understanding of people's need for fellowship, "church" began to expand beyond the buildings into cell groups, living-room dialogues, house church, colonies. Also, the great network of Catholic schools, facing spiraling costs and finding their uniqueness eroded in a more tolerant society, began to crack. There are signs now of the remaining schools holding a line, but in an amazing short time, five years or so, so many became centers of one sort or another.

Consider one major archdiocese alone—the Archidiocese of Detroit, presided over by John Cardinal Dearden, first president of the National Conference of Catholic Bishops. The Archdiocese had not opened a new school since 1965, a check of the school program in 1973 showed. The number of elementary schools dropped from 245 to 169 in the past four years, and the number of high schools from 79 to 50 in the same period. Elementary school enrollment dropped from 118,727 to 72,622 in four years, high school enrollment from 39,069 to 28,309. In the Detroit area, the closed schools are being used as centers to teach catechism, as community college classrooms, as teen and retiree centers, and, in one case, a new Protestant parochial school with an enrollment of 400 has taken over a former Catholic high school in Pontiac, north of Detroit. The Detroit Board of Education is using eight former Catholic school buildings, and Wayne County Community College is using four former Catholic schools in the Detroit area.

THE FUNCTIONAL CHURCH BUILDING

In Rockford, Illinois, most of fourteen pastors interviewed by the *Register-Star,* said "the church of the future probably will have to be a fully multiple-use building to be a paying proposition." An example is Christ the Carpenter United Methodist Church now under construction. "Besides a church for worship services and the usual auxiliary church meetings, the building also will be a day-care center for children of working mothers and a cultural enrichment center for the South Rockford neighborhood. Other churches, like Second Congregational, First Covenant, Westminster Presbyterian, and Court Street United Methodist are used extensively by non-church groups from Alcoholic Anonymous to garden and weight-reducing clubs. Some churches have rented their educational buildings to public school systems."[11]

The ecology movement—and energy crises (see Chapter IV)—is forcing the churches and religion toward the "functional" concept of religion buildings as centers, or whatever. Thus, a Californian theologian, Dr. George Rupp, told a general assembly of the National Council of Churches, in Dallas, in 1972, that the thirty-three denominations of the NCC should "go on record as opposing all further construction of church buildings." He said the times demand "simplicity, frugality and self-sacrifice." He pointed out

[11] DePew, George, "Church of Future May Have New Look," *Sunday Register-Star,* September 6, 1970.

that earth cannot sustain continued growth and that a sense of justice calls for a more equal distribution of resources. "The most crucial tendency that must be confronted is the materialism that pervades American life," he said. "Instead of acquiescing to Western preoccupation with material products, the church must again work to focus human energies on what Paul the apostle calls the fruits of the spirit—on enterprises which only minimally deplete resources and cause pollution . . . It seems to me that only a moratorium on the church's exhorbitant and unnecessary investment in physical plants can render credible our rejection of indefinitely continued economic expansion." He said it would be better for new religious groups to meet in homes, community halls, or schools, or share facilities with other churches.[12]

There developed a reaction against the word "church" itself. "It has always been a mistake to call buildings 'churches,'" said E. A. Sovik, architect and lay theologian at a Conference on Worship '73 in Minneapolis. "The church is a body of people, the community of believers. The place may be called a meeting room or a hall, or we may find another name. . . . If such a place is to be a really useful tool, it must be a place of extreme flexibility." Sovik suggested that the place be called a "centrum." He added:

There will be some special items of furniture required for any non-cultic use of the centrum, and when it is used as a place of worship, some specifically liturgical equipment will be needed. All of it, the table, pulpit, candlesticks, fabrics, cross, utensils, symbolic devices and accessories need to be portable, as portable as the equipment in the Israelite Tabernacle. I confess there is something attractive to me about the image all this portability provides—the image of a pilgrim community that moves in and out of the sheltering centrum. It is the people and these artifacts which serve their actions that make of the centrum from time to time a good house for worship. . . .

I think we must come to the conclusion that it is really better for Christians not to have places that are specifically and exclusively built to be places of worship. Such places inevitably tend to stabilize, fix and stultify the forms of worship. There is too great a temptation to let the building and its artifacts

[12] Cornell, George, "End All Building, Churches Urged," Associated Press, report from Dallas, the *Detroit News,* December 6, 1972.

control the liturgy, and there is too small an opportunity for the imagination and thoughtfulness of those who plan and perform liturgies. . . .

Religion in the future may not only reflect both the emphasis on home worship and the use of centers, but blend the two ideas. That is, the home itself could become the center for ritual. Certainly the Jesus People have demonstrated the possibilities of this, and I have sat on floors of upper rooms from San Francisco to Toronto and watched these young people break bread and share a chalice in a familylike informal setting. And some families on their own conduct their private communion services, as Pat Boone tells me his family does in a second-floor room of their Beverly Hills home. And some seventy young Jesus People have been baptized in Boone's swimming pool.

Futuristic designs for homes and for other places where meetings might be may help encourage the administering of ancient sacraments. Consider baptism, popular among Near Eastern cults and Roman military cults even before the time of Christ. Looking through a "modern living" section of a newspaper and finding futuristic housing designs, with water as a theme, it takes little imagination to wonder if sometime perhaps the inclination to use water in ritual, coupled with a resort consciousness, and a planning of new housing around fountains and water, might perpetuate home water ritual. Betty Frankel, a garden writer, described the home of Dan Wood and his family in Farmington Hills, Michigan. In his back yard is a free-form swimming pool. "Unlike so many home swimming pools, which look like an afterthought, the Wood's pool and the landscaping around it are thoroughly integrated. Each would be incomplete without the other. Together they create a picturesque scene." The children "can dive from the top of a stone cliff, scoot down a winding slide, splash beneath a waterfall, or just paddle around to their hearts' content. . . . Water is a natural focal point. Subtly, but surely, it draws your attention. Dan Wood believes that 'water is just about the prettiest thing you can have in a yard.' Also: 'The lower your pool is set, the more water you see.' "[13] If religion comes more and more to the home, or if home religion augments a stadium or central rally, the home setting in all of its splendor, as

[13] "A Little Bit of Hawaii in Back Yard," *Detroit Free Press*, August 11, 1973, p. 1-B.

enticing as any river or creek natural setting of frontier religion, becomes a natural place for baptism. (But, of course, baptism in the home setting does not need the full waterfall regalia. I was amused when during the 1972 election campaign I checked out erstwhile candidate George McGovern's former parish as a Methodist seminarian in Diamond Lake, Illinois. In one case, in his pastor days, he took a kitchen bowl, filled it with water, and baptized one family which had handicapped members in the home.) In Robert Heinlein's *Stranger in a Strange Land:*

> Mike sent a glass into the bathroom, had the tap fill it, return it to Jill. Mrs. Paiwonski watched with interest; she was beyond being astonished. Jill said to her, "Aunt Patty, this is like being baptized . . . and like getting married. . . ."
> Jill took a sip. "We grow ever closer." She passed the glass to Mike.
> "I thank you for water, my brother." He took a sip. "Pat, I give you the water of life. May you always drink deep." He passed the glass to her.
> Patricia took it. "Thank you. Thank you, oh my dears! The 'water of life'—I love you both!" She drank thirstily.
> Jill took the glass, finished it. "Now we grow closer, my brothers."[14]

It would be folly to argue that any persistent ancient sacraments, such as "sharing food and drink around a table" or "using water or other liquid to initiate," would fade away in a new age. But one can wonder how such ancient, almost ingrained rites might come out in a future of changed mankind, changed society, and changed religion.

[14] (New York: Berkeley Pub. Co., 1972; c. 1961, Robert Heinlein), pp. 271–2.

CHAPTER X

A Scenario

RELIGION 2101: THE MONKEY RITE
*or, Whatever Happened to the Pewsitters
and Sunday-Dress-Up People?*

Look down to the earth from the sky. Look down to the hills
to the low and nearly barren hills. Look down into the valleys.
Away from the centers. Away from the 100-million member
city states. Look down to the planned, populated country side.
Look down into the village, AG56D88.

The rains from controlled clouds have come, as they always do,
the treasured water, so welcomed, so rejuvenating. The sun is
bright still on the sparkling hills. Look down along the sun's rays,
along a narrow settled canal bathed in the sun's last aura, so
welcomed, so warm.

Look down into a long valley of the future. See the windowless
sixty-story tower—the office and government center standing watch
over a long threadlike community. The tower is casting a shadow
in late evening that makes the tower shadow and long town look
like two hands on a clock.

Look lower now along the rectangular glass houses, stacked above
the channel, one on ground level, the next one up a story, and
so they go on—like match boxes in a row, touching the corners of
the neighbors' houses, here, then there.

Zero in closer. See the 135th tinted house firm against its beams
above the channel. There is a stirring here. There is excitement.
Happiness. A boy moving, a boy about to be initiated into the

most important faith of the land, the Church of the Celebration of the Holy World Cosmos.

Not that religion is all that important. The government keeps it under control. The tube tower back near the sky—it has an office of cosmos religious affairs. A furrowed old bureaucrat, nobody can remember his name, sits there, plunks down rubber stamps that can spell life or death, to a religion and to a religious individual. He looks kindly on the Celebrators. But he frowns on others, remnants, who keep alive strange old traditions. In a way, the Celebrators themselves are ancient. They still hold to a Jesus of a forgotten lore. Some say the water rites and a food rite connected with the faith have the most ancient of origins.

To the man in the tower and others, the Celebrators are useful. They keep a dying race healthy by physical exercise, a part of their beliefs. The Celebrators are free of political ambitions. They find joy in a travel-less society. They are a mark above the old-fashioned zealots who feel they must traverse the world to win converts, who feel they must follow worship as they follow a clock, who have a mean look as they study hard.

The Celebrators survived the last world revolution. That's when the city state of Bo-Wash, a federation of 100-million people on the Eastern seaboard, fired up by old-time religious people sought to seize the world. The rebels raised old flags and chanted old creeds. Almost to a man their leaders were wiped out. Only a few of the old religious zealots are left. Popularly they are called "Pewsitters," for it is said of them, "how they love to sit and worship on straight hard pews." Their leaders put on black robes. Their followers put on ancient head pieces, bright decorations on a long slip of cloth around the neck over a white shirt, and black or gray leg garments, and matching open-front, half-length heavy garment, and leather foot pieces "hats, ties, trousers, coats, shoes," the items used to be called. The Pewsitters look to a one deity for whom they have no precise name. The Celebrators look to more.

Look closer now, at the house and the boy. His name is Davel. And like most youths reaching the age of twelve, he can now be a member of the Celebrators. And he wants to so very much. Joy and celebration are to be his life. Politics and negative thoughts would be his sins. He is about to be trained to forego negative thoughts. They do arise, but once trained, he will become part of a rigid control system. He will be sheathed with a new power of faith, sanctioned and blessed from on high, and trusted with a new practical instrument, a small laser gun with power to zap a dissenter into nothingness. The guns in this society are for the faithful true Celebrators, the powerful.

Davel is about to become a Son of the Skies. Almost half of the group of shaven youths will be girls, but little attention and no distinction is paid to sex. As an initiate now becoming an elder, Davel will listen more intently to the sounds of the stars, he will talk with sons of gods and Jesuses around the universe. Davel has some powers of detection. He has gone through "psi-catechism" for a year. He has also been a good camper on earth and in orbit. He has helped others, while never compromising his faith nor mixing with the dangerous wing of the Orthodox Pewsitters: the "Rocks," who are disciplined not to move when they sit on pews, who also take terror into their hands when they are out in the community. That terrorist kind of Pewsitter brings death to the world, and the new Celebrator initiates are immediately trained to counteract their kind instinctively. The Celebrator elder is both an usher and a policeman. He can be entrusted to safeguard the national faith and security.

Of course, there are harmless Pewsitters, called the Simple Pewsitters, and the government lets these dress up quietly in regulated museums on the second part of Sat-Sun, one of two double days of leisure. The simple Pewsitters have also been known to smile.

Davel is not afraid to mix with the good wing of obedient Pewsitters who conform to the museum laws. He has learned to tolerate the law-abiding good docile Simple Pewsitters. But he has also been taught to abhor the angry militant Orthodox Pewsitters, represented by the Pewsitters Defense League.

Look closely now to the glistening boxlike house on the second level, not yet enveloped with darkness, about there, yes, about two thirds of a mile down the long glass-house row. Davel lives there.

He feels alone today. The day has been long. His smooth bare head, recently shaved, a shade lighter than his sun-wrapped body, is ready for ritual. He thinks of a Pewsitter friend, Marvin. Will Marvin be allowed by his cranky Pewsitter parents to be initiated into the Celebrators?

Davel is sitting in the "nest." Think of it as a great big upper, upper double bedroom, with one large wall-to-wall cushion. Nestled here and there are members of all shapes and sizes and all ages, some sleeping, some stirring, like Davel, late in the lazy day of rest and tripping on the government blue pill. He rolls over, dodges other members of the nest, scoots and sorts of hops over to the slow-moving belt that runs along one edge of the nest. Apples, oranges, nuts, flavored bread chunks—he picks here and there, nibbles on one, lets it go, takes a banana, peels it back in one stroke, down it goes, and he flips the peel back on the never-stopping conveyor belt. The new fruit, he thought, sure has the brown-sugarlike protein cakes produced from oil and other old-fashioned food beat.

He scoots out to the edge, and looks down from the high loft into the floorless house. It is almost the outdoors. Like all the dwellings it is right over the water. There are no floors. Beneath is the inviting channel (although some of the units have floors—Pewsitters usually do). Here and there in Davel's house are little island platforms at different heights. For Davel, and the hale of body and limb, there are loops and rungs on which to swing and on which to dart around the room. Should he slip he would not hit one of the little platforms, but splash down into the sparkling channel; he would climb back out and then leap about the house. Davel loved to catapult down into the water. Now he sat on the edge of the great nest.

His muscles flexed. He was eager to swing in this house built for the strong of limb. The house and the water village were typical of villages in the new world created from off-shore land of old Bo-Wash. For a long time, important people had warned that the man animal, becoming dependent on the metal machines of a computer society, would lose his limbs from too much lack of movement. So it was important as well as fun to belong to the Celebrators, the people best preserving the human animal. There would be no evolving to legless and armless people with people like Davel and his household.

The nest, no longer stilled. . . . The late afternoon siesta was over. Infants cried. And old, old relatives—made mostly of metal and plastic—moved and fussed and gave hoarse commands largely ignored. Davel had few favorites among these "GGGMM's" and "GGGFM's"—the "great great grandmother machines" and the "great great grandfather machines." Oldsters, using the many new wonders of new synthetics and metal, inevitably ended up more artificial than human. Yet they retained a certain consciousness and most of these "GGGMM's" and "GGGFM's" seemed to remember who they were before their parts replacement program began long ago. They, of course, could not swing about as tree animals, but rather went about by hooking onto a pulley system in the house. But the old folks were useful, helpful, controllable, and somehow Davel's mothers and fathers in the household seemed to remember something special about each of the old machines. Perhaps his parents and he himself would be like them someday, too.

With the agility of the most adroit beast of forgotten jungles, the naked boy of the house without a floor swung from ring to ring. No sooner had he grasped the tall off-centered ring, he let go. Down into the water in the channel he went. But as quickly, he grasped the side and sprang out. With a great reach, he secured a low-level ring, and swung back up to a perch.

Several mothers and at least one GGGMM could be heard talking out loud. Davel got the message. They wanted to be sure he was ready for the great initiating rite. He could sense several other members of the household thinking on him, that he had better be ready.

"I wonder if Marvin will be there," said the shaven head boy, who would soon take on awesome religious responsibilities.

Suddenly there were some more thoughts, probably from two or three of the GGGMM's or GGGFM's in the house—"Stay away from Marvin, that boy, Davel, do you hear?" . . . "Those Pewsitters. . . ." The thoughts continued to burst in on him. "You can't trust any of them." . . . "Their memories are too long." . . . "You can't trust any of the Pewsitters." . . . "Marvin's brother, Woodrow, is on the dangerous list." . . . "Get the message, Davel, get the message, Davel. . . ."

"Those damn machine relatives," Davel said, and swung on up by way of two rings and one intermediary platform to the far upper corner, across the jungle-gym big room, opposite from the nest loft. Beneath him the water was gray like a moonlit night, dimmed in this tinted glass house, protected from the sun. The tiny staggered platforms, wet from his splashing and swinging around, now stood out in the deepest orange, red, and blue hues. Davel sat on the cold green cement "communication corner" platform, dripping wet, but feeling the spirit and freshness of a new day, the way a Celebrator and a new initiate-elder of the sect should feel.

On the screen on the small communicator platform in the upper corner, he tuned in the face and thoughts and voice of Marvin, a half-dozen glass houses down the way.

"Marvin, it's me," said Davel.

"Hi," a round face, chubby youngster, with freckles and closely cropped hair, said.

Davel pushed back along his wet head, pretending to wring the hair that was gone. "Going to be there, Marvin?"

"Where?"

"You know."

"Yeah. . . ."

"Well?"

"Yes, but I can't be initiated."

Davel looked into the screen. He reached down and scratched like some tree animal that once lived on old earth, when trees— he hadn't seen many—were as thick as the artificial polypropylene grass.

Marvin looked puzzled. "We're not Celebrators, you know. I want to be one. I know all of the stuff. But we're Pewsitters, and we have to dress up, and we have to look straight ahead, the same time every Sat-Sun. I wish I could do what I wanted to do . . . what you're doing."

"Yeah, Marvin. . . ." He was interrupted.

From outside loud came the great waterfall roar, transmitted out from the tube tower. It would soon be time for "church" in this A.D. 2101 society whose dominating religion was the Celebrator cult. Twice a week, or sometimes once a month, they met— Davel was never quite sure when. But usually on one of the four days, including Sat-Sun, when the underground precision works and other factories were shut down.

The waterfall roar dimmed. . . .

"Davel?" Marvin said.

"Yeah."

"Let's see how much of the Church of the Celebration of the Holy World Cosmos creed I know. . . ."

"OK."

Marvin's eyes looked out intently into Davel's from the communicator screen. Davel met Marvin's eyes in concentration, and Davel listened to a confession of faith, all the time feeling the presence of other minds in the back of his mind, allowing the conversation, but monitoring it all the same.

"I believe in the Gods and the Fathers and the Jesuses, the God the Father, the Son, Jesus number One of history. . . . I believe . . ."

"He descended . . ." interrupted Davel.

"Where did he go, Davel?"

"Oh, that's a long story . . . he came here, of course . . ."

"And now?" asked Marvin.

"Well . . ."

"Let's skip the creed."

"There's more to it," said Davel.

"The commandments," said Marvin. And he began: "Thou shalt have no other gods before us. . . ." Marvin stopped and looked up. "There are a lot of gods, aren't there? . . . What's a god? . . ."

Davel just listened.

"And don't bow down to any images. . . ." Marvin continued with the commandments.

"Right."

"You know, they aren't all that different from the Pewsitters commandments that came down from a mountain once, when Moses came down from a visit to the sky. . . ."

Davel agreed. "But our commandments—they come from the same places. . . . We just add some 'S's'. . . ."

And now Davel reflected his catechism training well. "There was the name Elohim once for God or gods. It was plural, it meant gods. And when God was thought of as singular He had many names. And the one He liked best was 'I am that I am.' And that's what we say. 'We are, and we are.' Gods are, and gods are. I and we. This is a big universe . . . and when I went out on that last Celebrator youth retreat on the camp city orbiting near the moon, I tried to count the stars all the way out. You can't. . . . I like to think of each star as a god and all that live on them as little gods. . . ."

"That's not right," Marvin said.

"Oh, that's my idea anyway," Davel said. "But the Celebrator teachers don't mind if we think that. We just try to live together, men and gods, all are equal, all have a share, all make life a little better for somebody else. . . ."

"You don't travel. . . ."

"Look who's talking—Pewsitter! . . . You walk to a museum, and sit down!"

"You move around in a cage! . . ."

Davel was getting mad and he felt some probes in his mind from the GGGMM's and the GGGFM's and all the household people in the nest.

"I don't want to argue with you, Marvin . . . of course, nobody travels much, since the last Armageddon of men and gods. People are like oceans. When they move, they come in like a tide, and sweep the shores. Take a sand house, Marvin . . . a moving sea destroys it. . . . You can't have a lot of people moving about like a tide. We, and you, too, none of us travel much. But we have fun, and you folks ought to get off of your dead ends, and be patriotic, and have a house like this, and be strong, and physically fit as Chairman Chief of Sky and Earth, Ms. Agatha Rendezvous St. Cloud, and her committee says. . . ." And Davel scratched his back like a tree animal.

"Ask me some questions," Marvin said.

"How many religions are there?" and Davel felt a twinge, almost a shock, as the psychic powers of his relatives in the house centered on him, but nevertheless they let him talk.

Marvin's face furrowed, and he thought, and he began . . . "Well, the Pewsitters and the Celebrators. . . . Then there are the old Eastern animist Society which is the combined religion of two old continents, Africa and Asia; then there's a small Moses religion; a small Mohammed group; the Holy Papal Orthodox Catholic Church, another combination, led by a 'pontiff,' as they call him and his wife. Now, among the Pewsitter groups . . ."

"Sects . . ."

"Churches . . ." said Marvin. And he went on: "There are two kinds, the Simple Pewsitters and the Orthodox Pewsitters—we're the first kind, law-abiding." He straightened his shoulders proudly.

"Your brother belongs to the second. . . ."

Marvin winced. "He hasn't done anything wrong. . . ."

"I wouldn't bet on it." Davel paused. "Blow up any buildings lately?" and Davel's head hurt and the screen nearly went off, but his voice was taunting, and its tone probably made a difference, as the forces in the house let him continue talking to Marvin, his "suspect" friend.

Marvin looked as if he was going to cry, and his voice came softly over the screen, and Davel could barely hear Marvin say it, "I want to be a Celebrator." And the picture of Marvin on the screen suddenly was brighter than ever.

"Marvin, do you know the Alien creed . . . ?"

"I think so." And Marvin appeared to be biting on his lower lip, thinking hard. Marvin began:

> Life to all
> Sky for all.
> God is in the sky.
> Gods are in the skies.
> Man and God,
> They are together.
> "I am come that you might have joy,"
> Jesus number One said. And every boy
> And every girl, every
> man and woman, and the machines
> Great great grandparent machines,
> The household of life
> The household of the world
> We trust in the All.
> We listen to the aliens,
> We are aliens, too, to the Yonder,
> But we would be brothers
> To our friends of the Galaxy
> To our friends of the sea
> To our friends of life.
> Perish violence and strife
> Wipe out the destroyer
> Quickly from the earth.
> We are Celebrators of life.
> And, don't sit still.

And, together the two boys said the Lord's Prayer of Jesus number One, with the "S's" of the Celebrators:

"Our Fathers which are in heavens, hallowed be thy names. Thy kingdoms come. Thy wills be done in earths, as they are in heavens. Give us these days our daily breads. And forgive us our debts, as we forgive our debtors. And lead us not into temptations, but deliver us from evils, For thine are the kingdoms, and the powers and the glories, eon unto eon."

And Davel had a good feeling and Marvin seemed to glow from the screen. The screen then faded out by the wills of those others in the household. Davel waved, as Marvin faded, and Marvin's words, "See ya," faded with him.

A din of noise was coming from the nest, across the great room of the glass cagelike house above the channel. Davel sat, remembering some other little prayers, a bit nervous about his new responsibilities:

> Water and sun
> Substance and Stars
> Many there are.
> Faith is fun—
> Meaning is one.
> > Down with Darkness,
> > Down with roofs,
> > Down with the indoors
> > and hardwood floors.
> > Down with the straightened pew
> > for only a few,
> > Celebrate, Great Universe.
> > Live forever. Live in us. . . .

Davel put his hand over his heart, then leaned forward, and pulled and picked at his toes. He wished Marvin well. Marvin, caught in the old world, he in the new.

Davel could feel all the forces and inner voices of the household converging on him. He could even hear the GGGMM's and GGG-FM's clattering along on their pulleys. He stroked his ritually shaved head, stood strongly, and leaped about the room wildly from ring to ring, stopping on a platform here, then there. Somersaulting once, and leaping halfway across the house, he grabbed a ring. He sprang to the nest. Soon he was in the line-up to leave the house.

Within minutes, Davel was on his way out of the house, in single file, with two dozen others. He and the other young ones broke ranks and swung down to the ground by the rings—the parents and GGGMM's and GGGFM's took the slide down. There were a few groans at the bottom of the slide, then all were on their way, most of them in single file.

The low Western sun was warm and touched Davel's shaved head with benediction. On the ground surface, the flat solar discs curved up to the sky transmitting energy underground to the uniform temperature caverns of workshops and wide tunnels of shops and businesses.

Davel wore a ring on his fourth toe on his right foot. The ring, an amalgam of sodium, mercury, and gold, was a gift from the GGGMM's and GGGFM's of the household. It had a "C" for the faith of the Celebrators engraved on it. And the ring was all he wore. And the sun soon made all of his body warm, and the ring, irritated his toe in the heat. The irritable ring with the sodium hydroxide reaction was a reminder of the attention he would need to give to his sacred initiation. Inside the great stadium of worship he would receive his white robe with the horizontal rows of "C" encircling the garment.

The amount of clothing in this less-pretentious age of controlled climate was left to individual tastes. The GGGMM's and the GGGFM's were fairly well covered, maybe leaving bare a real arm or leg once in awhile to show they weren't all machine parts. A rule said that people over one hundred years of age and absolutely those who passed the 50 per cent mark of replaceable parts must be fully clothed.

The GGGMM's and the GGGFM's wore water-repellent clothes on the days of worship in the great Clam stadium, for each person entering the massive stadium was baptized as he entered. A roaring spray poured over each one like a waterfall. Children and youths such as Davel came naked, their mothers and fathers of the household mostly wore the ceremonial one-piece sack. They too were naked as they ducked into the entry baptismal waterfall. The garment was put into a small waterproof handbag. Once out of the water entry, they donned the sack garment again.

Just before he stepped into the spray, Davel saw Marvin and Marvin's serious household, including Marvin's brother, Woodrow. Marvin, like the rest of the Pewsitter clan, had a heavy dark rain cap and rain coat. The frowns on the faces of Marvin and his family betrayed the great hostility these Pewsitters who still practiced their old faith had for the government-approved Celebrator religion.

Once beyond the spray, the dark outer side of the Clam stadium gave way to pearl-bright whiteness inside. There loomed suddenly a rugged path, like a construction zone. Everybody started stepping over holes and ditches on the ground. Some years ago a conveyor belt used to take people into the inner whiteness of the Clam stadium. But in the government's new policy of physical fitness, the old conveyor belt had been taken out. But the little holes and ditches were not hard to overcome. One big step or a little leap got one across easily, and even the GGGMM's and GGGFM's delighted in showing they could negotiate these little obstacles.

Once inside the Clam arena, it was a world of movement. A round platform slid out, then downwards, and, once twenty feet off the ground, it rested suspended above a lower platform and lectern. A series of bars and rings formed a jungle gym approach to the higher platform. The new young initiates like Davel would have to show prowess swinging up to the platform. Moving also was the top of the Clam stadium, closing now, only to be opened later in a burst of ritual that would bring the stars almost into the laps of the worshippers. Various rings and parallel bars descended to large areas of the strange stadium, so the spectators who were a part of the physical fitness "save the limbs" program could swing back and forth from one loop to another or hang by their feet from a rod as they listened to the rites. There were still tiers of seats, however, and some of the GGGMM's and GGGFM's preferred these with their clackety-clack bodies. And, of course, the Pewsitters scrambled to the straight-back seats in which to sit in the rite that they cared little for. But for them to be absent marked them for special displeasure by the government, and besides, some of these Pewsitters were not all that inactive at the rallies. Certainly Woodrow, Marvin's brother, was not on a government dangerous list for nothing. In these big gatherings, some of the more zealous Orthodox Pewsitters wanted to make their displeasure known publicly as they shouted epithets quickly or a few tenets of their faith for everyone to hear.

The times were serious. And Davel knew, and the people all knew that some people still had to die for their faith—religious or political beliefs. The Celebrators were the accepted ones. The Pewsitters, the rebels. The history screens at school told Davel that the minorities always suffer some persecution, even slaughter. Fed to lions, burned at the stake, put into gas chambers—that was the history of life. Davel was thankful that his society sought only to obliterate individuals, a few here and there and that it was fast. Even the old liquid spray guns that made people a heap of ashes were gone, and now the sudden total obliteration of laser guns. There was a lump in the new boy initiate's throat. He would tonight in a first duty of an initiate become an usher and hold the "bleaker" —one of those laser guns entrusted to the faithful usher to use when directed. He hoped he would never have to use it, although, again, it might be fun. It gave him cause to think.

Davel kept on walking as members of his household found places to their liking in the stands. The mothers and fathers and brothers and sisters, many found a bar or ring from which to hang by their feet, or to dangle by an arm.

Davel walked on toward the high platform. He could hear the moaning and groaning, feel strange conflicting thoughts directed into his mind, could hear invisible laughter, could sense invisible pains and yearnings. He walked by the stands of the mutants. These non-people, some descendants of people, some highly gifted, some of them androids of one sort or another, a few of them licensed robots and cyborgs, others, the many limbed, the non-limbed—a reminder to the Celebrators of the value of holding faithfully to the new "save the limb" exercise program. These mutants—the out-casts of society—entered the stands docilely. Other Celebrator priest-police turned the lock on an iron gate after the last of the mutants entered the section, only to have it unlocked from time to time to gently boot a late-arriving mutant into the section. A two-headed android with twenty-three ears—Davel counted them—was the strangest mutant of all. Oh well, it takes all kinds, Davel thought.

There suddenly emerged some shouting from the Pewsitters part of the stadium, and Davel could see laser guns raised here and there by the elders of the church and a bright searching light beamed over to the section. Over in some far corner, he could sense some action. There came a rebel's shout, "Repent, ye sinners, in the name of the Lord!" It must be a Pewsitter. But the person did not persist, and the shout seemed to fade away. The light over there dimmed, then disappeared. Davel moved on toward the plat-form.

Davel grabbed the lower ring beside the platform, swung with enthusiasm to another ring, then grabbed onto a bar rod, flipped around in full circle, then sprung up to another ring, and another, and lit on the platform. There was cheering from all around. Other youths began to reach the platform, each also triggering a round of cheers from households and others caught up in the emotion of launching promising young Celebrators destined not only to preserve a society but to move it along in the years ahead to new levels of happiness.

Davel and the other two dozen initiates on the platform sat behind little scooterlike hovercrafts; each equipped with the things of ritual and discipline. Each had a cartload of small boxes of fish and bread lunches, for the happy supper, or communion. There were hooks with which to reach up to bring down the slim long hose-like funnels. The faithful would throw a credit number coupon into the sucking current as an offering.

The hovercraft had a small screen for communication on the dashboard, and on the side, one of those adjustable barrel laser guns, a tool of every usher—new initiate elder or seasoned elder.

The ritual began with a releasing of motley "birds of the earth"— sparrows, pigeons, and songbirds—amid a colorful display of lights. People were encouraged to feed the birds which later would escape to an open sky and settle among the homes of the channel. Little children attending for the first time were given tiny fishes of colorful varieties for keeping in their homes or releasing into the great fresh water channel. And they had smiles and the crowds cheered. A shout came from Pewsitters: "Suffer the little children to come unto me— damn the fish!" The shout was ignored, but it did serve to heighten the level of tension.

Great hymns to the stars were shouted by the Celebrators swing- ing from rings and rods, their songs mixing with unearthly but exciting electronic tones. Then the great top of the Clam stadium opened—it opened to the stars. Davel was awed, and the lights went out and he felt he sat with the stars. The "uhs" and "oms" and "hu's" in the audience, softly, and reverently showed that many shared the same feeling.

The new Scriptures, found on an orbiting alien unit, originating so many eons ago, from the beginning of cosmic time, was read amid awesome appreciation of the lights in the night, and an old Psalm from earth, with some pluralizing, was read. Davel rec- ognized it from his catechism training:

"O Lord our Lord, how excellent is thy name—and all thy names—in all the earth! who hast set thy glory above the heavens. . . .

"When I consider thy heavens, the work of thy fingers, the moon and the stars, which thou hast ordained; What is man, that thou are mindful of him? and the sons of man, that thou visitest them? "For thou hast made them a little lower than the angels, and hast crowned them with glory and honor."

Then there came quiet. A voice urged total silence as "whispers" from the distant stars magnified by a monstrous telescopic radio bowl were heard. Immediately there were star-flung hums and whispers, unintelligible. They increased in volume, and there were prayers and familiar chants of "O Great Universe" and "O Great Minds," and the "S" sound. None of these came very loud, which made it even all the more startling when from the Pewsitter section came a shout of a four-letter word, and one ray of light lit up a corner of the Pewsitters. There were silhouettes of elders and laser guns in positions. There would be terror yet tonight, Davel thought, but it could be met, and he eyed, or rather reached out and felt the gun on the hovercraft before him. The service went on—his mind wandered—there were psychic thoughts of beneficence sent toward him from his household. He opened his mind to the whispers and hums and occasional peeps-peeps of the sky. He was all and one with All. What a blessed night. Then he heard:

"Initiates—children of All—listen to the stars. Never forget them. Trust them. Seek them. Never look back. Look outward. Look to your fellow creature. Lead the way to the paths of righteousness. Keep the paths clear, never destroy unless necessary, act with the wisdom of the stars, for now and for ever more. Initiates, in this darkness, in the white light of the stars, you will all now, as we chant the many sacred sounds, the most blessed of all the "S" sounds, be ready—be robed. . . ."

And there came cheers in the darkness, then a settling down of the great stadium crowd to the "S" and "om" and "hu" and other sounds, and Davel felt a soft robe dropped over him. His arms were gently pulled through. Then came a touch of a scratchy substance on his head, and the star-dust cross on his head would glow, as now he could see also the fluorescent whiteness of his robe. When the last youth was so anointed, there was a pause, and a quietness, and even the Pewsitters did not dare make a sound. Then suddenly the main lights went back on and the chief elder stood at the rostrum below, looked up and grinning, bellowed,

"Welcome Initiates, welcome to the Church of the Celebration of the Holy World Cosmos, welcome, you are no longer initiates, but elders of the Holy Church." And he shouted as his enthusiasm triggered cheers abroad, "WELCOME!!!"

Now Davel grinned, as did the other youths, and they danced and they swung down on the rings and landed up again in their places. They were told to man the hovercrafts and prepare to serve the one and true church. Davel had learned the hang of the short distance, darting, multi-directional vehicles in school. Practice in the stadium the previous week familiarized him with the ushering routines and positions. It was so much easier to get around the hordes by hovercraft.

Scripture from the aliens along with earth Scriptures were read as the communion rite began. Davel, up in the air on his hovercraft, took his position halfway between a corner of the Celebrators and an enclave of the somber Pewsitters. Marvin, standing by his stoop-shouldered brother, Woodrow, looked up and waved.

Davel smiled at Marvin, then began to drop the communion boxes over the whole area. The Celebrators received them with a shout and laugh, while the somber Pewsitters merely took them, opened them slowly, and had hardly started eating by the time the Celebrators had eaten the last morsel. The great suction tubes were lowered to take back the discarded debris. Marvin, who had caught the lunch dropped gently to him directly from Davel, looked up and beamed at Davel, and Davel knew his friend would like to be up there on a hovercraft, initiated too, if only his parents would let him. Woodrow, next to Marvin, however, was a study in bleakness. He was not eating, just looking down.

The wine of communion dripped from the ceiling pipes and the faithful who caught the drops in their mouths, some of the Celebrators hanging upside down on bars and rings, did so in glee. Davel looked up and shared in the drops of communion and bliss also. Then as the final measure of communion ended and preparation was made to hear messages beamed in from other Clam stadiums in distant colonies and city states, a murmur began to grow among the Pewsitters.

The stooped Woodrow, next to Marvin, was looking around nervously. The murmur grew, in this interim period, and understandably, for now came the most abominable act to the Pewsitters. The moment of the blue pill, the final act of communion, a privilege to many. The pills that brought a sense of ecstasy, and peace, that lasted for days without affecting health, in fact stimulating the body to greater exercise and activity, as well as deeper sleep. The flat pills were ready on the long tapered sticks back at the platform. Davel took one of the long rods with him, and hovered near the crowds as he offered the final token of communion. He watched the Celebrators take the pills easily. The Pewsitters would have none of them. All over, the Pewsitters grumbled. "No blue pill," many, many chanted together. Woodrow, suddenly a bundle of electric motion, screamed: "An abomination!" Still stooped, his head was raised in an agony of anger: "An abomination unto the Lord! Woe, woe, woe! . . ."

Davel's communicator was bleeping. "Usher-initiate-elder Davel. Attention. Prepare to act. An elder will be there with you quickly. Sight fifth row, second from rail. Prepare to act. He is the one shouting. . . ."

And Woodrow was like a pierced animal. "Abomination! Abomination!" he screamed at the top of his lungs.

"Prepare to act, prepare to act . . ." the signal came. There was restlessness all around and the support promised to Davel did not come. He might have to act. At the same time from across the stadium came a sickening, glaring light, a zip-zip sound, and Davel knew that somebody had already been "obliterated."

"Prepare to act. . . . We have surveillance indicator report. Said party, fifth back, second right has an organic bomb ready to hurl. Your gun will obliterate all of his mischievousness—his distorted mind, voice, and potentially violent and dangerous act. . . . Prepare to act!" the bleeper now screamed. "Ready! . . ."

Davel was over position. He looked down. Marvin stood in a beam narrowed down from the roof lookout on the little area. He cowered, and peeked with one eye up to Davel. Woodrow in the beam also, was almost in a dance, stooped, his mouth cocked up, distorted to the sky, yielding "Abomination! Abomination!"

"NOW . . . Fire! . . ."

And Davel did. A boy became nothing in a burst of light. Beside the spot of the obliterated boy, the voice of another, Woodrow, faded as a part of him also disappeared, and the rest of him crumbling, he could still mutter, "Abomination, abomination . . ." barely audible in the hush. But gone altogether was the younger brother. Davel's aim had not been quite right. "Marvin, Marvin!"

shouted Davel. "I hit Marvin!" And indeed there was no more Marvin, only the empty spot, and a torn half form next to where Marvin had stood. Woodrow, half of him, muttering, "Abomination, abomination."

A back-up older elder, now beside Davel, fired again, and the sound of "abomination" disappeared altogether. Other Pewsitters, intimidated, quiet, huddled as far as they could from the barren death scene where two brothers had stood.

A final chant came over the great stadium, a benediction, from the stars, beneath the stars, phrased by a chief elder, "In the name of the Fathers, Sons and Holy Ghosts, the Skies, and All there is . . . from eon to eon."

Davel sat a moment back on the platform, the voices of his household came into his mind, some offering sympathy for his friend, some commending his bravery, all congratulating him on his new position of proved excellence in the active mother Church of the Celebration of the Holy World Cosmos.

Davel left his robe, swung back down, and soon he walked, spirit-wounded, not thinking, not talking, out into the evening that had become night. Single file, all of the household went back to the house.

They took part in a final rite of blessing, swimming designs in the channel water, beneath the floorless glass house, beneath the stars.

When it was over, Davel did not go immediately to the womb of the nest.

The voices of the household did not disturb him. Davel sat on the upper communicator platform perch, before an empty screen, and cried.

APPENDIX:
A Listing of Futurist Groups

Academy of Contemporary Problems
505 King Avenue
Columbus, Ohio 43201

American Association of Retired Persons
1225 Connecticut Avenue, N.W.
Washington, D.C. 20006

American Genetic Association
1028 Connecticut Avenue N.W.
Washington, D.C. 20036

Aspen Institute for Humanistic Studies
600 Fifth Avenue
New York, New York 10020

Association Internationale de Futuribles
52, Rue des Saints-Pères
75007 Paris VII, France

Carnegie Endowment for International Peace
345 E. 46th Street
New York, New York 10017

Carolina Population Center
Chapel Hill
North Carolina 27514

Center for Advanced Study in Organization Science
University of Wisconsin
Milwaukee, Wisconsin 53207

Center for a Voluntary Society
1507 M Street N.W.
Washington, D.C. 20005

Center for Integrative Studies
School of Advanced Technology

State University of New York
Binghamton, New York 13901

Center for Parish Development
Naperville
Illinois 60540

Center for Peaceful Change
5 North Hall
Kent State University
Kent, Ohio 44242

Center for Public Interest Management
201 I Street S.W.
Washington, D.C. 20024

Center for the Study of Automation and Society
Athens
Georgia 30601

Center for the Study of Church Organizational Behavior
McCormick Theological Seminary
800 W. Belden
Chicago, Illinois 60614

Center for the Study of the Future
4110 N.E. Alameda
Portland, Oregon 97212

Centro de Estudios del Futuro de Venezuela
Dividendo Voluntario para la Communidad
Edificio IESA San Bernadino, Apartado 12500
Caracas, Venezuela

Centro Studi Investimenti Sociali
Corso Vittorio Emanuele, 251
Rome, Italy

Club de Amigos de la Futurología
Puertafferisa 23
Barcelona 2, Spain

College of Environmental Design
Department of City Planning
University of California
Berkeley, California 94720

Commission on Minnesota's Future
101 Capitol Square Building
550 Cedar Street
St. Paul, Minnesota 55101

Committee for Collective Security
307 E. 44th Street
New York, New York 10017

Committee for the Future, Inc.
130 Spruce Street, Suite 17-B
Philadelphia, Pennsylvania 19106

Committee on the Challenges of Modern Society
North Atlantic Treaty Organization
Brussels 1110, Belgium

Committee on the World Food Crisis
1315 16th Street N.W.
Washington, D.C. 20036

Division of the Future
Dreyfuss College
Fairleigh Dickinson University
Madison, New Jersey 07940

Environmental Design Faculty
University of Calgary
Calgary, Alberta, Canada

Environmental Studies Division
University of Waterloo
Waterloo, Ontario, Canada

Environmental Studies Faculty
York University
Downsview, Ontario, Canada

European Centre for Population Studies
Pauwelaan 17
The Hague, The Netherlands

European Cultural Foundation
Jan van Goyenkade 5
Amsterdam, The Netherlands

Experimental Cities
11747 Bellagio Road, Suite 8
Los Angeles, California 90049

Food and Agriculture Organization (United Nations)
Via le delle Terme di Caracalla
Rome, Italy

Forecasting International, Ltd.
Arlington
Virginia 22210

Forecasting Research Center
Technical University of Wroclaw
Wybrzeze Wyspianskiego 27
50–370 Wroclaw, Poland

Free Church (directory, new experiments)
Box 9177
Berkeley, California 94709

Future Associates
Shawnee Mission
Kansas 66201

Future Research Associates
12 Shattuck Street
Nashua, New Hampshire 03060

Future Research Institute
Portland State University
P. O. Box 751
Portland, Oregon 97207

Futures Conditional
34 W. 33rd Street
New York, New York 10001

Futures Group
124 Hebron Avenue
Glastonbury, Connecticut 06033

Futures Information Network
World Institute

777 United Nations Plaza
New York, New York 10017

Futures Research
14 Martha Court
Centerport, New York 11721

Futures Society
University of Bridgeport
Bridgeport, Connecticut 06602

Futuribili
Via della Consulta, 50
Rome, Italy

George D. Dayton Foundation
505 Seven Thirty Building
Minneapolis, Minnesota 55402

Hudson Institute
Quaker Ridge Road
Croton-on-Hudson, New York 10520

Incentive SpA (research on third world)
Viale Liegi 33/B4
00198 Rome, Italy

Industrial Management Center, Inc.
1100 Red Bud Trail
Austin, Texas 78746

Institute for Juvenile Research
1140 S. Paulina
Chicago, Illinois 60612

Institute for the Future
2725 Sand Hill Road
Menlo Park, California 94025

Institute for the Future
Riverview Center
Middletown, Connecticut 06457

Institute of Behavioral Science
University of Colorado
Boulder, Colorado 80302

Institute of Religion and Human Development
Texas Medical Center
Houston, Texas 77025

Institute of Social Research
Colombo 7, Ceylon

Institute of Social Research
USSR Academy of Sciences
Novo-Cheremunski 46
Moscow 117–418, USSR

International Future Research Conference (Secretariat)
Institutionen for Matematik
Kungl. Tekniska Högskolan
Stockholm 70, Sweden

International Peace Research Institute
University of Oslo
Blindern, Postboks 1070
Oslo 3, Norway

International Society for Technology Assessment
Van Calcarlaan 24
Wassenaar, The Netherlands

Istituto per le Ricerche di Economia Applicata (IREA)
Via Venti Settembre 1
00187 Rome, Italy

Istituto Ricerche Applicate Documentazioni e Studi (IRADES)
Via G. Paisiello 6
00198 Rome, Italy

Italconsult (Aurelio Peccei, founder, Club of Rome)
Via Giorgione 163
Rome, Italy

Joint Action in Community Service, Inc.
1730 M Street N.W., Room 500
Washington, D.C. 20011

Joint Strategy and Action Committee (JSAC)
475 Riverside Drive, Room 1700 A
New York, New York 10027

Laboratory for Prospective Research
University of Bucharest
Str. Mihail Moxa 3–5
Bucharest 8, Romania

Leisure Studies Program
College of Social and Behavioral Sciences
University of South Florida
Tampa, Florida 33620

Low Impact Technology
73 Malesworth Street
Wadebridge, Norwall, England

Man and His Urban Environment Project
Room 5600/30
Rockefeller Plaza
New York, New York 10020

Mankind 2000
1 Rue aux Laines
Brussels 1000, Belgium

Marine Programs
University of Hawaii—Holmes Hall
2540 Dole Street
Honolulu, Hawaii 96822

Max-Planck-Institut
Riemerschmidstrasse 7
813 Starnberg, West Germany

Missions Advanced Research and Communications Center
Monrovia
California 91016

Modern Utopian—Utopia USA (a catalogue)
Box 36604
Los Angeles, California 90036

National Assembly for Social Policy and Development, Inc.
345 E. 46th Street
New York, New York 10017

National Center for Resource Recovery
1211 Connecticut Avenue N.W.
Washington, D.C. 20036

National Center for the Exploration of Human Potential
8080 El Paseo Grande
La Jolla, California 92037

National Center for Voluntary Action
1735 I Street N.W.
Washington, D.C. 20006

National Council on the Aging
1828 L Street N.W.
Washington, D.C. 20036

National Institute for Building Research
Box 27 163
Stockholm 27, Sweden

National Opinion Research Center
University of Chicago
Chicago, Illinois 60637

Nethers Community School and Future Village
Box 41
Woodville, Virginia 22749

New Guinea Research Unit
Box 1238, Boroko
Port Moresby, Papua (New Guinea)

New Worlds Training and Education Center
2325 Porter Street N.W.
Washington, D.C. 20008

Norwegian Society for Future Studies
Box 8401
Hammersborg, Oslo 1, Norway

Occupational Health Department
United Mine Workers of America
1437 K Street N.W.
Washington, D.C. 20005

Office of Planning and Program
National Council of Churches
475 Riverside Drive
New York, New York 10027

Office of Technology Assessment and Forecast
U. S. Department of Commerce
Washington, D.C. 20231

Parapsychology Foundation
29 W. 57th Street
New York, New York 10019

Plan Europe 2000
European Cultural Foundation
Jan Van Goyenkade, 5
NL-Amsterdam 1007, The Netherlands

Planning and Forecasting Consultants
941 N. Wilcrest Street
Houston, Texas 77024

Program for the Study of the Future in Education
School of Education
University of Massachusetts
Amherst, Massachusetts 01002

Psychosynthesis Research Foundation
40 E. 49th Street, Room 1902
New York, New York 10017

Radical Research Center (alternative press list)
Bag Service 2500
Postal Station E
Toronto, Ontario, Canada

Regional Research Laboratory
Horhat
6 Assam, India

Research and Development Services
National Board of YMCA
291 Broadway
New York, New York 10007

Research and Prognostics Committee—Poland 2000
Polska Akademia Mank Warszawa Polaw Kultury I Manki
00–901 Warsaw, Poland

Research Foundation for Eastern Wisdom and Western Science
8131 Berg/Starnberg—Postfach 36
West Germany

Rockefeller Foundation
111 W. 50th Street
New York, New York 10020

Saskatchewan NewStart
101 River Street East
Prince Albert
Saskatchewan S6V 5T2, Canada

Saucer and Unexplained Celestial Events Research Society
  (SAUCERS)
P. O. Box 2228
Clarksburg, West Virginia 26301

Science Fiction Foundation
North East London Polytechnic
Barking Precinct
Longbridge Road
Dagenham, Essex RM8, England

Science Fiction Research Association
7 Amsterdam Avenue
Teaneck, New Jersey 07666

Science Policy Research Unit
University of Sussex
Nuffield Building Falmer
Sussex BN1 9 RF
Brighton, England

Secretariat for Future Studies
10320 Stockholm 16
Sweden

Section of Innovation and Experimentation
The United Methodist Board of Education

P. O. Box 871
Nashville, Tennessee 37202

Section on Behavioral Systems
Laboratory of Brain Evolution and Behavior
National Institute of Mental Health—Building 110
Nihac, 9000 Rockville Pike
Bethesda, Maryland 20014

Selskabet for Fremtidsforsking
(Society for Research on Futures)
Skovfoldet 2S DK—8200 Aarhus N.
Denmark

Society for International Development
International Headquarters, Dept. F
1346 Connecticut Avenue N.W.
Washington, D.C. 20036

Society for the Investigation of the Unexplained (SITU)
R.D. 1
Columbia, New Jersey 07832

Socio-Technologies AB
Bromma
Sweden

Spiritual Community (alternate religious efforts)
Box 1080
San Rafael, California 94902

Strategic Studies Institute
U. S. Army War College
Carlisle Barracks, Pennsylvania 17013

Strategie di sviluppo
Montedison
Largo Donegani ½
20121 Milano, Italy

Strategy and Tactics Magazine
Simulations Publications, Inc.
Dept. 480
44 E. 23rd Street
New York, New York, 10010

Survival Institute of the Future
P. O. Box N 1131
Nassau, Bahamas

Task Force on New Concepts in Urban Transportation
University of Minnesota
Minneapolis, Minnesota 55455

Technological Developments Holding Corporation
Izmir
Turkey

Tech Utilization Center
IIT Research Institute
10 W. 35th Street
Chicago, Illinois 60616

Teilhard Centre for the Future of Man
3 Cromwell Place
London SW7 ZJE, England

Tomorrow's World
P. O. Box 43
Babson Park, Massachusetts 02157

Training Research and Development Station
Manpower and Immigration
154 Eight Street East
P. O. Box 1565
Prince Albert, Saskatchewan, Canada

Transportation Technology, Inc.
Denver, Colorado 80216

Twenty-First Century Media, Inc.
606 Fifth Avenue
E. Northport, New York 11731

United States Atomic Energy Commission
Division of Controlled Thermo-nuclear Research
Washington, D.C. 20545

Urban Studies Center
Tulane University
New Orleans, Louisiana 70118

Vocations for Social Change
46 Inman Street
Cambridge, Massachusetts 02139

World Association of World Federalists
63 Sparks Street, Suite 601
Ottawa, Ontario, KIP 5 A6, Canada

World Federalist Youth
Norrebrogade 36
2200 Copenhagen, Denmark

World Future Society
4916 St. Elmo Avenue
(Bethesda) Washington, D.C. 20014

World Health Organization
Avenue Appia
1211 Geneva 27
Switzerland

World Law Fund
11 W. 42nd Street
New York, New York 10036

World Meteorological Organization
41 av Giuseppe-Motta
1211 Geneva 20, Switzerland

Zentrum Berlin für Zukunftsforschung (ZBZ)
Hohenzollerndamm 170
D-1000 Berlin 31, West Germany

Zero Population Growth
4080 Fabian Way
Palo Alto, California 94303

INDEX